Latino Lives in America

Latino Lives in America

Making It Home

Luis Ricardo Fraga
John A. Garcia
Rodney E. Hero
Michael Jones-Correa
Valerie Martinez-Ebers
Gary M. Segura

TEMPLE UNIVERSITY PRESS
Philadelphia

Temple University Press
Philadelphia, Pennsylvania 19122
www.temple.edu/tempress

Copyright © 2010 by Temple University
Published 2010

Library of Congress Cataloging-in-Publication Data
Latino lives in America : making it home / Luis Ricardo Fraga . . . [et al.].
    p.   cm.
    Includes bibliographical references and index.
    ISBN 978-1-4399-0048-2 (hardcover : alk. paper) — ISBN 978-1-4399-0049-9
(pbk. : alk. paper)
    1. Hispanic Americans—Economic conditions—21st century. 2. Hispanic
Americans—Social conditions—21st century. 3. Hispanic Americans—Politics
and government—21st century. 4. United States—Ethnic relations. I. Fraga, Luis
Ricardo.
    E184.S75L36233 2010
    973'.0468—dc22

                                                                    2009038138

♾ The paper used in this publication meets the requirements of the
American National Standard for Information Sciences—Permanence of Paper
for Printed Library Materials, ANSI Z39.48-1992

Printed in the United States of America

4 6 8 9 7 5

Contents

Acknowledgments

We gratefully acknowledge the funders who made our research possible. Gil Cardenas, Director of the Institute of Latino Studies at the University of Notre Dame and a board member of the Anney E. Casey Foundation, gave us the opportunity to first meet to develop our initial project prospectus. Paul Brest at the Hewlett Foundation provided our one-year planning grant. Jacqueline Berrien at the Ford Foundation gave us our foundational grant upon which we were able to build. We gratefully acknowledge the additional financial support provided by Geri Manion, Carnegie Corporation; Aixa Cintrón, Russell Sage Foundation; Lande Ajose and Amy Dominguez-Arms, Irvine Foundation; Ken Meier, Program in Equity, Representation, and Governance, Texas A&M University; Edward Murguia, Mexican American and Latino Research Center, Texas A&M University; the Joyce Foundation; the Kellogg Foundation; the National Science Foundation; and the University of Iowa.

Our National Advisory Board provided crucial guidance in developing the survey. The members of our Board were Larry Bobo, Harvard University; Bruce Cain, University of California, Berkeley; Robert Huckfeldt, University of California, Davis; Pei-te Lien, University of California, Santa Barbara; Ken Meier, Texas A&M University; Vilma

Ortiz, University of California, Los Angeles; Lisandro Pérez, Florida International University; Kenneth Prewitt, Columbia University; Ricardo Ramírez, University of Southern California; Denise Segura, University of California, Santa Barbara; Christine Sierra, University of New Mexico; and Carlos Vargas Ramos, Hunter College of the City University of New York.

A magnificent team of research assistants was critical to our being able to complete our work. The members of our team included Francisco Pedraza, Helena Rodrigues, Seth Greenfest, Jenny Founds, Ann Frost, Sarah Sponaugle, Jeanette Tejada, Salvador Peralta, Gabriel Sánchez, Marcela García-Castañón, Carmen Arozco-Acosta, Renee Reyna, and Ali Valenzuela.

Several individuals provided support at various stages of our work. They include Luis Arteaga, Latino Issue Forum; Lisa Krisher, Georgia Legal Services; Dario Moreno, Center for Metropolitan Studies, Florida International University; Luis Nogales; Rebeca Rangel; and Professor Maria Velez, University of New Mexico.

We would also like to gratefully acknowledge our spouses, partners, and children. We are fully aware that it is your support that gives us the time to pursue our research. Thank you from the bottom of our hearts. We love you.

Latino Lives in America

▮▮ The Growing Presence of Latinos in the United States

n early spring 2006, an inspiring and impressive demonstration of Latino political action poured into the streets of American cities to advocate for a comprehensive reform to the existing immigration regime in the United States and against an approach—captured in House of Representatives Bill 4437 (*Border Protection, Antiterrorism, and Illegal Immigration Control Act of 2005*)—built on the criminalization of undocumented immigrants and their supporters. Marches occurred in more than 125 cities between March 10 and May 1, and included an estimated three million people. A general strike on May 1 shuttered dozens of food processing plants across the heartland, closed schools and businesses, and shut down countless construction sites in the United States. Collectively, these marches and the strike represented the largest single civil rights action in American history.

As much as these actions were both inspiring and impressive, the adjective most used by social scientists who are students of Latino life in the United States is "surprising." That is, almost nothing we "know" about Latinos from the work of social scientists and humanists would have predicted these events. These actions were surprising in any number of ways. First, they suggested Latino communities to be far more politicized and mobilizable than current scholarship had suggested. Second, they demonstrated more substantial pan-ethnic solidarity than might otherwise be expected. There appears to have been significant Puerto Rican and Cuban participation, despite the distinct legal arrangements that make immigration a nonissue for these two groups. There appeared to be significant participation and support by native-born citizens of the United States, belying the claim made by some immigration opponents that Latino citizens are not supportive of unauthorized immigrants. Surveys taken by the Latino Policy Coalition and others suggested widespread approval of the actions by Latino citizens and noncitizens alike.

Perhaps most importantly, however, the marches arguably signified critical and interesting predispositions among Latinos. To some degree, the marches simultaneously communicated dissatisfaction with current and proposed policy while also implicitly demonstrating a level of trust in the political system. Clearly, the marchers were unhappy with both the immigration status quo and the proposed legislation. But, by taking to the streets, they also signaled their belief that political action within the U.S. political system *can* yield policy change, a surprisingly efficacious stance. And finally, the marches, the demands, and the trappings of the action (replete with countless American flags) consciously and unconsciously communicated a collective commitment to making a life in the United States. Though clearly undertaken as a political strategy, the marchers' actions and even their very presence served to stake a claim to formal and informal inclusion in the American polity. It was, in the last analysis, a demand for membership.

We might see the marches as the culmination of the political process begun in 1994 with the Latino reaction to California Proposition 187, which prohibited providing most state services to those suspected of being undocumented immigrants. And *some* of the literature on Latino politics, since the late 1990s, had begun to identify some of the small but important changes in Latino political life that may have culminated in the events of 2006 (Fraga and Ramírez 2003; Pantoja, Ramírez, and Segura 2001). But we would be wrong not to recognize that our academic understanding of the Latino community, broadly construed, stands at odds with what was observed that spring. The preponderance of existing work documented a population that was politically disconnected, slow to mobilization and generally inattentive to politics, fractured along national-origin lines, and more likely to be the targets of political action than the actors themselves. Whatever else the marches of 2006 may have accomplished, they made it clear that our collective knowledge of Latino political orientations was, at best, incomplete and, quite possibly, dated beyond usefulness.

This project, begun well before the marches took place, proceeded largely from that assumption. That is, we began in the spring of 2002 with the creeping suspicion that things had changed, were continuing to change and changing quickly, and that political science may have, to a large extent, missed these changes. The decade of the 1990s witnessed the emergence and proliferation of statewide ballot initiatives, generally or specifically targeted at Latinos. Simultaneously, the immigrant population was exploding while immigrants of a previous wave, whose status had been adjusted by the 1986 Immigration Reform and Control Act (IRCA), entered the electorate in surprisingly high numbers. Latino communities were emerging in places that had little or no experience with immigration, chasing jobs in Southeastern carpet mills, Southern poultry plants, Midwestern slaughterhouses, and in construction throughout much of the country. Latino politicians sought and won elective office in growing numbers and in a larger array of locations than previously. A Republican candidate for president made outreach to Latinos a signature effort of his campaign; simultaneously, nativist elements of his own party made anti-immigrant politics a popular feature of GOP campaigns and rhetoric—all of which is to say that the political, social, economic, and demographic landscape had changed with results we were beginning to witness.

It is to these developments, and their implications for Latino life in the United States, that this project is addressed.

Demonstrable Changes in Latino Life— Has Political Science Missed the Boat?

Our take on the peculiar features and important aspects of the Latino communities in the United States today is driven in large measure by three important characteristics of social scientists and their impact on what we know and can learn. First and foremost, academic training emphasizes the existing body of knowledge as the baseline from which we begin any new effort at discovery. The "literature," with its long-held assumptions and well-established findings, serves as the foundation for new investigation. Attempting to move past the literature is difficult, and the logic of the Kuhnian epistemology that dominates contemporary social science suggests that evidence must be particularly strong if "received knowledge" is to be overturned.

The literature on Latino political behavior has evolved substantially in recent years (Fraga et al. 2006b). However, much of what we know about Latino political behavior, the long-held findings and foundational claims, is driven by data collected in the 1989 Latino National Political Survey (LNPS). The population of Latinos in the United States has changed drastically since the collection of those data. In fact, when we consider that the population of Latinos in the 1990 census was 22.4 million persons, some of whom have passed on in the intervening years, compared to 43.2 million in 2006, the universe of potential respondents to the LNPS represent fewer than half of the universe of Latino residents of the United States today. This is not to say that none of the findings of the survey regarding Latino political and social attitudes and experiences applies today. Certainly many things have stayed the same (which is interesting in and of itself, and we have more to say about this in this chapter). But with such a dramatically enlarged and new population, other things may have—indeed, *must* have—changed. Geographic, ethnic, and generational diversity collectively reshape the range of potential experiences—social, economic, and political—that together account for Latino life in the United States. So although some things remain largely as the literature suggests, there is at least the potential for others to have changed drastically.

What exactly has changed and with what effect?

First, the Latino population is much larger and represents a larger share of the national population. The 2006 American Community Survey of the U.S. Census Bureau estimates that Latinos make up 14.8% of the U.S. population while African Americans are 12% (U.S. Census Bureau 2006). Unlike African Americans, however, Latinos are projected to grow as a percentage of the population; African Americans are expected to remain at their current proportion. One projection estimates that by 2050 Latinos will make up almost 25% of the population; Caucasians may be a slim majority at 52% of the nation's population. It is projected that Latinos might make up as much as 33% of the population in 2100 (U.S. Census Bureau 2002).

Second, the national origin of the U.S. Latino population is increasingly diverse. People of Mexican origin have been in the United States in sizable numbers since at least the end of the war between Mexico and the United States in 1848; Puerto Ricans became part of the United States in 1898 as a result of the Spanish-American War. Some people of Cuban origin have lived in the United States since its earliest days, but significant numbers have come to this country since 1960 as a result of the Cuban Revolution. In 1990, people of Mexican descent represented 60.3% of Latinos in the United States; Puerto Ricans made up 12.2%, and Cubans 4.7%. By 2006, those of Mexican descent increased to make up 64.2% of all Latinos; however, substantial immigration from the Latin Caribbean, Central America, and South America reduced the percentage of Puerto Ricans and Cubans to 9.0% and 3.4%, respectively. Dominicans now make up 2.8% of all Latinos; those from countries in Central America comprise 7.6%, those from South America are 5.5%, and those self-described as "Other Hispanic or Latino" comprise 7.7% (U.S. Census Bureau 2006).

Third, Latino population growth is driven by both continued immigration and native birth. IRCA regularized the immigration status of a significant number of people, none of whom were eligible to enter the citizenry, much less the electorate, when the first LNPS was conducted in 1989–1990. Subsequent research documented reluctance on the part of the Mexican American population to naturalize and generally found consistently low levels of political participation among those who did (DeSipio 1996). However, changes in Mexican nationality law and the natural progression of those newly documented to citizenship eligibility resulted in a boom in naturalization beginning in the early to mid-1990s. In California, for example, this boom was accelerated further by the politicization of ethnicity resulting from immigrant-targeted ballot initiatives and by immigrant-unfriendly provisions of the 1996 Personal Responsibility and Work Opportunity Reconciliation Act (PL 104-193), more commonly known as "welfare reform." However, the largest source of population growth has not been immigration, but native births. For example, although only 44.4% of all Latinos currently residing in the United States are native born, 85.6% of all Latinos under age eighteen years are native born, whereas 39.4% of Latinos over eighteen are native born.

Fourth, the 2000 Census shows that Latinos now have a clear national presence, no longer confined to the Southwestern states, Florida, New York City, and Chicago. In 1990, Latinos were the largest minority group in only 16 of the 50 states, and their share of the population exceeded 5% in only 15 states. In 2000, Latinos outnumbered all other minorities in 23 states, and their population exceeded 5% in 23 states. Table 1-1 lists the states that experienced the largest percentage growth in their Latino populations between 1990 and 2000. Although Latinos still represent relatively small percentages of their respective state populations, the top four states in terms of percentage growth were North Carolina (394%), Arkansas (337%), Georgia (300%), and Tennessee (278%), states without any history of significant Latino presence before the mid-1990s.

The importance of this geographic dispersion should not be underestimated. These population growth rates might appear inflated as a consequence of the very low starting point. But in states like Georgia, Nevada, and North Carolina, the growth is so substantial that the population numbers are sufficient to begin triggering federal Voting Rights Act claims for representation at the state legislative and—soon—congressional level. That is, the actual number of Latinos in these locales is beginning to have significant political implications.

TABLE 1-1 STATES WITH THE LARGEST
PERCENTAGE LATINO POPULATION
INCREASE, 1990–2000

State	Percent Change	Total Latino Population
North Carolina	394	378,963
Arkansas	337	86,666
Georgia	300	435,227
Tennessee	278	123,838
Nevada	217	393,970
South Carolina	211	95,067
Alabama	208	75,830
Kentucky	173	59,939
Minnesota	166	143,382
Nebraska	155	94,425
Iowa	153	82,473
Mississippi	148	39,569

Fifth, Latino voters are now the recipients of overtures from both major political parties and from national, state, and local candidates for public office. At least since the 1960s, Latino voters in states such as Texas and California have received targeted campaigning from candidates running in contested elections. This was the case when the Kennedy campaign established their Viva Kennedy Clubs and Richard Nixon pursued his "Hispanic Strategy" in his 1972 reelection campaign. In 2000, however, something unprecedented happened. The Bush campaign chose to make his knowledge of and respect for Latino communities a foundational part of his broader public image to portray him as a "compassionate conservative" to the entire country. Although it can be argued that this approach was more symbolic than substantive, it is hard to deny that the Bush campaign mainstreamed Latinos as potentially important players in American national politics (Fraga and Leal 2004). Moreover, Latino population growth has sometimes translated into electoral growth that has made Latino voters a key segment of electoral victories in important states. Although Latinos make up only a small percentage of the overall national electorate, they are located in states that are of strategic importance to both Republican and Democratic candidates. California is now one of the strongest Democratic states in the country because Latino voters, now estimated at approximately 17% of the statewide electorate, vote Democratic at margins of about 7 to 3, thus being key determinants of Democratic victories when the white vote splits relatively closely. Latino voters in Florida have been very significant components of close Republican and sometimes even Democratic statewide victories in recent elections. The continued growth in the Latino electorate in key states in the Southwest, including Nevada, Arizona, Colorado, and New Mexico, made these states key targets of 2008 presidential candidates. Do Latinos see themselves as key players in contested elections? How does one reconcile this apparent position of Latino voters as important to attaining winning margins of victory with the way that Latino immigrants are often targeted for deportation in much of the current immigration debate?

Sixth, the number of Latino and Latina elected officials has grown consistently over the past twenty years and there is every reason to believe that their number will continue to grow at significant rates.

The National Association of Latino Elected and Appointed Officials counted 4,004 Latino elected officials in 1990. By 2006, that number was just over 5,600, a nearly 40% increase. The plurality of these officials serves on school boards and city councils, local levels of government responsible for critical services affecting Latino children and the quality of life of Latino families. Latinos have also increased their presence in state legislatures. In California, for example, Latino members of both the Assembly and the Senate are a critical component of their respective Democratic caucuses. By 2008, California had its third Latino Speaker of the Assembly. In that year, three Latinos served in the U.S. Senate: Ken Salazar (D-CO), Robert Menendez (D-NJ), and Mel Martinez (R-FL). Bill Richardson, a Latino of mixed Caucasian and Mexican heritage who is the current governor of New Mexico, was a declared candidate to be the Democratic nominee for President of the United States in the 2008 presidential primaries. In 2009, Sonia Sotomayor was confirmed as the first Latina justice on the Supreme Court. How does this growth in Latino political representation affect senses of Latino political efficacy? As a result of this increase in descriptive representation, do Latinos feel more a part of American society? Do they see politics as a way to further enhance their chances for upward mobility in the United States?

The dramatic changes we have just recounted—rapid population growth, national origin diversification, geographic dispersion, clear growth in Latino political incorporation as voters and as elected officials—all portend significant variation in the social, economic, and political experiences of America's Latino population. New settlements in the South and rural Midwest expose Latinos to entirely new social contexts with interesting results—some predictable, some less so. Similarly, the growth of second- and third-generation cohorts suggests the emergence of a Latino population whose experiences with American society, grasp of American politics, and sense of power in American politics may differ considerably from earlier cohorts. The mixing of previously distinct (and geographically distant) national-origin communities such as Mexicans, Puerto Ricans, and Cubans, as well as the arrival of larger numbers of new communities such as Dominicans, Salvadorans, Colombians, and others, raises new questions about pan-ethnic identification, cooperation, and competition, a demographic reality almost unheard of just 15 years ago.

It is, indeed, likely that all of these changes will have some effect on Latino attitudes, views, and social experiences. The first challenge in this project, then, was for us to set aside our long-held expectations, expectations generally fortified by the academic literature, but driven by a social and political reality long-past.

The Presence—and Significance— of Continuity

A second characteristic of social scientists is to regard social change as interesting—more interesting, in fact, than social continuity. Few papers find their way into the pages of the *American Political Science Review* or the *American Sociological Review* whose findings can be summarized as entirely consistent with previous work and with intuitive expectations—no difference, no change, nothing new. For that reason (and others), there is a fetishism of change in the social science community that actually might be inherently misleading in other ways. Specifically, by focusing on change and its legion of potential causes—demographic and otherwise—we overlook the many circumstances of Latino Americans today that look very much like they did a generation ago. This level of continuity should be interesting, however, because it serves as potential evidence of important social forces that we must address.

Specifically, with significant change in the geographic diversity of the Latino population, the presence of more and more varied generations, and the growth of Latino political power, the persistence of one or more social indicators—for example, Latino poverty or high school dropout rates—must, of necessity, suggest the presence of social forces *not* endogenous to the demography. That is, the absence of change on important measures of social well-being, political engagement, or any other dimension highlights an underlying "sameness" in the experiences of Latinos in the United States across time and space.

From where might this similarity of life experiences originate? Some might suggest some form of cultural deficiency; that is, one or more cultural elements common to Latinos across national-origin groups and across generations and cohorts that shape outcomes on key measures. The evidence for these claims has always been suspect and the evidence to the contrary palpable (see Hero 1992).

Alternatively, persistently poor showings on a variety of social indicators may suggest the presence of one or more structural disadvantages, structures that transcend generations and exact a toll on most Latinos—those coming of age in the late 1980s and those today, twenty years later—in a similar manner. Likely candidates may include white flight from school systems, persistently hostile reception among Anglos (non-Hispanic whites) in the United States, and other opportunities foreclosed.

Whatever the cause, it is our contention here that social constancy is as interesting and important as social change. Our second challenge in this project, one as important as the first, was not simply to assume that everything we knew was wrong, outdated, or even eroding significantly. Some of the received knowledge of the earlier generation of work likely still applies.

Confounding Elements of Complexity in Latino America

Examining these elements of continuity and change is made somewhat more difficult by the exceeding complexity of the phenomena at issue. It may seem trite and somewhat obvious to identify complexity as an issue—after all, most social phenomena are complex. We suggest, however, that specific characteristics of Latino populations introduce levels of complexity that complicate and confound our efforts to capture the nature of Latino life in the United States today. Specifically, diversification by generation, national origin, and legal status, as well as widely disparate perceptions of Latino identity and place in American society, make generalization treacherous and conclusions profoundly contingent.

A number of examples illustrate this point, we believe. A significant share of foreign-born Latinos in the United States—and a share of both our focus group subjects and survey respondents—are unauthorized immigrants. When we query subjects about their comfort level in their new communities, their perceptions of government responsiveness, or their willingness to engage non-Latinos in social and political relations, the answers must be contingent on this question of status. An answer detailing significant social alienation or distrust in government means different things coming from a U.S. citizen of Latino ancestry than it does from an unauthorized immigrant, whose alienation or mistrust might well be justified or, from the standpoint of survival and safety, even advisable.

A second example raises the important issue of nationality differences and how they might interact with immigration and opportunities for transnational communities. Cuban immigrants, as a consequence of U.S. policy, face a very different and more accepting immigration regime than Mexicans on the one hand, but have a much more difficult time maintaining contact and family relations with individuals back in Cuba on the other. Contrast both of these experiences with that of Puerto Ricans, whose status as U.S. citizens affords them the greatest political rights of any group and the freest opportunity for contact, travel, and circular migration, opportunities that are far more difficult for unauthorized Mexican immigrants and essentially impossible for many Cubans. The effect of these differences can cut in surprising and unexpected ways. When we examine questions of community building and civic and political engagement in the United States among those born elsewhere, the opportunity is undoubtedly greatest for Puerto Ricans. But the motivation to build a life and community here in the absence of meaningful access to circular or reverse migration—may well be greatest for Cubans or unauthorized Mexicans.

Generation and identity with pan-ethnic labels such "Hispanic" and "Latino" vary in important ways as well. Some third-, fourth-, or nth-generation Latinos in the United States may have entirely different perceptions of American society and their place in it when compared to newcomers; alternatively, they may have surprising empathy for the circumstances of newcomers if collective memories of the immigration experience—or direct social or familial connection with others of more recent vintage—sensitizes them to these realities. Similarly, identification with pan-ethnic labels varies across individuals and may be driven by the proximity of Latinos to other national-origin groups, levels of political awareness and interest, or even something as simple as familiarity with racial and ethnic terminology in American society. To the extent that collective political action and interests presuppose an awareness of commonalities and a sympathy of interests, variation in generation, empathy for the immigration experience, and sense of pan-ethnic solidarity will inevitably shape individual Latinos' perceptions of the American experience.

Our point, of course, is that we cannot merely describe "a" Latino experience but, rather, because of clearly identifiable and important social, legal, and political forces, we must identify a variety of modalities of Latino experiences and the forces that shape them. Throughout this effort, we endeavor to illustrate when and where these complexities challenge our received knowledge and circumscribe our conclusions.

Searching for Community

Returning for a moment to the immigration marches in 2006, we noted earlier that one important and symbolic element of the marches was an effort on the part of those participating to stake a claim to membership in American society. Apart from the obvious, including flags and the like, marchers carried signs regarding work, family, and community. Slogans illustrated the specific roles filled by immigrants in American society, the assertion that our current immigration regime was unjust, and perhaps most poignantly, reminders that apart from Native Americans, we are *all* immigrants. Apart from the proximate message calling for significant reform of the immigration process, the intent of the messages was clear: The marches were a call for inclusion.

Building a community in the United States is a theme that appears frequently in the coming chapters. We illustrate in considerable detail how Latino aspirations in U.S. society are remarkably reminiscent of the "American dream." We discuss the progress and difficulties Latinos face in creating pan-ethnic identity and consciousness, a matter of considerable importance in locales where there is considerable diversity in national origin among the Latino population. We are reminded at this juncture of a comment made by an elected official in Miami. He reported considerable angst among Cuban American leaders about the growth of non-Cuban Latino populations in South Florida. He wanted us to tell him how to mobilize and incorporate these new populations into the pre-existing political machine—in short, how to make a Cuban political power base a "Latino" political power base. The salience of this concern was evident on his face. A few moments later, another group participant, discussing the issue of identity and pan-ethnicity, raised a somewhat different concern. He was Bolivian, his wife Cuban. "What is our daughter?" he wanted to know. Easy—"*Cuban!*" answered the elected official, sporting a big smile (emphasis most definitely in the original).

We also examine the sometimes pleasant and sometimes hostile interactions with non-Hispanic neighbors, co-workers, and even in-laws, and the persistent recognition that language, accent, skin color, and name often continue to conspire to exclude many from the full realization of that American dream. Can Latinos be part of American society if they are unwelcome? Can civic and political incorporation occur if socioeconomic mobility is difficult or, for some, even impossible?

Finding a home in America is shown to be more urgent than we might otherwise realize. Though a large share of Latinos in the United States are foreign born, it is safe to say that, for many, you really can't go home again. Several of our foreign-born subjects, in different ways, communicated a growing unease with the communities and societies they left. Different subjects had different takes. One man expressed a desire to return home to Mexico but lamented that his children would never stand for it. Others reported going to their home country for a visit and then immediately being anxious for the visit to end, either because of physical discomforts and deprivations or merely a sense of not belonging. Still others—especially women—flat out reported feeling that life and opportunities were better for them in the United States.

The lesson drawn from their words and others is that, while Latinos and Latino immigrants are most certainly changing America, America is—in important ways—changing them too. Whether the processes of assimilation and acculturation are chosen or merely passively experienced, Latinos in the United States, even foreign-born Latinos—are *not* Latin Americans. They are something different, having experienced at least a partial metamorphosis in the United States. "Latino" is an inherently American identity. Latino or Hispanic identity, and the lives, views, and preferences of those to whom we refer, cannot be understood outside the context of U.S. society and politics. Exactly how that identity is formed, shaped, and differs from other Americans is something we discuss in detail in the coming pages.

Change, Continuity, Complexity, and Community

With the discussion of community, our thematic structure is complete. In this effort, the six of us set out to illustrate the forces shaping the formation of the Latino community in the United States. That process of community formation is simultaneously a search for self-definition on the part of the almost 50 million Americans of Latin American ancestry and a search for acceptance and inclusion by the remaining 250 million non-Hispanics in the greater economy, society, and polity. In that exploration of community, we take particular note of how aspects of that search and the challenges faced reflect the continuity of nearly identical experiences of Latinos in previous generations, and how—at least on some dimensions and particularly with respect to the sheer magnitude of the Latino population and its impact—those experiences might have changed considerably. In all instances, we try to situate the experiences reported within the unique circumstances and variations that complicate our examination but ultimately, we hope, enrich our understanding.

Our Focus Group Approach

It is because of these multiple challenges that a focus group methodology was our first resort in identifying and mapping the contours of Latino life in America. While survey research was our ultimate goal and a more familiar terrain for most of us, we worried that we did not have enough information about the instances of continuity, change, and complexity or a full understanding of exactly how Latinos were creating lives and communities within the United States. We did not wish to write yet another questionnaire based on erroneous assumptions—in this case, that little had changed, or that everything had.

To that end, we began our project in a straightforward way, by gathering information through simply speaking with a broad and diverse array of ordinary Latinos in America. We hoped to gauge their sentiments and views on life—economic, social, and political—in the United States. Most of the material we discuss in the coming pages comes from these formal focus groups conducted among those everyday folks. Naturally, our impressions are also informed by extensive interactions with policy advocates, leaders of community-based organizations, elected officials, academics, union officials, immigrant advocates, civil rights attorneys, and others in and around various Latino communities across the United States.[1]

Focus groups are a research technique whereby data is collected through group interactions on topics determined by the researcher (Morgan 1993: 130). These can be conducted in more or less directive interview styles and with more or less structured question formats, depending on the purposes of the particular project.

This methodology is used widely across the social sciences and related fields, including communication studies, education, marketing, and public health (Morgan 1996: 132). While Morgan notes that some form of group interviewing has no doubt existed from the very beginning of the social sciences (Morgan 1996: 129; Bogardus 1926; Merton, Fiske, and Kendall 1956), interest in the use of focus groups in the social sciences has expanded significantly only since the 1990s (Krueger 1994; Knodel, Havanon, and Sittitrai 1990; Stewart and Shamdasani 1990; Vaughn, Shumm, and Sinagub 1996). As a consequence, focus group research is still seen as a relative newcomer in the social sciences.

In part because of their recent adoption and application in the social sciences, focus groups are most often seen used in conjunction with other research methods, particularly surveys, either to help develop the survey instrumentation or to aid in interpreting survey results. They are used to generate hypotheses and to stimulate new ideas, creative concepts, evaluations, and impressions (Bishoping 1999; DeMaio et al. 1993; Forsyth and Lessler 1991; Morgan 1988, 1996; Stewart and Shamdasani 1990). Barbour notes that in addition focus groups are often used to ensure that the questions being asked are appropriate, easily understood by respondents (Barbour 2005: n 7–9), and contextually relevant (Barbour 2005: n 10). Focus groups are also useful in designing culturally sensitive survey methodology (Barbour 2005: n 11–12; Bishoping 1999). In fact, these reasons were part of the original purpose for the inclusion of focus groups as part of the Latino National Survey (LNS) project: Focus groups were included to help develop the study's framework and instrument.

However, focus groups have also increasingly been used on their own as a "self-contained" method (Morgan 1996: 130; Sigel 1996). Group interviews can be seen, in some respects, as an intermediary method between personal/individual interviews and surveys with a broader range of respondents. Focus groups allow researchers to get reactions "from a relatively wide range of participants in a relatively short time" (Morgan 1996: 134). On the one hand, they provide greater breadth than individual interviews, although individual interviews might allow greater "depth"—that is, more time with each interviewee (Crabtree et al. 1993: 134). On the other hand, while focus groups on the whole do not allow for participation of the numbers of respondents typically included in survey research, in exchange they offer researchers some insight into the subjective experience of individuals, beyond simply a recitation of their opinions, attitudes, and attributes. As one leading researcher noted, "Focus groups are useful when it comes to investigating what participants think, but they excel at uncovering *why* participants think as they do" (Morgan, cited in Barbour 2005: n 38; Morgan 1996: 139; Morgan and Kreuger 1993; see also Fern 1982).

The focus groups conducted by the research team for the project presented here offer precisely this convergence of both breadth and depth. The team used a common protocol to guide discussion in fifteen focus groups—with more than 150 participants in nine cities across eight states—that were designed to include either Spanish- and English-speaking respondents, in different regions of the country, with differing compositions by generation and country of origin. The number and range of the participants in these Latino focus groups are unique in the social science literature. While the focus groups were originally conducted to aid in the development of a larger survey of Latino residents in the United States, it quickly became clear that the transcripts they generated were a significant data source in and of themselves.

Focus groups have other strengths as well. As other researchers have pointed out, focus groups allow access to hard-to-reach groups (Barbour 2005: n 1; Morgan 1996: 133). The LNS, with its focus on Latino residents in the United States, faced a considerable potential obstacle in the number of Latinos in the United States who are undocumented. To our surprise, though never directly asked in the focus group protocols, many of the focus group participants freely volunteered information about their legal status in the United States. Presumably the relative comfort among participants taking part in a group conversation among Latinos facilitated these confidences.

The group dynamics present in this form of research are also one of its strengths: "What makes the discussion in focus groups more than the sum of separate individual interviews is the fact that the participants both query each other and explain themselves to each other" (Morgan 1996: 139). Morgan and Kreuger emphasize that this interaction provides valuable data on the extent of consensus and disagreement among participants (Morgan and Kreuger 1993), an attribute of the data used to full effect in this book project.

Two central concerns about focus groups relate to the generalizability of their findings and their comparability to findings using other methods. Several studies have analyzed these differences (Folch-Lyon et al. 1981; Saint-Germain et al. 1993; Ward et al. 1991). In each case the authors found that focus groups confirmed the findings uncovered using other methods (primarily surveys), differing only in going beyond the survey data by providing more in-depth information and detail on the topic at hand (Delli Carpini and Williams 1994; Morgan 1996: 137). There is, nonetheless, a tradeoff between the two approaches of focus groups and surveys: Focus groups allow for more depth than surveys, allowing open-ended responses to questions and eliciting responses that get at participants' interpretation and meaning that are simply not possible in surveys; however, the limitation is that focus groups can typically cover only a fraction of the topics typically covered by a survey and the findings are not usually suitable for quantitative analysis.

In sum, this book presents the results of a unique data set—the results of fifteen focus groups conducted across the United States with Latino residents, including foreign-born—both legal and undocumented immigrants—and native-born. These data provide more range than allowed by the typical interview-based project and not only give key insights into Latino residents' thoughts about community, language, discrimination, ties to their countries of origin, and the like, but also provide some sense of participants' explanations of their reasoning and motivations, something not achievable through structured survey data alone.

Table 1-2 shows the date and time, language in which the discussion was conducted, targeted ancestry, and location for each of our focus groups; Table 1-3 summarizes the demographic characteristics of the participants. In retrospect, the choice of cities and locations, the allocation of various acculturation segments for the groups, and

TABLE 1-2   SUMMARY OF LOGISTIC DETAILS OF LNS 2003
            FOCUS GROUPS

Group	Date	Time	Language	Ancestry	Location
A	May 3	11 A.M.–12:30 P.M.	English	Mexican, Central American	Houston
B	May 3	1:30–3 P.M.	Spanish	Mexican, Central American	Houston
C	May 5	6–7:30 P.M.	English	Mexican	Los Angeles
D	May 5	8–9:30 P.M.	Spanish	Mexican, Central American, Other	Los Angeles
E	May 9	6–7:30 P.M.	Spanish	Mexican	Dalton, GA
F	May 10	12–1:30 P.M.	Spanish	Dominican, Puerto Rican, other	New York
G	May 10	2–3:30 P.M.	English	Puerto Rican	New York
H	May 12	6–7:30 P.M.	Spanish	Cuban, South American, other	Miami
I	May 12	8–9:30 P.M.	English	Cuban, other	Miami
J	May 19	2–3:30 P.M.	English	Mexican	Muscatine, IA
K	May 19	7–8:30 P.M.	Spanish	Mexican	West Liberty, IA
L	May 15	6–7:30 P.M.	Spanish	Central American,	Washington, DC
M	May 15	8–9:30 P.M.	English	Central American,	Washington, DC
N	June 19	7–8:30 P.M.	Spanish	Central American	Washington, DC

LNS = Latino National Survey

the diversity of national origin achieved combined to deliver a good set of respondents that is reasonably representative of the U.S. Latino adult population. For example, the gender and age diversity approximate that of the larger Latino population. Also the proportion of participants from each national-origin group reflects the proportional ranking of national-origin groups in the United States. Of particular importance, the participants represent the full spectrum of "generational distance," including second, third, or higher generations of U.S.-born as well as immigrants in the full continuum of exposure to the United States—from "newcomers" who have spent a small fraction of their lives here to "transplants" who have been in the United states much of their lives. However, Latinos with little or no formal education and annual incomes below $15,000 are somewhat under-represented among the group participants whose education and income levels are known.[2]

TABLE 1-3   DEMOGRAPHIC CHARACTERISTICS OF
FOCUS GROUP PARTICIPANTS

Demographic	Description	Number	Percentage
Gender	Male	66	51
	Female	64	49
Age	Less than 30	41	31
	30–39	35	27
	40–54	33	25
	More than 50	18	14
	Not known	3	2
National origin	Mexico	58	44
	Puerto Rico	17	13
	Chile	1	<1
	Cuba	7	5
	Colombia	5	4
	El Salvador	9	7
	Nicaragua	5	4
	Guatemala	8	6
	Dominican Republic	3	2
	Peru	3	2
	Spain	2	1
	Ecuador	1	<1
	Panama	2	1
	Paraguay	2	1
	Bolivia	1	<1
	Uruguay	2	1
	Venezuela	1	<1
	Mixed Latino	4	3
Nativity	U.S.	42	32
	Not U.S.	88	68
Generational	Third or More Generation	23	17
distance*	Second Generation	19	15
	First Generation Transplants	38	29
	First Generation Transitionals	29	22
	First Generation Newcomers	22	17
Education	Less than 9 years	14	11
	9–11 years	14	11
	12 years	29	22
	13–15 years	28	21
	More than 16 years	35	27
	Not known	11	8
Income	Less than $20,000	19	15
	$20,000–$39,999	47	36
	$40,000–$60,000	31	24
	More than $60,0000	23	17
	Not known	11	8

*Definitions: *First Generation Newcomers*: Born in a foreign country; spent <¼ of life in United States. *First Generation Transitionals*: Born in foreign country; spent ¼ to ½ of life in United States. *First Generation Transplants*: Born in a foreign country; spent at least ½ of life in United States. *Second Generation*: Born in United States with at least one immigrant parent. *Third Generation*: Born in United States with both parents born in United States. (Note: These figures do not include a 15th focus group conducted with working-class Latino participants in Washington, DC.)

Obviously, a set of fifteen focus groups in diverse communities cannot adequately fill all the possible sociodemographic cells. Some of the gaps we identify are among the most difficult to recruit for focus groups or for social research in general. However, in Washington, DC, we benefited by inadvertently ending up with valuable input from persons employed in the public sector, who provided opinions not found as commonly in other places. Similarly, in Houston, we benefited from having a group of fairly assimilated Latinos who tried hard to appear "Latino" by participating in the Spanish language groups when clearly English was their dominant language. To some extent, these participants provided us with another view of the complexity and diversity of Latinos and of the potential tendency for some reverse acculturation.

Beyond demographic characteristics, it is worth noting that the groups had wide variation in manner of self-expression; there were highly marginal and vulnerable persons (largely due to their immigration status) who were almost afraid to be interviewed, and there were very vocal and sophisticated persons who were highly engaged in social and political activity. The groups also contained persons whose lives are totally segregated from American society and persons who are totally at ease in the majority culture.

The Latino National Survey

These focus groups were completed to better inform the final development of the questionnaire that was used in our 2006 LNS. The LNS was a forty-minute telephone survey of 8,634 self-identified Latino/Hispanic residents of the United States. It was in the field from November 17, 2005, to August 4, 2006. The questionnaire had approximately 165 items, including questions about policy preferences, political behavior, political attitudes, and a wide set of sociodemographics. Respondents were given the opportunity to speak either English or Spanish at the beginning of the survey. All interviewers were bilingual.

Representative samples of Latino households were drawn from fifteen states and the District of Columbia metropolitan area. The fifteen states were Arizona, Arkansas, California, Colorado, Florida, Georgia, Illinois, Iowa, Nevada, New Jersey, New Mexico, New York, North Carolina, Texas, and Washington. This group includes states with historically large concentrations of Latinos and those with Latino populations that have arrived more recently. Approximately 87.5% of all Latinos in the United States live in the above described areas. As indicated in Appendix A, some state samples were further stratified by specific substate geographical areas to facilitate within-state comparisons. Each state sample is a valid, stand-alone representation of the respective state's Latino population. A minimum of 400 respondents were drawn from each state. California had a minimum of 1,200 respondents; Florida, Texas, and New York had 800; and Illinois had 600. Each state's sampling error was ±5%. The national margin of error is approximately ±1.05%. All reported data are weighted to be nationally representative.

We use data from the LNS and from other selected national surveys to supplement the narratives that emerge from our focus groups and, when appropriate, to establish a baseline to demonstrate how much continuity and change across selected dimensions of Latino life in the United States are present. Additionally, we are able to use data from the LNS to demonstrate how representative the focus group narratives are of more systematic trends in experiences and views within Latino communities.

Latino Realities in Contemporary Society

The data drawn from the focus groups alone represent thousands of comments, questions, and points of emphasis made by our diverse pool of subjects. They are rich in ways we did not anticipate, and more than once ideas and arguments emerged that were completely unanticipated by the six of us. In short, we learned a lot from the narratives our subjects offered regarding their lives and the lives of their friends and families. While it is tempting to report on everything our subjects offered, we choose instead to identify the distinct themes and topics of emphasis that emerged from these narratives of Latino lives in the contemporary United States. The scope of these areas of examination serves to portray essential elements of the status and experiences of Latinos in a variety of settings, communicating in different languages, and from different backgrounds and national origins.

A note about national-origin differences: As many commentators and researchers have pointed out, differences among Latinos from different national-origin groups can be as significant as those between

Latinos and other ethnic or racial groups. Cuban Americans, for example, have consistently expressed a closer affiliation to the Republican Party and a more conservative bent on some public policy issues than Latinos of Mexican origin. Mexican immigrants, for their part, are considerably more conservative on social issues than either Puerto Ricans or Cuban Americans. In the chapters that follow we point out national-origin differences whenever they appear relevant. Some chapters highlight similarities and differences among Latinos from multiple national-origin groups. Chapter 6, on Latinos' transnational ties, for instance, mentions Puerto Rican respondents' comments about their relationship with both the United States and New York City. But in general national-origin differences were muted in the focus groups, even when the groups drew from several national-origin groups. Sometimes, unfortunately, this was because national origin could not be discerned from the transcripts, which did not always allow us to identify individuals' national origins from what was said. It is also the case, however, that in some groups national-origin differences were entirely absent. For example, Latino residents in the Midwest are overwhelmingly of Mexican descent, so national-origin differences simply never come into play in our discussion of Latinos in rural America (Chapter 5). This is all to say that we were deeply attuned to the differences, as well as to the possible commonalities, among the participants in these focus groups, and the chapters that follow paint a picture that we hope captures the Latino population in the United States with all its nuances and complexities.

In Chapter 2, Trying for the *Americano* Dream: Barriers to Making the United States "Home," we examine the extent to which our focus group participants identify the quintessential "American dream" as their life goal, and their experiences—good and bad—in trying to achieve that outcome. We begin by comparing their opinions with those of other working Americans on what the American dream means and the perceived barriers to its achievement. We then trace how subjects informed us on questions as diverse as how residential segregation, job opportunities, legal status, and education shaped this path to inclusion, social mobility, and the American dream. We move beyond socioeconomic mobility, then, to examine what our subjects had to say about actually "being" American. We again look at a variety of aspects of assimilation and incorporation, including linguistic, marital, cultural, and structural elements. We consider the role that assimilation plays in the pursuit of life goals by looking specifically for indicators of assimilation in the respondents' reported behavior and in their evaluations of other Latinos' success at achieving their dreams.

We turn our attention in Chapter 3 to what is likely the most salient element of both socioeconomic mobility and assimilation: the education system. In Education: Latinos' Great Hope, America's Harsh Reality, we examine the policy arena that continues to most directly affect the chances for Latino upward mobility in the United States. We begin by noting the importance that Latinos give to education, as captured in a number of national surveys; the tremendous growth in Latino presence among public school students across the entire country; and the way that current education reform efforts specifically affect opportunities for Latino educational attainment. We do this to highlight three specific dimensions of assessment of educational systems in the United States revealed by our respondents: (1) the importance Latinos ascribe to education in determining their chances at upward mobility, (2) how schools affect assessments of the quality of neighborhood life overall, and (3) the perceived quality of education in large urban school districts where many Latinos attend public schools. Unlike some previous findings that suggest that elements of many Latinos' cultural values are at odds with academic achievement, our respondents reveal a set of values, experiences, and expectations regarding education and American public schools that is fully consistent with mainstream American values.

Chapter 4 focuses on the other principal impediment both to social mobility and to incorporation, specifically prejudice and discrimination. In Exploring Discrimination and Intergroup and Intragroup Relations among Latinos, we briefly review previous evidence from surveys, then explore our participants' perceptions of intergroup and *intra*group relations, including their personal experiences of discrimination. The focus group discussions demonstrate a wide range of differing views on these issues. We hear signs of despair and continuing frustration regarding both relationships with other Latinos and with other racial and ethnic groups generally. However, we also hear voices asserting positive change and improvement. Immigrants seem to be more optimistic than members of later generations, but overall the focus groups portray a sense of the complexity and great variety of views on these matters. In addition to illustrating perceptions of discrimination, the comments by participants suggest hypotheses that should be tested in future studies.

In Chapter 5, New Homes in New Communities: Living in Rural America, we explore how Latino settlement in rural and agricultural communities—in the Farm Belt, the South, and the interior Pacific Northwest—clearly illustrates both the continuing problems facing Latinos, but also some of the positive changes stemming from changing patterns of immigrant settlement. On the one hand, white flight from public schools, severe residential segregation, patterns of political exclusion, and a complete lack of political representation echo the experiences of generations past and suggest that long-rehearsed patterns of political contestation between Latinos and other Americans will be reenacted in these new settings. On the other hand, Latino inmigration has meant substantial economic and population growth in long-declining areas and noticeably reinvigorated local economies and industries. Coupled with the low crime and quality schools in some of these areas, as well as social engagements with non-Latinos that are often positive or at least more nuanced than in other areas of the country, the day-to-day life of many of these new arrivals is perceptively better than in other, more established locations and in past periods of Latino settlement.

In Chapter 6, Transnationalism and the Language of Belonging, we explore the ties Latinos maintain with their countries of origin. The dramatic increase in Latin American immigration to the United States, the barriers these new Latino residents encounter as they try to achieve the American dream, and the ease of communication and travel to immigrants' countries of origins would all seem to point to the likelihood that immigrants would retain strong ties to their countries of origin. This, we were surprised to learn, is not necessarily so. We find in our focus groups a surprising amount of ambivalence about immigrants' connections with their countries of birth. While Latino immigrants do, indeed, maintain affective ties to their countries of origin, these ties serve to refresh immigrants' memories of the reasons that impelled them to leave in the first place and are a particularly salient indicator of how their lives, beliefs, and expectations have changed. Indirectly, then, transnational ties appear to reinforce Latinos' sense of attachment and belonging in the United States. Transnationalism and assimilation, then, are not only complementary, but may actually be mutually reinforcing.

In Chapter 7, The Evolving Latino Community and Pan-ethnicity: Explorations into the Confluence of Interactions, Networks, and Identity, we examine relations between the various Latino national-origin groups and, in particular, the growing sense of pan-ethnic identification. We begin with a brief discussion of the concept of pan-ethnicity, including how it has been characterized and measured in the past. Then, we turn to the focus group narratives to identify the principal elements of community among Latinos and how those ties are reflected in daily life. If a pan-ethnic community has, in fact, emerged, we want to find out whether it is a consequence of shared values, language, social networks, or something altogether different. We also want to know how national origin and other salient identities may interact with or relate to pan-ethnic consciousness. Similar to the findings of past research, the focus groups reveal that identity and social networking based on country of origin continues to be a prominent feature in the lives of many Latinos. However, we also see that the prominence of national origins has not precluded the development of pan-ethnic and American identities. Moreover, the content and weight of both participants' comments and LNS responses indicates the clear presence of a pan-ethnic (Latino) community that is self-conscious and politically meaningful.

We conclude the book in Chapter 8 by integrating these findings with an eye to the future. In Conclusions: Paradoxes along the Way to Making America Home, we assess the process of contemporary Latino incorporation in the United States, a process that is best understood as a series of paradoxes and tensions. We highlight the numerous contradictions discovered in the beliefs and experiences of Latinos and consider what this means for their future success and acceptance in mainstream America.

The strength of our study, as well as the source of its inspiration, is that we "hear" from ordinary Latinos "in their own words." The analytical questions that we pose serve to underscore the complexities of living as a Latino in 21st century America, and increasingly of living in America for many citizens and residents of the United States. The responses of our participants are filled with insights, frustrations, expectations, and dreams. The questions also serve to organize our understanding of these important phenomena. Most important, however, are the verbatim responses of the focus group participants. Together, the extended conversations with Latino focus group participants, in combination with references to selected survey data, provide a window into the continuity, change, and complexity of the growing and diverse population of Latinos in the United States. This book digs beneath the surface of journalistic takes and ten-minute polls to provide an in-depth view of the experiences of Latinos and the way they think and talk about themselves as individuals, their identities, their families, their communities, and the larger nation of which they are such a growing part.

Appendix A: Latino National Survey (LNS) Geographic Sample Strata within States

Jurisdiction	Geographic Needs	County
Arizona	Complete state	All counties
Arkansas	Complete state	All counties
California	Los Angeles Metro	Los Angeles, Orange, Ventura
	Inland Empire	Riverside County (western part), San Bernardino County (southwestern part)
	San Diego Metro	San Diego County
	Central Valley	Fresno, Kern, Kings, Madera, Merced, San Joaquin, Stanislaus, Tulare
	San Francisco Metro	Alameda, Contra Costa, Marin, Napa, San Francisco, San Mateo, Santa Clara, Solano, Sonoma
Colorado	Denver Metro	Adams, Arapahoe, Boulder, Broomfield, Denver, Douglas, Jefferson
	other Colorado	Remaining counties in state
District of Columbia	Washington-Arlington-Alexandria, DC-VA-MD-WV Metropolitan Statistical Area	District of Columbia; Calvert County, Charles County, Frederick County, Montgomery County, Prince George's County, MD; Arlington County, Clarke County, Fairfax County, Fauquier County, Loudoun County, Prince William County, Spotsylvania County, Stafford County, Warren County, VA; Jefferson County, WV; Alexandria city, Fairfax city, Falls Church city, Fredericksburg city, Manassas city, Manassas Park city, VA
Florida	Miami Metro	Broward, Miami-Dade, Palm Beach
	Orlando Metro	Orange, Osceola, Seminole
	Tampa Metro	Hillsborough, Pinellas

Jurisdiction	Geographic Needs	County
Georgia	Atlanta Metro	Cherokee, Clayton, Cobb, DeKalb, Douglas, Fayette, Fulton, Gwinnett
	other Georgia	Remaining counties in state
Illinois	Chicago Metro	Cook, DuPage, Grundy, Kane, Kendall, Lake, McHenry, Will
	other Illinois	Remaining counties in state
Iowa	Complete state	All counties
Nevada	Complete state	All counties
New Jersey	Complete state	All counties
New Mexico	Complete state	All counties
New York	Complete state	All counties
North Carolina	complete state	All counties
Texas	Dallas–Fort Worth	Collin, Dallas, Denton, Tarrant
	Houston Metro	Brazoria, Chambers, Fort Bend, Galveston, Harris, Liberty, Montgomery
	San Antonio Metro	Bexar, Comal, Guadalupe
	El Paso Metro	El Paso County
	Rio Grande Valley	Cameron, Dimmit, Hidalgo, Kinney, Maverick, Starr, Val Verde, Webb, Zapata
Washington	Seattle Metro	King, Kitsap, Pierce, Snohomish
	Yakima Valley	Yakima
	other Washington	Remaining counties in state

2 Trying for the *Americano* Dream

Barriers to Making the United States "Home"

n a focus group in Los Angeles, the moderator asked our participants, "Can you ever imagine immigrating to Mexico and becoming a citizen?" The immediate response from multiple people was an emphatic NO! "Why not?" asked the moderator. One man explained: "It's the freedom here, the economy. There's no pay there." Another man simply stated: "It's the American dream." The "American dream" is a term that has been in usage for a long time by persons throughout the United States. It is a subjective expression that means different things to different people but usually implies achieving a successful and satisfying life as a result of hard work (Adams 1934; Cullen 2003). While many people measure their achievements in life in material terms, such as earning a high income or owning a house, others' perceptions of living the American dream are more abstract, typically described in terms of having personal freedom, enjoying equal rights, and ensuring safety or security for self and family (Hochschild 1995). The allure of the American dream has been pointed to as the motivation of countless generations of immigrants who came to the United States to escape the lack of opportunity and poor quality of life in their home countries. Yet, critics of Latino immigration, especially immigration from Mexico, warn that unless Latinos better assimilate into mainstream society, they will not be sharing in the "Americano dream" (Huntington 2004a).

What does "living the dream" mean to Latinos? What are they willing to do to achieve that life? What role does assimilation play in their efforts to achieve their life goals? In this chapter, we endeavor to answer these questions. Before we examine what the dream means for our focus group participants, we first examine more systematically how most people in this country think about the American dream. Then we briefly review the conceptual development and controversy of assimilation and consider whether Latinos view "assimilation"—or at least some sense of assimilation—as their path to the American dream. Finally, we look at the extent to which Latinos are integrating into majority society—becoming part of the American fabric—by focusing on select aspects of cultural, structural, and marital assimilation as evidenced in the attitudes and behaviors of our focus group participants and some of the aggregate indicators from the Latino National Survey and other studies.

Definitions, Barriers, and Attaining the American Dream

As points of comparison, before we discuss what "living the American dream" means to Latinos, we should have some idea of what the dream means for most Americans. Besides their definitions, we should know what they feel are barriers to obtaining it and to what extent they believe the dream is attainable, both personally and for other people. Two national surveys, conducted independently in 2004[1] and 2007,[2] focus on each of these topics.

The targeted populations of the two surveys were distinctly different. The 2004 survey was designed to ensure a broad representation of the total U.S. adult population. Demographic comparisons of the surveyed respondents with U.S. census data suggest the 2004 survey was highly successful in capturing the views of the general population. The 2007 survey was intended to measure the attitudes of workers in non-supervisory positions. The demographic profile of 2007 respondents was obviously less representative of the general adult population, but these comparatively younger, less educated, less affluent, and primarily blue-collar and service industry employees more closely match the aggregate characteristics of the U.S. Latino population (Ramirez and de la Cruz 2002).

In the first survey, 1,002 respondents were asked: "How do you personally define the American dream?" and were allowed to provide up to three definitions. Financial security/stability was the most frequently provided response (24%). Good jobs/careers and personal freedom tied for the second most commonly provided answer; both were cited by 14%. Having a family (13%) and living comfortably (12%) rounded out the five most mentioned definitions (National League of Cities [NLC] 2004). However, significant racial/ethnic, generational, and social class differences were apparent in the collection of definitions.

"Having choices" or "freedom" was significantly more likely to be mentioned by non-Hispanic whites 18- to 29-year-olds, college graduates, and those with household incomes over $75,000. "Financial stability" was the top definition voiced by nonwhites, blue-collar workers, and those making less than $30,000. "Good health" was the dominant factor in older respondents' version of the dream (NLC 2004: 6).

When given a predetermined list of definitions and asked to select only two, respondents' priorities changed somewhat but components of the dream remained essentially the same. "Living in freedom" became the top definition (33%), followed by "being financially secure (26%), "a quality education for my children" (17%), "having a family" (17%), and "enjoying good health" (16%). Having "a good job" (9%) dropped out of the top five, placing a somewhat distant sixth among the offered definitions, which also included "owning a home" (8%), "living in a good community" (6%), and "a secure retirement" (6%). One quarter of the respondents volunteered that everything on this list was part of their American dream (NLC 2004: 28).

When respondents were asked to select two of the most serious barriers or obstacles to achieving the dream from a list of ten items, "poor quality public education" was the most frequently chosen answer (27%). The remaining top five selections were "not being financially secure" (22%), "inability to find a good-paying job" (19%), "limited access to health care or health insurance" (17%), and "racial or ethnic discrimination" (14%). Interestingly, in a separate question, respondents were asked whether they agreed with the statement "Where I live (community, city, or town) has limited my ability to achieve the American dream" and 31% agreed (NLC 2004: 29, 31).

According to this survey, however, Americans remain optimistic about their personal situation: Two thirds of the respondents said they were currently living the American dream. Among those who reported they were *not* living the dream, a majority were still somewhat (33%) or very confident (19%) that they eventually would. They had considerably less confidence in others' abilities; 67% agreed with the statement "The American dream is becoming more difficult for average people to obtain," and 70% also agreed that "It is becoming much harder for young families to achieve" (NLC 2004: 30).

In the second comparison survey, a national sample of 800 nonsupervisory workers[3] was asked an open-ended question of what the American dream meant to them; 37% provided answers that focused on the basics of personal economic security, saying that it meant "having a good job," "being able to make a comfortable living," and the more general answer of "financial security." Having a good place to live or raise a family was also cited by 29% of the respondents. Other less frequently offered definitions included personal freedom (15%), owning a home (14%), and having opportunity/choice in life (9%) (Lake Research Partners [LRP] 2007: 6–7).

When asked to assess the importance of American dream-related or life goals identified by others, 80% ranked "having a job that pays enough to support a family" as extremely important, 75% ranked "having affordable quality health care on a dependable basis" as extremely important, and 74% said "having the means to ensure his/her children have the opportunity to succeed" was also extremely important. After these three economic concerns, "being treated with respect" was the next most important component of the American dream for these workers (71% ranked extremely important) (LRP 2007: 8).

When asked to name the number one reason the American dream was becoming more difficult to reach, 49% gave income-related reasons (for example, low wages, high cost of living, lack of good jobs). Tied for second place, about 10% said the primary obstacle was politics or was the government's fault, while an equal percentage cited changes in Americans' morals or work ethic. In third place, 8% cited problems in education.

Although a majority believed the dream was still obtainable, three quarters of those surveyed felt it was becoming harder to achieve. In sharp contrast to the 2004 survey, in which two thirds reported they had already obtained the American dream, only 18% of these working-class respondents felt they were currently living the dream (see Table 2-1). Nearly 70% felt that policies of the government would determine the future for the American dream.

A closer inspection of the results of both surveys suggests one obvious divergent pattern in respondents' answers. Social class (education, job type, and income) significantly constrains individuals' definitions of the American dream as well as perceptions of its attainability. The answers of college-educated, white-collar workers with more affluent incomes suggest that the sense of individual freedom, having options and making choices, are key ingredients of the American dream. Most believe they will or already have attained the dream. In sharp contrast, for those without college degrees, in blue-collar jobs making considerably less money, the goal of being able to financially provide for their family and their future is foremost in their minds when they describe what it means to be "living the dream." Many believe this goal is attainable, but very few feel like they have achieved it. How do these two distinct visions of the American dream compare with those held by Latinos?

TABLE 2-1   COMPARISON OF THE REPRESENTATIVENESS OF SURVEY RESPONDENTS AND ANSWERS TO AMERICAN DREAM QUESTIONS, AMONG 2004 NCL AND 2007 LRP SURVEY RESPONDENTS

Comparison	2004 Respondents	2007 Respondents
Representativeness of survey respondents	General population including more white collar	Exclusively blue-collar, working-class
Most frequently cited definition of American dream	Living in freedom	Economic security
Most frequently cited barrier to American dream	Poor quality of education	Income/employment concerns
Percentage who believe they have achieved the American dream	66%	18%

NCL = National League of Cities; LRP = Lake Research Partners

Living the *Americano* Dream

Unlike the surveys, in which respondents were asked direct questions, the focus groups were not specifically solicited for their thoughts on the American dream. However, the notion of wanting the dream and the process or actions required for achieving it emerged *independently* as a theme in focus group conversations across the country. At least four participants made specific reference to the concept, and there were numerous comments—regarding participants' life goals or ambitions, barriers that impeded their efforts, and the progress (or lack thereof) that they thought they had made in attaining those goals—that can be used to depict what living the *Americano* dream means to Latinos.

In major ways, the dream seems to have the same meaning for Latinos as it does for other working-class Americans. With a few exceptions, most notably the English-language focus groups in Washington, DC, the demographics of our focus group participants closely mirror the demographic profile of respondents in the 2007 survey. And, like the workers surveyed in 2007, our participants' comments also focused most on the comforts that come from having good-paying, steady jobs. They want to own homes in safe neighborhoods with high-quality schools for their children. They also want to be respected and treated fairly. Freedoms associated with the First Amendment were important to only a few.

The central focus of the dream for Latinos is the financial security that comes with regular employment. Foremost, they want *good jobs*. Every focus group assessed particulars of their personal employment status and the general climate of jobs available to Latinos. With the exception of a few who originally came to this country to further their education or to flee dangers of political instability at home, most participants acknowledged that Latinos came to the United States primarily to find work. This is certainly not a surprise (Alba and Nee 2003). Recently arrived immigrants reveled at the fact that they were able to find "many good-paying jobs." Later generations, and some of the immigrants who had spent significant portions of their lives in the United States, prized finding jobs that paid well too, but they also were more likely to wish for (and if they had it, to express satisfaction with) a positive working environment (that is, providing "benefits," "good relations with co-workers," "respect and trust from supervisors," and having jobs that they preferred over "jobs that no one else would do"). In Dalton, GA, for example, respondents noted their preference, not just for any work, but for what they perceive as *good* work:

> Pablo, immigrant (Dalton, GA, S):[4] I have not seen any difficulties. I like it here, jobs are well paid and because they are not out on the fields.
>
> *Valdemar, U.S. born (Dalton, GA, S):* I like it because the majority of jobs offer good benefits, like medical insurance.

Another component of the *Americano* dream, a part that is greatly dependent on getting good-paying jobs, is being able to move *away from rough parts of town* or to move *out of the barrios*. A conversation thread found in groups held in all the major cities was the desire to avoid or escape the "noise" (from too many "people crowded together," "bottles breaking," and "gunshots"), the "drugs," the "gangs," and other bad elements. Contrary to recent commentary that recent Latino arrivals choose to remain in ethnic enclaves separated from the Anglo population (cf. Huntington 2004b), a majority of those in our focus groups wanted away from the places that had "too many" of their co-ethnics. We see examples in the Miami and New York City focus groups:

> *Multiple respondents (Miami, S):* "Little Havana is a bad neighborhood." "It's really bad. . . . Now there are gangs and thieves." "There's so many [Latinos]." "You can't leave your house. People just sit in their house." "The houses they depreciate there." "The culture is depreciated; there's criminals and drugs." "I want away from there." *(Collective agreement):* "Yeah."
>
> *Ivan (New York, E):* What I like is that there are not many Latinos. It is very quiet, I feel that there is peace. I don't hear the noise . . . so it is peaceful.
>
> *Victor (New York, E):* I like the neighborhood where I live now because it is quiet, it's clean. Everyone is working people. It is quiet most of the time. I lived in Harlem for 28 years and the reason I left is because I had two big bullet holes on my wall, and I said I better get out of here before I get killed because of these guys out there selling drugs. I said I had to

work hard. Back then I used to do things foolishly, but now I save my money and use it wisely. I LIKE where I live now.

A third component of the *Americano* dream is the goal of *home ownership* in a community that is good for raising a family. With very few exceptions, participants indicated how much they valued being able to purchase a home in a quiet neighborhood that had safe streets and good schools for their children. Every focus group had people mention their goal (either desired or realized) to live in a place that was "quiet," "tranquil," and "safe" enough for "children [to] play outside" or where they could "walk the street at night" without fear.

> *Eric (New York, E):* Where I live now is day and night from where I grew up. Even now when I go to visit my mom, who still lives in the projects, it is LOUD, there are people all over the place, music, throwing bottles. . . . I don't want to go back. I am working very hard to buy a house.
>
> *Nicholas (Houston, E):* Now I got it GOOD . . . I moved out [of Alief, TX] and over by I-464. Just bought a brand-new house. It's quiet. . . . We got a three-bedroom home and it's quiet. I love it! I don't hear sirens. I love it! . . . I know I don't have children yet . . . but I always wanted something where I knew my kids would grow up safely and in a good area.
>
> *Roberto (Miami, S):* The tranquility in the streets. My kid can play ball in the street. . . . The unity of family is important where I live, neighbors with families. It is safe and you get a sense of security.

Quality education for their children or themselves is another integral part of the *Americano* dream. Contrary to some popular opinion that Latinos have low expectations and low priorities for education (Badillo 2006), participants in all of our groups referred to the importance of education, especially "having good schools for their children" and "more education" for Latinos in general.

> *Elsa (Muscatine, IA, S):* I am proud to see Hispanic students on honor rolls and to see more Hispanic young adults attending college.

Francisca, immigrant (Houston, S): [S]ome Hispanics are better prepared than others, right? At least for me. I studied
nursing, and for 10 years I worked to support myself as a
voluntary [nurse], over there [in Mexico]. . . . When I came
here I felt comfortable when I saw a Hispanic, but I have
seen that because they are better prepared with English
and all, is like they treat us with inferiority. Now that I
have my kids I want them to study and prepare themselves
to go farther than me.

The final part of the dream for Latinos is to *be treated fairly
and respectfully by others.* In every focus group there was discussion about perceived discourteous behavior or discrimination from
Anglos and other Latinos (we look more closely at these comments in
Chapter 4). However, these discussions were often balanced by comments regarding positive interactions and how much they appreciated
it when these occurred. The following experience provided by a naturalized Latino in Houston conveys both the sting felt by discriminatory treatment and the sincere appreciation for a salesman who
treated him well:

Fernando (Houston, S): Once, I was helping one of my cousins
to buy a car. . . . When we got there we saw a Hispanic guy.
We said to ourselves, "We are lucky; he is going to give us
a hand." We felt supported. We came close, he saw us and
ignored us; he didn't help us. I think because of the way
we were dressed and maybe because he thought we were
Hispanics and we might not have money, or he thought we
didn't have enough to put down about $500, or who knows,
but he did not want to help us. Then, an African American came and asked, "How may I help you?" So, we told
him that we would like to buy a car. He said, "Okay," he
helped us very well, much better that we expected, and on
top of that he gave us a discount on the car. My cousin gave
the money to pay for the car in full and, in cash, as appreciation for his help my cousin gave him $500. He went in
front of the Hispanic that was working there and told him,
"For not wanting to help him, see what he gave me?" Just

because of [our] appearance he [Hispanic salesperson] didn't want to give us a hand.

Barriers to Achieving the Dream for Latinos

Barriers to achieving the American dream as identified in our focus groups overlap somewhat with those cited by the survey respondents in the previous studies, specifically problems with both the quality of schools and discrimination. However, other noted obstacles were more likely to be immigrant-specific concerns. The most frequently cited barrier is a problem for many immigrants from non-English-speaking countries, English proficiency. Another widely acknowledged barrier, sometimes expressed as an individual concern but more commonly identified as a barrier for Latino immigrants in general, was legal status, either their lack of citizenship or lack of documentation.

With respect to the top obstacle, there was universal agreement across the focus groups that limited English proficiency decreased the likelihood of achieving success with respect to jobs and equal treatment. The following examples directly illustrate how participants tied job advancement and upward mobility with having good English speaking skills:

> *Mario (Washington, DC, S):* Language is the most difficult barrier. Moving up and making more money depends on speaking good English.
>
> *Cubia (Washington, DC, S):* If you don't know English, you work in jobs that nobody wants with low pay and sometimes no pay.
>
> *Nicholas (Houston, E):* The guy that's been there the longest is Mexican. . . . The fact that he hasn't moved up, like the other guys that are equal to him at that time is because the fact that he doesn't speak English well. . . . That's what's holding him back.
>
> *Ivan (New York, E):* I think they [immigrants] would have to speak English. If you don't speak English you will not get a good job. I studied [in] high school and it was different when I came here because of the accents, but English is the key.

Legal status or, more specifically, the lack of documentation to regularize their status, was a topic of personal concern for only a few participants. However, multiple people in every focus group said that they personally knew Latinos who were undocumented and described the difficulties faced by these individuals regarding matters of employment, education, and place of residence due to their illegal status. Others also lamented the fact that they, or their spouse, were not U.S. citizens, and that this put them at a disadvantage in the workplace and in going to college:

> *Arturo (Washington, DC, S):* When you don't have papers it is harder to find work and people who know or think you don't have papers will treat you bad.
> *Randy (New York, E):* If you don't have a green card you can't get into a university.
> *Man (Los Angeles, E):* They take advantage of the Latino workers. They don't pay them the salaries they are supposed to get paid. I know a girl working three different jobs. She doesn't get the pay she deserves. She is illegal and they take advantage of it.
> *Marie (Houston, S):* I know my husband would have kept his job if he were a citizen.

Concern for the poor quality of education noted by survey respondents was echoed in the comments of focus group participants, especially those who had direct experience with the secondary schools in large urban areas such as Houston, New York City, and Miami. Their comments regarding problems identified with these urban school districts are highlighted in Chapter 3, Education: Latinos' Great Hope, America's Harsh Reality. However, it is also important to note that participants in these same cities were very satisfied and appreciative of the opportunities provided by higher education in their areas. For example, a common theme in their comments was the acknowledgment that both participants and their children were "doing better financially because [they were] now able to go to college" and "achieved greater success in their careers because they went to college."

Latino Optimism for the Attainability of the *Americano* Dream

Like most of the surveyed Americans, Latinos think the American dream is becoming harder to achieve, but overall they are optimistic about the prospect of attaining it, for themselves and for Latinos collectively. For example, in a New York focus group, the moderator asked participants, "What is the future of the Latino here in the United States?" The replies were.

> *Multiple respondents (New York, E):* "Whatever you make it." "Good, if you know how to defend yourself and know what you are doing." "Good, there are lots of opportunities with education, so anyone who comes can do it." "The opportunities are there, but you have to look for them. They will not find you. You have to be willing to do whatever it takes" *(Collective agreement):* "Yeah."

One comment from an immigrant in Los Angeles is especially illustrative of the optimism shared among many of the foreign-born respondents:

> *Immigrant man (Los Angeles, E):* As time goes by, they [Latinos] can elevate their position. I started in warehouse sales and moved up making more money. Dreams don't die; they only die if you don't pursue them.

Perhaps the best indicator of the continuing appeal of the American dream for foreign-born and U.S.-born Latinos alike is found in their commonly expressed preferences to remain in the United States when asked whether they (focus group participants) could see themselves returning or moving to home/ancestral countries on a permanent basis. The response of an immigrant from Chile captures the sentiment expressed by many foreign-born:

> *Graciela, immigrant (Washington, DC, S):* This place is everything I dream for and more. I like very much living

here. It is beautiful, tranquil. My son has a good job, he is
happy. . . . My son's children will go to the university. . . . I
am staying here.

Second-generation and higher respondents generations were even
more direct in expressing their commitment to remaining in the
United States to attain their long-term goals. As reported in the intro-
ductory remarks of this chapter, whenever the moderator asked sec-
ond- and third-generation Latinos whether they could ever imagine
themselves immigrating to their family's home country, their immediate and unanimous response was an emphatic "NO!" Moreover, the
follow-up conversations clearly supported the conclusion of one participant, who reported: "The quality of life I want is only found in the
United States."

Is Assimilation Part of the American Dream?

Given these understandings of Latinos' aspirations about the American dream, especially their focus on economic success and security,
do their views on related topics suggest that assimilation is seen as
(implicitly or explicitly) part of, essential, or instrumental to their realization of "living the dream?" Is the extent of assimilation itself suggestive of some movement toward the American dream? To explore these
possibilities, let us begin with a brief discussion of the complex concept of assimilation. We can then consider Latinos' understanding(s) of
the concept as well as the extent to which Latinos appear to be thinking, acting, and experiencing social outcomes that seem compatible
with movement toward assimilation and, in turn, toward something
approaching the American dream.

The Complexity of Assimilation

There is no simple or widely agreed upon definition of "assimilation"
except to say that it refers to a multigenerational process by which the
"characteristics of members of immigrant groups and host societies
come to resemble one another" (Brown and Bean 2006). Early articu-
lations of the concept (still in vogue among Huntington and others who
believe in a single Anglo-Saxon Protestant culture) were normative

and prescriptive. Assimilation was characterized as a "straight-line" progression whereby all immigrants eventually conform, abandoning their original cultural attributes and adopting the behaviors and customs of the Anglo-Saxon majority as they advance both socially and economically (Park 1950; Warner and Srole 1945). Milton Gordon's *Assimilation in American Life* (1964) more accurately described a process that was considerably more complex, involving numerous dimensions besides culture and the possibility of different outcomes besides Anglo-Saxon conformity. Later scholars of assimilation no longer claim that conformity is even necessarily a desirable outcome (Portes and Rumbaut 2001).

Today, the classic model of assimilation ("straight-line") has essentially been eclipsed by a variety of alternative theories of how the process occurs (for example, "bumpy-line," "segmented," "two-way"), with differing opinions on which dimensions of assimilation are most important for immigrants and minorities to survive and thrive within the larger society (Alba and Nee 2003; Gans 1996; Portes and Zhou 1993). Still, most scholars agree that certain factors can delay or even block assimilation. Two of these factors include racial/ethnic discrimination and governmental policies that limit social and economic mobility (Brown and Bean 2006).

Cultural Assimilation

According to Gordon (1964), *cultural* assimilation, or alternatively "acculturation," is likely to be the first adaptation to occur when immigrants come into contact with the majority population. Acculturation refers to the *two-way* process whereby both immigrants and majority citizens adjust their values and behaviors, as opposed to the classical view of assimilation that the direction of change is only one way, whereby immigrants change their appearance, diet, language, religion, social customs, and core values to comply with those of the majority. Some cultural practices (for example, attire, eating habits, and social customs) are considered more easily surrendered than others (for example, core values or religious identity), but "changing" is not necessarily a subtractive process. Gibson (1988) argues that assimilation/acculturation is *selective* and should be viewed as additive in purpose; that is, minority individuals make deliberate decisions to adopt certain

TABLE 2-2   IMPORTANCE OF LEARNING ENGLISH/RETAINING
            SPANISH ACROSS GENERATIONS (IN PERCENTAGES)
            AMONG LNS RESPONDENTS

| | Learn English | | Retain Spanish | |
Generation	Somewhat Important	Very Important	Somewhat Important	Very Important
First	5.5	94.5	9.9	90.0
Second	9.5	90.3	12.5	87.4
Third	12.9	86.8	18.9	80.7
Fourth	13.7	85.7	25.5	73.9

LNS = Latino National Survey

practices of the majority that they think are useful to their future success. They also work to retain salient ethnic cultural traits. In turn, the majority often adopts from the minority culture whatever they find appealing.

English proficiency is widely considered to be the most important aspect of cultural adaptation if immigrants are to be successful outside of their ethnic enclaves, but immigrants may also value the retention of their native languages (Alba and Nee 2003). We can see evidence of this longing to "have it both ways" in LNS respondents' answers to contrasting questions on learning Spanish and maintaining Spanish (Table 2-2). Especially among the foreign born (first generation), overwhelming majorities think it is very important to learn English while also thinking Spanish maintenance is very important: 84% and 89%, respectively.

The goal of being equally proficient in both English and Spanish was also very evident in the comments of the focus group participants. Immigrant participants were keenly aware that they had problems communicating effectively in English, and many expressed the desire for their children, if not for themselves, that they would "get better" or "good at" speaking English. However, most of the Spanish speakers also wanted their children and grandchildren to be bilingual. U.S.-born participants were especially mindful of the economic advantages of being bilingual:

Della (Miami, E): Every time you look in the paper you have
    to be bilingual.
Jose Luis (Muscatine, IA, S): It is important to be bilingual. My
    brother lost his Spanish. He went to school and became

a lawyer [but] he had to change jobs because of his location and Spanish was the language most used and he didn't know it.

Participants in the English-language focus groups frequently expressed regret at not having made more of an effort to learn or maintain their Spanish and also to pass it along to their children. An exchange in one of the focus groups in New York is illustrative of this sentiment:

> *Christopher (New York, E):* We want them to think like all the other races. . . . We want them to learn English. As long as there are grandmothers around, you are going to learn Spanish. It will be heard. That is what would happen to me. I wanted to shy away from Spanish, but I couldn't. . . . I am glad now for it.
>
> *Eric (New York, E):* That's the thing, while we are American, born here, we can't forget our heritage. My daughters, I try to teach them Spanish; I bought DVDs to teach them Spanish. They only speak English, and I am trying to tell their mother as well because you can never forget your heritage. We are American, and we do have to speak English well, but don't forget where you came from.
>
> *Shirley (New York, E):* I think with every generation you lose more and more. I read and write Spanish, but growing up, my mother—born and raised in Puerto Rico—taught us Spanish and we learned our English in school, which to me was an advantage because here in New York, they know how to speak it but not write it, and it is good to know it all. . . . I do get disappointed with myself for not teaching my daughters.

Interestingly, the level of English proficiency and Spanish retention among the U.S. Latino population is something about which there is a great deal of information. A great deal of longitudinal data is available on the topic from the U.S. Census Bureau and from other national studies. Basically, the data are consistent across these sources. Roberto Suro, former Director of the Pew Hispanic Center, aptly summarizes the findings from these data:

[A]bout three-quarters of foreign-born Latinos, the first generation, speaks only Spanish and the rest of the immigrants are
bilingual to some extent. The second generation—the children
of immigrants—are about evenly divided between English
speakers and bilinguals, with almost none reaching adulthood
speaking only Spanish. And, among Hispanics of longer ten-
ure in the U.S.—those born here, of American-born parents—
more than three-quarters speak only English and the rest are
bilingual to some extent, though often their Spanish is weak.
So we know for certain that a transition to English is taking
place across generations with a lot of bilingualism along the
way (Suro 2006: 3).

We also know something about another indicator of cultural assimilation that, according to Gordon (1964), is significantly less subject to
change: religious affiliation and practices. Religious identity was characterized by Gordon as an intrinsic trait that is "essential and vital to
a groups' cultural heritage" (Gordon 1964: 72). Change in their traditional affiliation (which is Catholicism for Latinos) to Protestant-
ism, the predominant religious identity of American society, could be
viewed as a convincing measure of cultural adaptation. We find evidence of this type of assimilation from a national telephone survey of
2,310 Latinos conducted in 2000 on religious life in the United States.
According to the survey:

- The first generation of Latino immigrants is 74% Catholic
  and 15% Protestant.
- The second generation is 72% Catholic and 20% Protestant.
- The third generation is 62% Catholic and 29% Protestant
  (Espinosa, Elizondo, and Miranda 2005).

We also see evidence of religious adaptation when we look at the levels of Catholicism across generations among respondents in the 2006
LNS. Looking at the first row of Table 2-3, we can see a modest but
steady decline in the numbers of Catholics with each generation. The
biggest drop in Catholics [or Catholicism] occurs between the third
and fourth generations.

TABLE 2-3   SELECTED MARKERS OF ASSIMILATION ACROSS
GENERATIONS (IN PERCENTAGES) AMONG LNS
RESPONDENTS

	First	Second	Third	Fourth
Roman Catholic	73.6	70.6	65.0	58.0
Participation in civic groups	14.1	23.4	29.3	31.7
Has mostly Latino friends	44.6	28.0	22.0	16.7
Military service	15.9	46.3	66.3	68.5
Education less than high school	48.7	23.1	18.4	17.3
Household income less than $35,000	53.3	35.6	28.5	34.2
Married to non-Latinos	13.5	28.9	38.9	49.1

LNS = Latino National Survey

As hypothesized by Gordon, the change in Latino religious affiliation is occurring more slowly relative to other aspects of cultural
assimilation. The difficulty or reluctance in changing religious practices was discussed by immigrant participants in the Washington, DC,
focus group who were fully bilingual and participated in our English-
speaking session:

> *Man (Washington, DC, E):* There is a church here in Alexan-
> dria in Spanish, but sometimes I go to the one in English
> even though the one in Spanish is easier to understand.
> The Americans that go to church still seem cold, while the
> Mexicans show they care.
> *Woman (Washington, DC, E):* I still can't learn the prayers in
> English.
> *Man (Washington, DC, E):* I had the same experience. I made
> my communion over there when I was 17, and all prayers
> were in Spanish. Then I came here and I had to learn them
> in English, and I can't relate to them. I know them though.
> *Woman (Washington, DC, E):* I learned them in Spanish, and
> I came here when I was 24, and I have found it very diffi-
> cult to learn them or say anything in English. I can't follow
> the Mass in English.

Changing religious affiliation is seemingly one critical indicator of assimilation, but it could be argued that it may be more important for Latinos to be attending churches with significant numbers of

non-Latinos. Participation in integrated mainstream organizations is an important component of *structural* assimilation, the entrance into or participation of minority individuals in primary groups and institutions of the majority society (Brown and Bean 2006; Gordon 1964). Whenever church or religion was discussed in the focus groups, there were always some participants who said the membership of the church they attended was mixed, including some that said their church was mostly Anglo. However, there were always other participants who said they felt "more comfortable" attending services that were conducted in Spanish or with their co-ethnics.

Structural Assimilation

Gordon deemed that once structural assimilation begins, it stimulates all other dimensions of assimilation. Activities as varied as participation in integrated social/civic/work organizations, friendships with persons outside of one's ethnic group, and U.S. military service are all indicators of structural assimilation. Increasing levels of education and home ownership are also proxy measures of structural assimilation (Brown and Bean 2006). We see evidence of increasing structural assimilation among the LNS respondents across generations along most of these indicators when we examine rows two through five in Table 2-3. The biggest change in each of these measures occurs between the first (foreign-born) and second (U.S.-born) generations.

The sharp decline in the percentage of those with less than high school education somewhat overstates the improvement in educational status of Latinos (primarily because the Latino dropout rate continues to be a serious problem), but the only indicator on this table that does not show steady improvement across generations is household income. There is substantial improvement between the first and second generations, reflected by the big drop in the percentage making less than $35,000, but the decline is small between the second and third generations and actually increases between the third and fourth generations.

Further evidence of structural assimilation was revealed when focus group participants discussed the race/ethnicity of their coworkers and friends and their degree of interaction with them. Many referenced in a very positive light the racial/ethnic diversity of their workplaces and neighborhoods. Many said that they socialized regularly with non-Latino co-workers and friends. Interestingly, however, those they considered "close friends" were more likely to be fellow Latinos. Participants in New York, Miami, and Los Angeles also noted that they felt "more comfortable doing different things" with their non-Latino friends, such as going to the gym, and had "more fun partying" or simply "hanging out" with their Latino friends. This suggests that their structural assimilation is selective. They are comfortable in integrated work and social settings, but at times they prefer to be with people from their own culture. On the other hand, recent immigrants and participants who had recently relocated to rural towns were more likely to live almost segregated lives, reporting that their co-workers, friends, and neighbors were all mostly Latino and that the attitudes of long-term residents were "not friendly."

Marital Assimilation

The incorporation of Latinos into the American fabric may be occurring primarily through marital or family integration. Over the past 30 years the number of Latinos marrying non-Latino spouses has more than doubled, from 600,000 in 1970 to 1.8 million in 2000. This is a significant trend since the same data show that many Latino immigrants arrive already married. Even with the surge in Latino immigration between 1990 and 2000, the percentage of Latino intermarriages remained fairly stable: between 23% and 25%. As the proportion of U.S.-born Latinos increases relative to the proportion of foreign-born, the percentage of intermarriages is predicted to climb even higher (Lee and Edmonston 2005).

The reported pattern of increasing marital assimilation is clearly shown across the generations of LNS respondents (see the bottom row of Table 2-3). Again, as with previously discussed indicators, the biggest change occurs between the first and second generation, but there is at least a 10% increase with each subsequent generation. By the fourth generation, over half of the respondents are married to non-Latinos.

These aggregate indicators are reflected in the marital circumstances of our focus group participants. Although approximately one third of the participants were single or divorced, many of these reported having parents or siblings who were married to non-Latinos. Having non-Latino spouses was very common among the U.S.-born married participants; about half reported they were married to non-Latinos. Out-group marriages were far less common among immigrant participants, with several reporting that they immigrated to the United States with their wives/husbands.

The significance of having a non-Latino American spouse for facilitating the process of becoming a part of the majority society is best illustrated by the comments of a Miami participant who immigrated to this country as an adult from Majorca, Spain:

> *Rosa (Miami, E):* I came here when I was 21 years old. . . . I am an outsider. My husband is American. He is from upstate New York. A little town in upstate New York and also has family in Pennsylvania. They never make me feel like an outsider. They try to talk to me slowly when I first came to this country and be friendly and give me all that food. I was like "Oh, my God. What is that? Give me some snails to eat." But they were friendly and everything. . . . They don't make me feel outsider.

It is equally significant to note that marriage to a non-Latino does not necessarily result in the loss of Latino cultural ties. Participants' comments seem to suggest that acculturation is the more common effect as families learned to appreciate, or at least accept, the customs and practices of the different cultures. The following, somewhat lengthy, Miami focus group discussion regarding the differences in holiday practices provides several acculturation examples.

> *Omar (Miami, E):* My wife is American. They're very relaxed like most people but when I say "party," I want to go to a Latin people party. Let's say for Christmas, celebrating Christmas with a Latin family is very different than an American family. I like it better with the Latin family, even though I spend most of the time with my wife's family because my parents are not here.

Toni (Miami, E): The customs are different. Like for Christmas, Christmas Eve for Hispanics is a big thing, whereas for Americans they celebrate more on Christmas day than Christmas Eve.

Joni (Miami, E): I have been here long enough to celebrate both ways but we keep our traditions. We do the *Noche Buena*, the Christmas Eve. We invite a lot of people.

Marisol (Miami, E): When it's work related, I will go with anybody. I work as a realtor and there are a lot of nationalities where I work. . . . But when it comes to something personal, I would rather stick with what I know and like, which is the Latin side of my life. When it comes to me and my family . . . the weird part is growing up here and being from another country is really sometimes you are like this: "Christmas Eve, Christmas day, what do I do?" Sometimes you end up doing both, which is a lot of fun. Because I love Thanksgiving, and I was raised in New York where Thanksgiving is Thanksgiving. But then I get down here [Miami], and they are having Cuban food at 11:00 at night. It's weird. When I was in New York, we knew we had to eat turkey, got dressed, the table was totally beautiful. Down here it's different.

Joni (Miami, E): I think it's because they like food and they like partying, because Thanksgiving is not part of Cuban tradition. And yet, Cubans and Hispanics in general celebrate Thanksgiving as if they have been celebrating it their whole life. They take advantage of both, their heritage and what they've learned in this country. Because there is no such thing as Thanksgiving over there. Take advantage of both.

Maria (Miami, E): My mother came to the U.S., my [American] father brought her to the U.S., and she was raised most of her life in Majorca. You celebrate Thanksgiving and you have a turkey and you stuff it with bread and it was so foreign to her. So she had to transition. She always put her spin on it. She always put chorizo in the sauces. . . . She had to incorporate in her Latin experience to celebrate American tradition.

Self-recognized Importance of Adapting to "American" Ways

As originally detailed in Chapter 1, the self-reported characteristics of participants suggest there is great variation in the level or extent of assimilation represented among the focus groups. Some participants who were in this country for less than one year and spoke only Spanish appeared to be just beginning the process, while others, primarily second- and third-generation participants who spoke only English, were clearly further along in the process of fitting into American society. However, recognition of the importance of assimilation or at least "accommodating American ways" was evident in similar comments made in practically every focus group we held. For example:

> *Woman (Los Angeles, E):* If you come from Mexico with attitude, you are going to have lots of problems. If you come willing to adapt, you won't have problems. . . . Pride is a big killer. Sometimes you will have to go down to go up. You might be the most educated person and start out as a housekeeper with a company, just to get your foot in the door.
>
> *Immigrant woman (Washington, DC, S):* When you come to the U.S., you have to accustom yourself or nothing. . . . Do whatever it takes.
>
> *Marisol, immigrant in U.S. 10 years (Miami, E):* I really believe that everybody should learn English personally. If you're here, you should speak English. If some people want the schools in Spanish, I think that's wrong. . . . You have to change.
>
> *Nicholas (Houston, E):* There ain't no leaders in the Hispanic [community] that you can talk to. So anytime you want to move ahead you have to talk to some other races. We ain't got no presidents. . . . There is nobody in office for us, you know what I mean? For us to even get there we would have to go through another race. You have to be able to adapt, you got to learn other things.

Conclusions

It seems that Latinos share the same vision as other working-class Americans of what it means to be successful and satisfied in life. Their focus is primarily on material success and economic opportunities and not on political freedoms or the more abstract ideas identified with those in the middle class. While some of our focus group participants appear to be very satisfied with where they currently live and work, most are still striving to reach their life goals. For the most part, participants' attitudes about the future for themselves and for Latinos in general are upbeat and confident.

Interestingly, in most cases, immigrant participants were generally more satisfied and optimistic than the U.S.-born we talked with. Perhaps because the U.S.-born were significantly more aware of the barriers to upward mobility, they were less optimistic and more cynical about the prospects of achieving their dreams as they defined them. They also seemed to be more aware that many of the obstacles were out of their control, such as the quality of schools and the attitudes of elected officials or residents (including other Latinos) in new receiving communities.

As previously stated, Latinos know they must adapt—at least in some ways—if they want to improve their status. They clearly recognize that they must learn to speak English (and to speak it well) if they are to have continued success in moving up the socioeconomic ladder. However, judging from the other information presented here, from a variety of credible aggregate sources, and from the individual comments from those in our focus groups, there are other signs besides English acquisition that Latinos are integrating into American society—through marriage, friendships, churches, and military service, for example. The ways that Latinos are becoming a part of the American fabric are similar to the behaviors followed by previous waves of immigrants (Sassler 2006); from this perspective Latinos' behavior reflects more continuity than change.

Yet, the decision to adapt (assimilate) is complicated by the fact that Latinos also want to maintain their cultural traditions, such as their Spanish proficiency (as we saw in their answers presented in Table 2-2). Further evidence of the complexity or contradictions in

TABLE 2-4 PREFERENCE FOR CULTURAL ASSIMILATION AND
DISTINCTNESS (IN PERCENTAGES) AMONG LNS
RESPONDENTS

	Blend into Larger Society		Maintain Distinct Culture	
Generation	Somewhat Important	Very Important	Somewhat Important	Very Important
First	27.2	60.4	16.8	78.3
Second	33.4	42.1	18.0	75.7
Third	36.9	37.7	20.3	74.2
Fourth	37.5	34.0	26.0	66.0

LNS = Latino National Survey

Latinos' feelings about assimilation can be seen in Table 2-4, which provides LNS respondents' answers to questions regarding how important they think it is for Latinos to attempt to "blend into the larger American society" and also to "maintain their distinct cultures." Large majorities in each generation say *both behaviors* are somewhat or very important. Moreover, support for blending into the larger culture and for maintaining a distinct culture is positively related ($r = .1415$); they are not viewed as either/or propositions.

The likelihood of Latinos fully incorporating into American society is obviously complicated. The pursuit of the American dream and subsequent Latino incorporation faces potential roadblocks—some mentioned by focus group participants, such as poor schools, legal status, and discrimination. The next two chapters look specifically at barriers Latino participants indicated they face on the path to [making the U.S. "home"] achieving their version of the American dream: the challenges in education and experiences of discrimination.

3 Education

Latinos' Great Hope, America's Harsh Reality

Education has long been understood as a primary means through which Americans of all backgrounds and incomes can gain the skills to realize the opportunities that are likely to lead to upward social, economic, and political mobility in the United States (Hochschild 1984, 1995; Hochschild and Scovronick 2004). Few would argue, however, that the American system of public education has worked equally well in this way for all groups, especially ethnic minorities, racial minorities, and immigrants (Tyack 1974; Tyack and Cuban 1995). To attempt to overcome these limitations in educational policy and practice, access to high-quality education has often been a primary goal of these groups and their advocates, motivated by the hope that the civic knowledge and marketable job skills that often come with education can serve as the foundation for increasing chances for upward mobility (Patterson 2002). Latinos are no exception in this regard. They have long worked to push American schools to provide their children better educational opportunities to realize the American dream (for example, see San Miguel 1987).

Our focus groups provide key insights to the ways that Latinos understand schools and the significance of education in their daily lives today. The focus group protocol did not ask specific questions about education. However, in response to general questions about neighborhoods and how they have changed, friendship networks, feelings of belonging, and policy issues important to Latinos, a sizeable number of our focus group participants chose to make explicit reference to education and public schools in the United States. This is a clear indication that education is important to Latinos today.

This is consistent with findings of recent national polls. A national survey of Latino public opinion conducted by Bendixen and Associates in 2004, for example, found that in response to the question "What do you think is the most important issue to you and your family today—education, jobs and the economy, health care, terrorism, or immigration?" just over a quarter (26%) of Latinos selected education as *the* most important issue. It ranked second only to jobs and the economy, noted by 30% of respondents, and was well ahead of the other issues: 20% selected health care, 15% immigration, and 6% terrorism (First National Poll 2004). The Pew Hispanic Center (2004b) reports that in their survey of Latino registered voters, education received the highest ranking as an issue that would be extremely important in determining the presidential votes of 54% of respondents. By comparison, the economy and jobs was ranked extremely important by 51%, health care and Medicaid by 51%, and the war in Iraq by 40%.[1] In our 2006 Latino National Survey (LNS), when asked to identify "the most important problem facing the Latino community today," education ranked third, having been chosen by 9% of respondents, behind illegal immigration at 30% and unemployment/jobs at 12% (Fraga et al. 2006a). This is a significant change from the relatively low ranking of education as the most important "national" or "local" problem as revealed by the Latino National Political Survey in 1989, in which only 3% of respondents cited education, well behind other social problems identified by more than 60% of respondents (de la Garza et al. 1992: 88–89).

It is important to remember that a larger share of the Latino population is of school age than is the case for non-Hispanic whites. The 2004 Current Population Survey estimated that 26.8% of all Latinos were between the ages of 5 and 19 and only 19% of the non-Hispanic white population was within this age range (U.S. Census Bureau 2004). Additionally, Latinos are the largest nonwhite ethnic/racial segment of students enrolled in public schools across the nation. In 2005–2006 there were 9,641,407 Latinos enrolled in public schools—19.8% of all students (National Center for Education Statistics [NCES] 2007). Moreover, Latinos represent the fastest-growing racial/ethnic segment of public school enrollment across the country, with a dramatic growth of 356% since 1968 (Orfield and Lee 2004: 13). By comparison white enrollment was 27.8 million (57% of all public school students) in 2005, reflecting a decline of 20.0% since 1968, and African Americans numbered 8.4 million (17.2% of all students); however, this was an increase of only 31% since 1968 (NCES 2007).

Just as dramatic as the national enrollment increases noted is the growing presence of Latinos in public schools in all regions of the country. For example, from 1972 to 2002 Latino student enroll ment doubled in the Northeast to 12.2% of all public school students, grew by over three and a half times in the Midwest to 7.1%, similarly grew by just under three times in the South to 17.4%, and doubled in the West to 38.6% of all students. As of fall 2005, Latinos comprised the largest percentage of students enrolled in New Mexico schools at 54.0%. They were also the largest plurality of students in California (48.5%) and Texas (45.3%). They also comprised sizeable percentages of the students enrolled in Arizona (39.0%), Nevada (33.6%), Colorado (27.1%), Florida (23.9%), New York (20.1%), Illinois (19.0%), and New Jersey (18.2%) (NCES 2007). Most Latino students attend schools in larger cities. For example, in 2006–2007 Latinos made up 73.3% of all students in the Los Angeles Unified School District. In that same school year, Latinos also comprised a sizeable percentage of students in Miami-Dade County (67.1%), Houston (59.3%), New York City (45.2%), and Chicago (38.3%).

However, there is a fundamental paradox between Latinos' aspirations and expectations that education will serve as a means of upward mobility and the reality of their educational experiences in the United States. Despite the history of Latinos working to expand educational opportunities for their children, despite the importance that Latinos give education as a policy issue, and despite the growing presence and dispersion of Latinos throughout many different American public schools, Latinos continue to have among the highest rates of enrollment segregation (Orfield and Lee 2004; Orfield and Yun 1999) and dropout rates (Greene and Winters 2006), as well as among the lowest levels of educational attainment of any major segment of the American population (Gánadara and Contreras 2009; Carnevale 1999; E. Garcia 2001; Macias 1998; Riley and Pompa 1998; Secada et al. 1998; Valdés 1996; Valenzuela 1999). This is not a new occurrence. There is a fundamental continuity in the detrimental educational experiences of many Latino students in the United States today.

Many interpretations have been offered that attempt to explain why this is the case. They range from general theories of genetic or inherent inability (Hernstein and Murray 1994) to social class reproduction (Bowles and Gintis 1976) to cultural deprivation or differences (Valdés 1996; Valenzuela 1999). Few give much credibility to explanations based on the limitations of genes. Cultural arguments appear to be somewhat more prevalent than class-based explanations, although many of those examining Latino education draw on both conceptual frameworks. Cultural explanations focus on family background and life experiences to understand school performance. According to this argument, the differences in language, customs, and values of Latino families versus those of white middle-class families serve to disadvantage Latino students because schools typically promote the culture of white middle-class America. Teachers and administrators generally view students as culturally *deficient* when their parents have limited English proficiency, few years of formal education, and little knowledge of or involvement with their children's schools. Latinos also suffer socially and academically when schools systematically ignore or devalue their cultural heritage and traditions. This line of argument concludes that the result is that Latinos' attitudes and behaviors with respect to education do not "fit" with those advanced by the education system (E. Garcia 2001; Valenzuela 1999).

Our focus group participants reveal that a cultural deficiency explanation for continuing patterns of low educational attainment among Latinos is misinformed. Three specific dimensions to assessing education and public schools in the United States are mentioned by our participants: (1) the importance of education to upward mobility in the United States, (2) how schools influence assessments of the quality of neighborhoods, and (3) the quality of education in large urban school districts. In each case we find that Latinos' views of schools and education are completely consistent with traditional, mainstream American values.

This is in marked contrast to views that Latinos do not want their children to achieve at high levels in American public schools and at odds with views that Latino parents do not engage with their children's schools (Quiocho and Daoud 2006). Although it is unclear whether this view was ever fully accurate, and therefore that current views of Latinos toward education represent a fundamental change in attitudes from what they were previously, what is undoubtedly clear is that it does not characterize the current Latino population in the United States. It is telling that our respondents demonstrate values that are fully consistent with traditional American values that place a very high priority on education as both an end in and of itself, and as a means of upward economic, social, and political mobility.

We refer to this alignment as "value convergence." Value conver gence is defined as the extent to which the expectations of education practitioners and education reformers, as well as expectations of Latino parents regarding themselves, their children, and the schools are consistent and complementary with one another at minimum and fully collaborative at best. We argue that value convergence is high between Latinos and education professionals. This is even the case for first-generation Latinos. We also argue that this convergence should set a rich foundation from which educators and Latino parents can work collaboratively toward improving Latino success in America's public schools. That current patterns of Latino educational attainment do not reflect patterns of consistent gain, and yet that Latino values and expectations remain very much aligned with American values, suggests that institutional barriers such as enrollment segregation, inadequate funding, and ineffective representation in policy decision-making arenas may be among the more significant factors limiting Latinos' realizing the American dream through increasing educational attainment.

Latinos, Value Convergence, and the Foundation for Education Reform

Participants in our focus groups discussed three dimensions of education and schooling in the United States. In this section we discuss each of these dimensions in turn with a special reference to the ways that their perspectives fit with traditional notions of what parents should expect of themselves, their children, and public schools. We find that Latino participants expressed views in clear agreement with what education practitioners often say they want from parents. These views were consistent across our participants despite differences in their own educational backgrounds, preferred use of Spanish or English, and region of the country in which they lived. Significant value convergence exists between our participants and traditional expectations of what it takes to succeed in the American educational system. Again, whether this is understood as demonstrating continuity in Latino attitudes toward education or as a significant shift in these views, this value convergence is clearly the reality for Latinos in contemporary educational policy and practice.

Education and Upward Mobility

Among the most accepted views of the value of education is the way that it can serve to improve one's chances to get ahead in American society. This is most apparent when one sees education in an instrumentalist way, such that more formal years of education mean a better job and a better job is likely to lead to gains in returns from employment over the long term. It has become even more accepted in contemporary American society to understand higher education as a critical component of a young person's chances to secure stable long-term employment in an economy where high-level skills related to problem-solving are in increasing demand. Without such formal education, a young person may be destined to a life of low pay and unstable employment with little chance of meaningful upward mobility. A number of our participants displayed this view of education as central to having a better chance to get ahead by leading to a greater ability to access a fuller range of the opportunities available in this country.

The hopefulness of this instrumentalist view of education was apparent. One participant stated, "There are a lot of opportunities with education, so anyone who comes [to the United States] can do it." Another participant phrased his view this way: "Education, to me it's the foundation of almost everything. If you're educated you're going to learn English and everything else in life." Yet another participant said, "Education—that's where you learn to get your job." In this regard a final participant indicated, "Education. If you have education you have access to more things."

This hopefulness of the value of education was especially clear when linked to the future opportunities for Latino children. A participant from Los Angeles noted, "Education—that's where it begins. It's the future of the child/next generation." A participant from New York also characterized her sense of the value of education to Latino children through the role modeling that those successful in formal education can provide. Interestingly, this participant linked this role modeling to the success Latinos have had in moving into positions of political influence. She stated, "Leadership and acceptance help with the education because as children see Latinos moving into power, the children see that there is something to education."

One final participant from New York indicated that education might be the foundation of any meaningful strategy to improve the status of Latinos in the United States. He said, "[E]ducation is definitely key, because without education, you can't reduce anything on that list [of problems confronting Latinos]."

The above comments indicate that education was very highly valued by Latino participants. Education was understood as a critical foundation to being able to access the employment and other opportunities available in the United States today. It is part of our common wisdom that education can play a key role in determining a whole range of opportunities for all segments of U.S. society, and perhaps especially for members of the working classes. Latino participants seemed to fully internalize important elements of this view. Again, value convergence is apparent. Participants valued education, valued it for their children, and even saw education as a potential key to strategies to address many of the challenges currently faced by Latinos in the United States.

Education, Schools, and the Quality of Neighborhood Life

The linking of the quality of public schools to the quality of life in a community has become a truism in American society in the post–World War II era. Among the major reasons that many Americans chose to withdraw from central cities and move into suburbs was the perception, and often the reality, that the quality of schools in many suburbs was noticeably superior to the education available in larger cities. Families with children have often indicated that moves were largely driven by perceived gains in educational opportunity available to children in better neighborhoods. By one recent interpretation, Americans are more willing to incur house-related debt today than ever before because of the potential benefit to their children in having access to higher quality public schools in more expensive residential areas (Warren and Tyagi 2003).

A number of our participants indicated that schools were central to their perceptions of a high or improved quality of life in the United States. They indicated that among the reasons they liked the neighborhoods in which they currently lived was the school district, schools, and education available to their children.

A participant in Houston stated, "I don't think I will move; it [this neighborhood] has good schools for my granddaughters." Another participant from Houston phrased it this way: "I like the school districts [in my community]. They have free tutoring." Two separate participants in Los Angeles similarly linked schools to the quality of life in their neighborhoods. One stated, "And, the school districts out there [in my neighborhood] are excellent." Another indicated that "Schools are close by the homes [where I live]." A participant in Washington, DC, similarly indicated that among the things she valued in her current neighborhood related to schools. She said that "The area where I live is also close to the train and schools. It is safe."

Interestingly, participants in two smaller communities, one in Georgia and one in Iowa, had very similar views of how education and schools were important to their understanding of the improved quality of life available to their children. A participant from Dalton, GA, stated, "I like the life I can give my children [here in the United States]—education especially." A participant from Muscatine, IA, similarly stated, "Before, the schools had too many students per class and kids lacked attention. The schools here [in this area] are better in that aspect."

The quality of education and schools served as an important indicator of the quality of life in neighborhoods and larger communities for the participants. These views are very consistent with traditional American ways of thinking about the desirability of a neighborhood in postwar America. Our Latino participants displayed these same traditional linkages of quality of schools to quality of neighborhood life. Again, these views serve to display a value convergence between how Latinos see education and life in the United States that is fully consistent with the views of many Americans generally.

Large Urban School Districts

A number of our participants who resided in large central cities expressed the same general concern that has become commonplace since the early 1980s and the publication of *A Nation at Risk* by the National Commission on Excellence in Education (1983). Building on this report, many practitioners, scholars, parents, and students have hoped that many school reforms would have their greatest impact in areas where there was the perceived greatest need: large urban school districts where lower-income students of color, including most Latinos, attend school. The cities of Houston, Los Angeles, New York, and Miami were specifically singled out as places where the quality of education was in great need of reform, according to a number of our participants.

The Houston Independent School District (HISD) received particularly negative assessments. One participant noted, for example, that "education is bad here in Houston. . . . They don't educate them [the children] the way they should be educated." Another participant noted, "[A]bout HISD, those school[s] are terrible. Those school[s] are bad and now that I have a granddaughter [in those schools], I think of those types of things." One critique noted the propensity of the HISD to practice what has come to be described as social promotion. He stated, "In HISD there were some kids that didn't even know how to read and they still passed them."

Another participant spoke at length about perceived deficiencies in the alleged attitudes and practices of administrators in the Houston schools. This prompted him to remove his child from the HISD. He stated, "HISD spends money on videos. HISD spends money on Hawaiian vacations. HISD spends money on steaks and all this PlayStation 2 and all of this. And none of the money is going to the schools. That's why the roof is falling apart. And you know they're tracking it down. They're finding this all out right now. . . . Yes; they are misusing the funds and not using them for the kids. That's why I got out of the HISD school district. Because I knew it would be bad for my son."

This propensity to use the poor quality of education in the Houston schools as a motivation to move and pull children out of the HISD was a point made by a number of other participants. One stated, "They have real good counselors in the [non-HISD] schools and they really make an effort to help your child, and when I lived over there in HISD, you couldn't get anything. The teachers didn't even teach proper English in the school." Another stated, "It's a separate school district so it's a lot better than HISD."

In an assessment of the Los Angeles Unified School District (LAUSD), one participant indicated a similar concern about staying in his current residence because it would require that his children attend schools in the LAUSD. He stated, "We are planning on starting a family, and I would like a better school district than the LA Unified for my kids."

The New York City Public Schools also received harsh critiques from a number of participants. One assessment was a general critique of the schools and compared them to those available in a number of suburbs in the New York area. He stated, "The schools in the rough areas are messed up and need renovation. Children are sharing textbooks, but not all teachers care the same way as the suburbs. They make more money and don't work with struggling families, and that is a big problem." Another assessment focused on the overcrowding that is apparent in a number of schools in New York City. He stated, "Another reason is that the population keeps growing, and the schools are not growing as fast as the population and you get overcrowded schools."

The schools in Miami also received a number of complaints, including general references to the quality of education, class size, and the changing nature of students who are attending schools in this city with a growing and increasingly diverse Latino community. One participant put the critique succinctly: "The quality [of schools] has gone down." Another stated in response to an inquiry regarding issues affecting Latino communities, "The schools. They've gotten worse because there's more students and the same number of teachers—how are they going to teach 38 kids? It's impossible." One final participant in Miami stated, "The problem is . . . My wife is a volunteer at school. No one respects her. If she reprimands a child, then their parents come and reprimand my wife for doing it."

The continuing challenges to Latinos presented by public school systems in central cities are reflected in the comments of our participants. None of these critiques are particularly surprising; however, they all indicate that Latinos have high expectations of the quality of education students should receive in public schools. Critiques of schools included a general assessment of quality, but also included specifics regarding questions of school expenditures, social promotion, quality of teaching, availability of textbooks, and overcrowding. It is important to note that there did not appear any consensus as to why public education was particularly challenging in central cities or what specific responsibilities Latino parents may have to working to improve schools. Nonetheless, it is clear that in assessing the quality of education in large urban school districts, value convergence exists between Latinos and the goals and expectations of many urban school reform efforts.

Education and the Future for Latinos in the United States

In 2003, the Pew Hispanic Center conducted a national survey of Latinos that focused exclusively on issues related to education. Interestingly, they report that despite continuing low test scores on achievement tests, relatively high dropout rates, and low rates of college completion, "Hispanics do not emerge from this survey as a disgruntled population that views itself as greatly disadvantaged or victimized" (Pew Hispanic Center [PHC] 2004a: 2). The Pew Hispanic Center also reports that Latinos, especially those who are immigrants, are more "positive" and "optimistic" about public schools than are whites or African Americans. They continue, however, that "a sizeable minority of Latinos takes a negative view of the state of public education" (PHC 2004a: 3). Approximately 29% of Latino respondents would give the public schools in their "community" a grade of C, D, or F, and a full 38% would give these grades to the public schools in "the nation as a whole" (PHC 2004a: 4). This favorable view of American public education is also revealed in the LNS, in which 32% of all respondents gave their "community's public schools" the grade of A, and another 38.1% gave them a B. Only 19% gave them a C; and very small percentages gave them a D (5.3%) or an F (5.5%).

Latino participants in our focus groups displayed a similar pattern of views. Our participants indicated that they valued education as a means to facilitate securing gainful employment and achieving upward mobility in the United States generally. The quality of schools was also a very important dimension related to their sense of the quality of their neighborhoods; good schools were an important part of how they characterized what they liked about where they lived. However, there were also statements indicating dissatisfaction with some schools, especially schools in larger central cities. General satisfaction with some systems of public education, high expectations of the value of education, and yet some very clear assessments of the need for some public schools to improve indicate that Latinos in our focus groups see education and schools as very important components of their lives in the United States.

The value convergence between the views of Latinos and traditional views of American public education are further reflected in findings from the LNS. Table 3-1 indicates the responses to how far the parent "would like" to see her child go in school, and Table 3-2 displays the responses to how far the parent "expects the child to actually go in school." In both tables what is clear is that Latino parents have very high aspirations *and* expectations of their children's educational attainment. Interestingly, this largely holds across generations. Nationally, 38.6% of all respondents would like to see their child graduate from college and 55.4% would like to see them attain a graduate or advanced professional degree. A smaller percentage of first-generation respondents—35.9%—would like to see their child graduate from college compared to other generations. Interestingly, it is in the fourth generation that the smallest percentage of respondents—39.9%—would like to see their child go to graduate school or receive an advanced professional degree. Similarly, 41.7% of all respondents "expect" their child to graduate from college, and 40.3% expect them to attain a graduate or advanced professional degree. Again, it is in the fourth generation that the smallest percentage of respondents—23.7%—expects their child to obtain a graduate or advanced professional degree. Nonetheless, Tables 3-1 and 3-2 reveal that only a very small percentage of

TABLE 3-1   PARENT ASPIRATION FOR CHILD'S EDUCATION*

	Graduate High School or GED	Vocational Training after High School	Graduate from College	Graduate or Advanced Professional Degree
Nation	4.0	2.0	38.6	55.4
Gen 1	3.5	1.9	35.9	58.8
Gen 2	4.7	2.6	42.2	50.4
Gen 3	2.3	2.8	47.7	47.2
Gen 4	9.4	1.9	48.8	39.9

*Question: How far would you like to see this child go in school?

TABLE 3-2   PARENT EXPECTATION OF CHILD'S EDUCATION*

	Some High School	GED	Graduate High School	Vocational or Job Training	Graduate College	Graduate or Advanced Professional Degree
Nation	1.5	1.7	10.4	4.4	41.7	40.3
Gen 1	1.5	1.9	9.9	4.0	38.8	43.9
Gen 2	2.1	1.7	8.9	4.2	48.6	34.5
Gen 3	0.2	0.0	10.8	6.9	50.6	31.6
Gen 4	2.1	2.3	16.4	5.6	50.1	23.7

*Question: How far do you think your child will actually go in school?

respondents nationally and across generations would like or expect their child to only graduate from high school or to obtain only vocational training after high school.

Tables 3-3 through 3-5 reveal that reported contact with school officials, including meeting with a teacher, attending a parent teacher association (PTA) meeting, and volunteering in the school, is high. This is a major change from the much smaller percentages of respondents indicating such engagement in 1989 in the LNPS (de la Garza et al. 1992: 120). Again, the LNS reveals that value convergence with traditional expectations of how parents should engage with the school is extremely high. Table 3-3 reveals that 90.2% of all respondents reported meeting with teachers; there is no significant variation by generation. Table 3-4 displays responses regarding whether or not the parent has attended a PTA meeting; a full 74% of all respondents indicated having done so. Interestingly the highest percentage—77.5%—was reported from first-generation parents and the smallest response—64.3%—from fourth-generation parents. Just over half of all respondents (52.4%) reported volunteering in the schools, as

TABLE 3-3   PARENT MEETINGS WITH TEACHER*

	Yes	No	Don't Know	Refused
Nation	90.2	9.7	0.1	0.0
Gen 1	89.5	10.5	0.0	0.0
Gen 2	88.9	11.1	0.0	0.0
Gen 3	95.5	3.3	1.2	0.0
Gen 4	91.9	8.1	0.0	0.0

*Question: Here is a list of things that some parents have done and others have not regarding their children's school. Which of these things have you done? Have you met with your child's teacher?

TABLE 3-4   PARENT ATTENDANCE AT PTA MEETING*

	Yes	No	Don't Know	Refused
Nation	74.0	25.6	0.3	0.1
Gen 1	77.5	22.0	0.4	0.2
Gen 2	64.4	35.6	0.0	0.0
Gen 3	65.6	34.2	0.3	0.0
Gen 4	64.3	35.7	0.0	0.0

*Question: Here is a list of things that some parents have done and others have not regarding their children's school. Which of these things have you done? Have you attended a PTA meeting?

TABLE 3-5   PARENT VOLUNTEERING AT SCHOOL*

	Yes	No	Don't Know	Refused
Nation	52.8	46.9	0.1	0.1
Gen 1	47.8	52.0	0.0	0.2
Gen 2	59.4	40.3	0.3	0.0
Gen 3	73.1	26.9	0.0	0.0
Gen 4	67.4	31.8	0.8	0.0

*Question: Here is a list of things that some parents have done and others have not regarding their children's school. Which of these things have you done? Have you acted as a school volunteer for your child's school?

reported in Table 3-5. This rate was noticeably lower in the first generation—47.8%—and highest in the third generation—73.1%. Parent engagement with the schools is high among our respondents. These responses indicate that large percentages of Latino parents meet teachers, attend PTA meetings, and just over half even volunteer in their children's schools.

Of special significance, the views of public education offered by our focus group participants and further supported by findings from the LNS are in clear alignment with mainstream American views of schools, education, and the critical role that these play in affecting one's life chances. This high level of value convergence suggests that, despite the growth in the size of the Latino population in the United States, the growing diversity of this community, and the significance of continuing immigration from Latin America to this overall growth and diversity, many Latinos view education in the same way as other Americans do.

The logic of a number of major current reform efforts assumes that communities, and especially parents with children in schools, must have attitudes toward education that fit within traditional notions of education and related expectations of upward mobility.[2] Program enrichment reforms, for example, include efforts to broaden curricula by making them more culturally inclusive, expanding programs of bilingual education, and even pursuing culturally sensitive methods of promoting English immersion. Each of these efforts assumes that once these changes occur, parents will be more easily engaged in the education of their children because both students and parents will be better able to identify with the school curriculum. This, it is assumed, will result in parents better appreciating what it is that the school is trying to teach their children. Value convergence drives anticipated benefits of program enrichment strategies.

Yet another major set of reforms, standardized performance assessment, such as that required under the No Child Left Behind Act (NCLB), also assumes a value convergence ultimately resulting from scores on tests. The score, such as that earned on a statewide performance test, is assumed to place pressure on students, parents, and schools to work to improve student performance. Whether the incentive is understood in terms of a potential reward or threat, the expected result is that an alignment of expectations will occur among parents, students, and schools. Similarly, the expected benefits of market-based initiatives, whether in the form of vouchers, charter schools, or some other form of enhanced school choice, are driven by assumptions about parental knowledge directly contributing to greater value convergence. Choosing which school your student attends requires information, and choice plans can only work when parents have sufficient, if not overwhelming, knowledge about schools (Chubb and Moe 1990; Henig 1994; Moe 2001; Peterson and Hassel 1998). Parents must also have the capacity to interpret this knowledge in ways that lead to choices that best serve their children.

Another major set of reforms calls for increased parental involvement, as part of a strategy of community-based empowerment to further enrich systemic reform. These efforts are fundamentally premised on the anticipated benefits of parents having greater knowledge of the educational process in schools. Schools are expected to benefit from the labor and other services that parents can perform, but a more critical contribution derives from parents, under this theory, better appreciating the difficult task that teachers and administrators have, as well as gaining knowledge as to how to better support their children in schools. Under this reform strategy, there is a very clear assumption of value convergence flowing almost organically between teachers' and administrators' expectations of parents and the expectations that parents will then have of themselves, of their children as students, and of the schools (Quiocho and Daoud 2006). Finally, democratic institutional reforms, such as increasing the election of Latino school board members and selection of Latino school administrators, is based on the assumption that parents as voters and advocates know how to best identify candidates to support (Fraga, Meier, and England 1986; Meier and Juenke 2005; Meier and Stewart 1991). The greater the likelihood that a candidate of first choice will be elected, the greater the incentive for Latino citizen parents, as voters, to study educational issues, assess candidates on the basis of their issue positions, and ultimately elect candidates who are more likely to address educational issues of direct concern to Latino parents. Again, the value convergence between expectations of parents, students, and schools drives the expected gains that are to result from such reform efforts.

The evidence from our focus group participants clearly indicates that reform efforts relying on value convergence to improve the quality of educational opportunities available to all students, including Latinos, so they can begin to realize the opportunities that can lead to upward mobility should have enthusiastic supporters among Latino parents. It would be unfortunate if this value convergence went unrecognized or was not fully utilized by school reformers and educational officials. Should this happen, the implications for Latino children will be clear: further increases in enrollment segregation, continuing high dropout rates, and the potential continuity of low academic attainment.

4 Exploring Discrimination, Intergroup Relations, and Intragroup Relations among Latinos

A s Latinos have become an increasingly large part of the American population, how they feel they are viewed and treated by others gains significance as a social and political issue—for the Latino population itself as well as the broader society. More specifically, perceptions of discrimination, prejudice, and unfair treatment are indicative of how Latinos understand the larger social structure and their place within it. Further, these perceptions have been shown to have implications for a sense of group identity, political participation and alienation (for example, civic engagement, lack of trust; Schildkraut 2007).

How do Latinos perceive their relationships with *other groups*, including discrimination from other groups, and what might that imply for their sense of community and belonging in the United States? Do they perceive discrimination *within* their own group—and what might this suggest for the sense of a pan-ethnic Latino community? Do current perceptions of discrimination among Latinos indicate continuity or change from what we know about these perceptions in the past? These questions—which have yet to be explored in the context of the massive Latino immigration of the 1990s—are the focus of this chapter.

The complexity of the phenomenon of discrimination is reflected in the findings of a major study by the National Research Council. The study concluded, first, that discrimination can be perpetrated by either individuals or organizations; second, that discrimination can be either intentional or indirect; and third, that in organizations direct forms of discrimination can take the form of statistical profiling, whereas indirect forms can simply be enmeshed in the organization's culture. In addition, discrimination can be seen either in the disparate treatment of minorities or in disparate impact, or results, even when discrimination is not immediately apparent. Finally, the effects of discrimination on individuals can be cumulative across arenas—so although discrimination may appear minor in any one domain, the impact of discrimination adds up across situations and across time (Blank, Dabady, and Citro 2004).

The complexity suggested by the existing research is reflected in our focus groups. The conversations indicate that discrimination experienced by Latinos is a complex, multidimensional phenomenon. We find, first of all, that Latino participants report they are targets of discrimination perpetrated by Anglos/whites. However, they indicate relatively modest levels of personal experiences of discrimination while at the same time reporting high rates of continuing discrimination against Latinos in general. Second, they also state that they are increasingly accepted in American society by both Anglos/whites and, interestingly, by African Americans. Third, perhaps unexpectedly, there are clear indications that intragroup discrimination—discrimination of Latinos against other Latinos—occurs and may be widespread. This chapter both reports and makes sense of the complexity of these findings on discrimination, suggesting that individual perceptions of discrimination diverge from perceptions of discrimination against the group, that individual views of discrimination are tied in with views of intergroup relations more generally, and that discrimination is more than simply about white Americans' view of Latinos.

Survey Research on Latinos' Perceptions of Discrimination

To better understand and compare Latinos' past and contemporary perceptions of discrimination, we turn to the findings of prior survey research as a useful starting point (even though the considerable and frequent difference in question wording across surveys can make direct comparisons difficult). In general, earlier studies tend to suggest that Latinos perceive some, but arguably not especially pronounced, discrimination from non-Latinos (cf. Hero 1992); that is, not the levels experienced historically by African Americans. For example, the Latino National Political Survey (LNPS), a national sample of Mexicans, Puerto Ricans, and Cubans conducted in 1989, included numerous questions about Latino citizens' and noncitizens' perceptions of discrimination (see de la Garza et al. 1992: 92–95, 171–174). A general pattern in the LNPS findings was that Latinos reported only modest levels of perceived personal experience with discrimination (roughly a third of the LNPS respondents said they had personally been discriminated against), while larger percentages of respondents reported discrimination against their national-origin group. Interestingly, citizens perceived higher levels of both personal discrimination and discrimination against Latinos in general than did noncitizens.

More recent surveys of Latinos have found significantly higher rates of perceptions of discrimination. The Pew Hispanic Center's 2002 National Latino Survey concluded that: "Latinos overwhelmingly say that discrimination against Latinos is a problem both in general and in specific settings such as schools and the workplace." Note, however, that the question asked in the survey refers to discrimination toward Latinos as a *group* rather than *personal* experience with discrimination, likely raising the percentages reporting discriminatory treatment. The study also found that a very large majority (83% percent) of Latinos also reported that discrimination by Hispanics against other Hispanics is a problem, and almost half (47%) feel that this is a "major problem." Latinos were most likely to attribute intragroup discrimination to disparities in income and education, though a substantial number also feel that Latinos discriminate against other Latinos because they or their ancestors are from a different country of origin.

The difference question wording can make is seen in the results of another Pew survey, conducted in five states in 2004. Asking about *personal* experiences with discrimination, the survey found that about three in ten Latinos reported that they, a family member, or a close friend have experienced discrimination from non-Latinos during the past five years because of their racial or ethnic background. Large majorities of the respondents reporting discrimination indicated that discrimination was particularly problematic in schools (75%), the workplace (78%), and in general, in preventing Latinos from succeeding (82%). Forty-one percent of the survey's Latino respondents reported receiving "poorer service than other people at restaurants or stores" at some point, 30% had been "called names or insulted," and 14% perceived they were "not hired or promoted for a job because of their race or ethnic background" (Pew Hispanic Center 2004b: 3). This same survey also found that Latinos discriminating against other Latinos is a problem, reported by about half of respondents across all five states (Pew Hispanic Center 2004b: 4).

On the whole, the Pew surveys indicate that respondents perceived high levels of discrimination from non-Latinos when the question was asked about Latinos in general or in group versus "personal" terms. The percentages reported for group discrimination were higher than those reported by the LNPS, but reported about the same percentages when asking about individuals' own experience of discrimination. The Pew surveys also find considerable levels of perceived discrimination of Latinos by other Latinos.

The results of the 2006 Latino National Survey (LNS), conducted by the authors, had some similarities and differences from the findings reported from these earlier surveys. Some of these, again, may be due to question differences. While the LNS asked a battery of questions about personal experiences with discrimination, with one or two exceptions it did not ask about perceived discrimination against Latinos as a group. Specifically, LNS respondents were asked about "the way other people treated you" and if the respondent had been "unfairly treated," for example, either by (1) being fired or denied a job or promotion, (2) being discouraged from moving into a neighborhood, (3) being denied service at restaurants or stores, or (4) being treated poorly by the police.

About a third (33%) of all those surveyed by the LNS indicated at least one instance in which they had been "treated unfairly" on one of these four dimensions concerning personal experiences with discrimination, as shown in Table 4-1. These findings are broadly similar to the results of both the Pew and LNPS surveys. However, taking each question one by one, the overwhelming majority of Latinos—ranging from 81% to 92%—answered "No" to each of the four questions, as shown in Table 4-2. At first glance this seems to indicate a very modest

TABLE 4-1 PERCEPTIONS OF BEING "TREATED UNFAIRLY,"
BY GENERATION*

| | Generational Status | | | | |
	1st	2nd	3rd	4th	Total
No	76.75	9.89	7.75	5.61	100.00
	72.29	56.02	54.14	48.13	66.76
Yes	59.08	15.60	13.19	12.14	100.00
	27.71	43.98	45.86	51.87	33.24
Total	70.88	11.79	9.56	7.78	100.00

*Answered "yes" to at least one discrimination question.
N = 8,601; Pearson $\chi^2(3) = 300.5019$; Pr = 0.000. Data from Latino National Survey, 2006.

TABLE 4-2 RESPONDENTS' PERCEIVED EXPERIENCES OF
PERSONAL DISCRIMINATION IN EMPLOYMENT, IN
HOUSING, BY CUSTOMER SERVICE, AND BY POLICE*

	Employment	Housing	Customer Service	Police
Yes	16.4%	5.9%	16.4%	14.0%
No	81.4%	92.3%	81.9%	84.4%
DK/NA	2.2%	1.8%	1.7%	1.6%
Mean	1.86	1.96	1.85	1.88
Median	2	2	2	2
Standard deviation	.41	.27	.40	.37

*LNS question:
Employment: Have you ever . . . been unfairly fired or denied a job or promotion?
Housing: Have you ever . . . been unfairly prevented from moving into a neighborhood because
the landlord or a realtor refused to sell or rent you a house or apartment?
Customer service: Have you ever . . . been treated unfairly or badly at restaurants or stores?
Police: Have you ever . . . been unfairly treated by the police?
DK/NA = Don't know/No answer. N = 8,634 for all questions.

perception of personal experiences of discrimination among the LNS
respondents on the dimensions taken individually.

There, is however, clear differentiation in these responses by generation (see Table 4.1); perceptions of experiences of being treated
unfairly increase from first-generation immigrants to later generations.
While only a little more than a quarter (28%) of those in the first generation (those born abroad) note at least one form of being treated
unfairly, this percentage almost doubles for respondents born in the
United States. Forty-five percent of respondents in the second and
third generations, and over half (52%) in the fourth generation indicated they had been treated unfairly either in their place of employment, in their search for housing, in restaurants or shopping, or by the

police. Because first-generation immigrants comprise two-thirds of all respondents in the LNS, and respondents of this generation tend to perceive little in the way of unfair treatment, the overall perceptions of unfair treatment reported in the survey are lowered. This implies that as the proportion of Latinos who are second and later generations increase in the future, there could well be an increase in overall perceptions of unfair treatment among Latinos.

The LNS, like earlier surveys, finds that about a third of all Latinos experience some form of discrimination firsthand and that first-generation Latinos are less likely to perceive being treated unfairly or to identify that treatment as "discrimination." Perceptions of discrimination against one's group—Latinos in general, or one's national origin group in particular—have been found to be significantly higher. To understand how Latinos think about the complexities of discrimination in American society, however, it is best to turn to their own thoughts and words. Fortunately, our focus group discussions provide a window on Latinos' own conceptualizations of these complexities.

Focus Group Discussions on Discrimination and Intergroup and Intragroup Relations

The focus group discussions underscore that Latinos' views regarding discrimination are diverse and sometimes apparently inconsistent, not unlike some of the findings suggested by earlier survey research. Our analysis of their comments is organized as follows. We first examine focus group participants' perspectives on *inter*group relations— their sense of "acceptance" or "discrimination" and prejudice by other groups, usually non-Hispanic whites. We discuss general observations and then perceptions about several specific dimensions, such as jobs and the workplace. Next we consider their perspectives on another set of intergroup relations—between Latinos and African Americans— which have increasingly been a topic in popular discussion. Finally we focus on participants' perceptions of *intra*group relations.

The conversations include general comments and perceptions of such issues as (1) the extent, or relative absence, of discrimination; (2) what types of discrimination occur, in what arenas of social life; (3) the perceptions of the reasons discrimination occurs; and (4) who perpetrates the discrimination. Views on these issues are not necessarily clearly or separately delineated in the participants' comments, however; that is, references to these may take place within or be intertwined in participants' remarks about various subjects. Such is the nature of spontaneous conversations.

Intergroup (Latino-Anglo/White) Relations

Our focus group comments offer a different perspective on these issues than the findings reported in surveys, while not necessarily contradicting survey findings. For instance, a considerable portion of the focus groups participants report having personally experienced or been witness to discrimination by someone outside of their racial/ethnic group, most often by non-Hispanic whites. This is generally consistent with the evidence from the 2006 LNS presented in Table 4-3, which delineates who respondents report committed discrimination toward them.

A number of focus group participants suggest that intergroup discrimination is the result of initial misconceptions about Latinos and that once others have interacted with them or after Latinos have proven their worth, the experience of discrimination diminishes and is mitigated. Reports of intergroup discrimination are often attributed to initial concerns from neighbors about living near a family of a different "race" as well as to stereotypes others have about the Latino community. There is some sentiment in the focus groups that intergroup discrimination is resolved by forced interaction, meaning that people cannot always easily change where they live and that even if others do not like living near a Latino family they may, in a sense, "have to" accept Latinos through ("forced") contact. On the other hand, in

TABLE 4-3	RACE OF THOSE BY WHOM RESPONDENT WAS TREATED UNFAIRLY*
White	64.7%
Black	8.4%
Asian	3.3%
Latino	12.6%
DK/NA	11.1%

*LNS question: In the most recent incident [of being treated unfairly] you experienced, what was the race or ethnicity of the person(s) treating you unfairly?
DK/NA = Don't know/No answer. N = 2,868.

several instances Latinos perceive that whites simply relocate to avoid contact (with Latinos). This too, is generally consistent with the evidence from the 2006 LNS, presented in Table 4-4, which indicates the personal attributes that LNS participants have that they think are associated with the discrimination they experience, perceptions echoed in focus group comments.

Latinos sometimes attribute initial discrimination from Anglos or others to their "not knowing any better"; Latinos sometimes assert that it is the responsibility of the individual Latino or Latina to show others that Latinos are responsible and worthy of acceptance. For example, one participant noted that after white neighbors had seen how Latinos take care of their homes, mow their lawns, and behave "respectably," whites were more willing to accept and interact with Latinos. Perhaps notably, focus group participants did not necessarily seem to resent that they must "prove themselves" in the first place. They accede to a reality that they may not accepted or given the benefit of the doubt to begin with, but seem to feel that such perceptions of them can be overcome and changed. In line with the idea of "proving oneself," many of the participants argued at times that it is their *group's* responsibility to prove their worth and to improve their lifestyles.

There are also mentions of white/Latino separation from each other even when they are in the same neighborhood (such comments were more common in some focus group sites than others). Though participants say it is the individual who is primarily responsible for the

TABLE 4-4 PERCEPTIONS OF REASONS
FOR BEING TREATED
UNFAIRLY*

Being Latino	29.8%
Being an immigrant	8.1%
Your national origin	7.7%
Your language or accent	13.2%
Your skin color	12.6%
Your gender	2.3%
Your age	3.7%
Other	15.3%
DK/NA	7.4%

*LNS question: There are lots of possible reasons why people might be treated unfairly. What do you think was the main reason for your experience(s)? Would you say it was because of . . . ?

DK/NA = Don't know/No answer. N = 2,868.

disparate status of Latinos in the United States, others also blamed Latinos as a group, while yet others referred to what might be called "structural inequalities" for any systematic discrimination, especially within the workplace. The discussions and descriptions of intergroup relations also included positive, hopeful outlooks that relationships had improved or would improve between those of differing races/ethnicities. Underlying both intergroup and intragroup discrimination are matters of acceptance and the tension between being a "good American" through emphasizing economic success and hard work.

In each of the focus group sessions, participants were asked questions about their feelings of acceptance or sense of discrimination against Latinos. The question was posed by the group moderator along the lines of: "In general, in your neighborhoods, and in your own situations is there a good acceptance of Latinos? Of Hispanics?" The responses by participants ranged from reports of subtle negative interactions to overtly hostile responses. For instance, a woman at the English language focus group in Washington, DC, gave a picture of subtly negative intergroup interactions:

> The majority [of non-Latinos] have good acceptance [of Latinos]. But you always have some people who kind of look at you and . . . you know. They don't say anything, I've never had anyone say anything to me or act differently but I have gotten that kind of look from people . . . There's a look of, they're just curious and notice somebody or a look of . . . I don't know how to explain it, not intimidation, it just makes me uncomfortable. That I know it's just not an accepting look. It's very few people, but there are people.

The more specific question about "discrimination against Hispanics" elicited comments about more directly overt discrimination, such as:

> Woman (Los Angeles, E): I've grown up in white neighborhoods for most of my life and I've been called "wetback," "mojada," you name it, I've been called it and it hasn't gotten any better.
> Woman (Muscatine, IA, E): We were the second family of two Mexican families in Muscatine when we got here. People

picked on me a lot; there was a lot of prejudice back then. There is not as much now, but it still exists: For example, a 23-year-old man called my son a "Spic" when he was at the community Y[MCA]. My son came home crying.

Participants also perceived several different decisions and behaviors that they took to be indicative of whites' negative attitudes toward Latinos. For instance, multiple individuals in focus groups in Dalton, GA, West Liberty, IA, and Los Angeles reported incidents of whites selling their homes when Latinos moved into their neighborhoods. While survey research, including the LNS, has asked about being "unfairly prevented from moving into a neighborhood because the landlord or a realtor refused to sell or rent you a house or apartment" (see Table 4-2 above), surveys have not generally asked whether white (or other) neighbors were selling their homes when Latinos moved into their neighborhoods. The focus groups provide evidence of such perceptions among Latinos. In addition, participants in West Liberty, IA, and Houston expressed views that Mexican/Hispanic students were treated differently than white students in public schools. We also heard comments regarding slights in participants' day-to-day activities as customers or as service providers. A woman at the Washington, DC, English-language focus group cited [mis]treatment when she shopped: "In [a store] the other day, *the man just totally walked by me* and helped an older white lady." At the English-language focus group in Houston, one woman recounted an experience as a salesperson:

[Y]ou can feel sometimes different from the way they treat you. . . . I was trying to help and I was really nice to them. And the lady, she had a mother and maybe she was like 70-something and the daughter was like 50. They were trying to return something. I was nice to them and I was trying to be polite and tell them that I could not return the merchandise and she got really mad and she told me, "*I don't know what you are doing here but you don't belong to America.*"

Thirteen percent of LNS respondents believe language was a reason for discrimination they experienced (see Table 4-4), and focus group participants discuss these concerns as well. At the same time, participant comments also reveal the complicated nature of language as a source of difference and frustration in a kind of "damned if you do and damned if you don't" dilemma. Speaking Spanish is sometimes the basis for perceived dislike; on the other hand, some were annoyed that they are assumed *not* to have English language skills. For example, one woman from the Spanish-speaking group in Dalton, GA, said: "Sometimes they tell you bad words for not speaking English." Another woman in the group chimed in that, "I felt insulted because they thought I did not speak English."

In addition to general and language-related perceptions of discrimination, there were numerous comments having to do with one's situation on the job or in the workplace. About 16% of LNS respondents thought they had experienced unfair treatment "regarding jobs and/or promotions" (see Table 4-2). Likewise, the conversation in the Spanish-language focus group in Houston suggests perceptions of hostile work environments:

> *Woman (Houston, S):* I work in an office where the majority of the employees are whites . . . well . . . I was born here, and I grew up here, all my life here, I know that *a lot of discrimination is going on here.*
> *Moderator:* At your workplace?
> *Same woman as above:* Of course. Well, what happens nowadays is that now [there is] more and more demand for bilingual people in the work force. If you know more than one language it is a "plus" for you. Now, they look for people that speak more than one language than one who doesn't, *but anyway the discrimination is there.*
> *Another woman (Houston, S):* About three months ago, I was in my cubicle that is in the middle and a guy come and asked me, "How are the Mexicans today?" and I told him, "Same as rednecks." . . . *There is a lot of discrimination . . . a lot.*
> *A third woman (Houston, S):* [There] *always has been* [discrimination].

Comments made in other focus groups both echo the views of the Houston focus group, and make both specific and implicit references to Latinos' situation in the social and economic structure:

Man (Los Angeles, S): Work is hard, and the less paid and harder working are the Hispanics. I've never seen a white person as a dishwasher.

Woman (Los Angeles, S): They also give them [Latinos] more work and less money, but they [Latinos] don't speak up, so they stay there.

Man (Los Angeles, S): I had a Cuban friend who spoke English very well, but he did not feel that they gave him one of the jobs because he was Hispanic.

Man (Washington, DC, S): [F]rom the moment I began [my job] there, my IQ dropped about 10 points once they learned I was Hispanic. They are not accustomed that I am Latino.

Woman (Los Angeles, E): I am 32; I was born in Ciudad Juarez, Mexico, and grew up and lived in the San Fernando Valley; been living there for 28 years up until about a year and half ago. . . . We moved up to canyon country and that's my home now. What I've found difficult there is racism.

Man (West Liberty, IA, S): I believe that the racism will never end as long as there are different races. I have seen a lot of discrimination at my workplace. It seems like the Americans do not want to see us do better. I have seen the Americans humiliating the Latinos because they don't want us to surpass them. There's an element of us not defending ourselves—because of the barrier of not being able to speak English.

While on the whole participants saw workplace opportunity linked to language and recognized the implications of language abilities, we also heard another side of this issue discussed. It is probably not surprising that the following exchange took place in Miami, at an English-language focus group, where these types of issues have been a source of tension between Latinos, whites, and blacks. Here, there is a suggestion that speaking Spanish, or, more directly, being bilingual might be advantageous for Latinos, though non-Latinos may be less enthusiastic about this.

Woman A (Miami, E): Here in Miami . . . I believe that [you] have to be bilingual in order to get a job.

Woman A (Miami, E): Every time you look in the paper you have to be bilingual.
Woman B (Miami, E): But what kind of jobs are we talking about? We are not talking CEOs of companies.
Woman A (Miami, E): Everywhere.

Some Latinos sense that discrimination is not always expressed directly and that different standards of evaluation exist for Latinos even if they do not perceive overt discrimination. The comments of a Spanish-speaking participant in Houston are revealing in this respect:

Woman (Houston, S): Hispanics at work have to prove themselves more than a white person.
Moderator: Nowadays, still?
Woman: Of course.
Moderator: In which way?
Woman: In the way that you have to show off what you are capable at work. You have to have discipline at work, not only in education; you really have to learn your job (tasks), know your job better than a white person because of the discrimination, so, the discrimination always has been here in the south.

Perceptions of Changing Relations over Time

While some participants felt there had been little change in the extent of discrimination directed toward Latinos, some thought discriminatory behavior was decreasing, but attributed the decline to the "necessity" of non-Hispanic whites having to come to grips with changes represented by the growing Latino population. While there is hardly a growing sense of "'community" between Latinos and whites suggested in these comments, there is perceived change associated with the social and economic realities that whites confront.

Man (Los Angeles, E): I just feel it [discrimination] is suppressed only because we aren't the minority anymore. It's hidden. . . . We are a majority and have a louder voice.

Woman (Los Angeles, E): Whether they like it or not, we have buying power now. They have to hear it.

Man (Los Angeles, S): I think here in Los Angeles [it] has gotten better because the majority of us here are Hispanics. I have heard in other places where there are less Hispanics, they try to scare them off so that they can go somewhere, whereas here in Los Angeles, there are so many of us that it is accepted.

On the other hand, some participants perceived clear changing and improving circumstances regarding discrimination by non-Latinos toward Latinos. This is apparent in comments at the Los Angeles English-language focus group, when the participants were asked if they thought Latino-white relations were "declining or getting better." The explanations for and evidence put forth in support of their assessments are also interesting.

Man A (Los Angeles, E): I think it [discrimination] is going to decline because of the growing Latino population. They accept us more. On a personal level, I've never really been that much discriminated against.

Woman A (Los Angeles, E): It's changed so that *they help each other more*. It depends on where you live; *if there's diversity they [whites and Latinos] get along better.*

Woman B (Los Angeles, E): Less [discrimination] now. Other than an incident when I was younger, I haven't been discriminated against to my face.

Man B (Los Angeles, E): Less. I've started to see a big difference from industry, education; you know, first time I've seen a Latin owner in baseball. . . . I'm seeing more Latins in music. To me personally, *I'm starting to see a decline [in discrimination].*

Woman C (Los Angeles, E): In my neighborhood, we are the only Hispanic family there. Most of my neighbors are Jewish. *But, no one treats us differently at all.*

Man C (Los Angeles, E): Less [discrimination]. Comparing what my father went through and what I went through, it's much less. It's more subtle, don't show it as much. As I see it Latinos are making a big statement in politics and in the music industry—*it's not about color anymore. It's what people like.*

Similarly, we also heard perceptions that there may once have been considerable discrimination, but that this has changed over time in the Houston area.

> *Woman (Houston, E):* I remember when my parents bought the house they live in now. They had a hard time buying the house; the people selling the house—their neighbors didn't want them to sell it to us. The neighbors came up to us when we moved in and told us to leave because we were Mexican and that we belonged somewhere else. I don't think that would happen now. . . . I don't have to be cautious anymore because [we are] accepted.
>
> *Woman (Houston, S):* At work . . . a long time ago, around the 70s and 80s, I remember when I used to work part-time. I worked in a press and we used to work like here in this table . . . inspecting books and always *we had the Latino group, the white group, etc.* And after that I went back to work permanently again. . . . I worked in an office *and it wasn't there anymore. . . . We all were equals. . . . Yes, we all were equals. . . . In that aspect it has changed; I have seen a change.*

There were also comments by some Latino focus group participants claiming that perceptions of discrimination held by fellow Latinos might actually be incorrect or is overstated or attributed to racial/ethnic background when it should be or in fact is linked to something else. We hear statements about "merit," rather than racial, considerations being central, and that economic opportunities do exist for Latinos.

> *Man (Washington, DC, S):* I worked for a bank as a teller/cashier, and *my* experience has been that my friends are excelling, and they are happy with that. I have a friend who has worked there for 6 months and she began as a cashier,

but she wanted to work as a receptionist, but the manager told her she couldn't because she needed more experience, but she took it as not getting the position because she was Hispanic. I personally think that it was because of the lack of experience, but she thinks it is because they are gringos that they didn't hire her for the position.

Another man (Washington, DC, S): Truthfully, if one does not have the experience, in most jobs you will not advance. I worked in a communications center for a while, and I remember a Hispanic woman going to apply, and she did not understand English well, and ended up being let go, and she complained to the office that it was because she was Hispanic, but it was because she did not do her job well. My point is that if you are not prepared, it doesn't matter what you are in this country.

Moderator: In your point of view, you don't see any discrimination against Latinos?

Woman (Washington, DC, S): Like I said before, *not in my work, because they trained people very well, but they don't learn, so it is not discrimination.*

One participant, in Houston, echoed sentiments similar to these Washington, DC, participants:

Man (Houston, E): To me . . . where I work, it's like *if you're a good employee, you're okay, but if you still don't do what your job is, it don't matter what your color is.* The guy that's been there the longest is Mexican. I see the fact that he hasn't moved up, like the other guys that are equal to him [in] time, [is] because [of] the fact that he doesn't speak English well. . . . If he can't do his job, I mean, that's where he should have bettered himself, you know. There's English classes, there's all kind of stuff that I had to get that he didn't do. . . . I see where that holds him back. He doesn't see that there's another guy, that's been there 8 years and [this guy has] passed him up. But I see why. This guy's more intelligent, he . . . holds himself better, he talks very—I mean, you go, he can have a conversation with people that this other guy can't possibly. You know, because it's just too hard for him.

Latino-Black Relations

Most of the discussion in the focus groups on intergroup relations was on Latino-white relations. However, another topic that has received increasing attention in research and popular discourse is Latino-black interactions (see, for example, McClain et al. 2006; McClain 2006; Kaufmann 2007). The 2006 LNS survey indicates that about 8% of the Latinos who perceived discrimination said it was from blacks (see Table 4-3). Here, we note some comments that were made on this subject in Houston and in Los Angeles; in the latter site the views surfaced in both the Spanish- and English- language focus groups.

Woman (Houston, S). Well, when I started to work here in Houston, it wasn't a lot of African Americans, but I always got along with everybody. Once, in another job, a discussion started between a Latin-Texan (Tejana) woman and an African American and I was there with her and I told her, "I don't owe you anything, because I didn't know any blacks until I moved to Chicago that has a big population." In t[there], Del Rio wasn't much [of a black population]. . . . The discussion ended right after that.

Man (Los Angeles, S): I came here with my father [to Los Angeles from Hollywood]. . . . I had problems with some of the people . . . because they were all black, and they did not like Latinos. I got into a fight there . . . so I came back to North Hollywood. The people here are nicer.

Man (Los Angeles, E): Well, when I was living in San Fernando, it was pretty much all Mexicans . . . and you don't really see any other types of nationalities. I did notice a couple of black people moving in there. . . . Mexicans reacted towards that really quick. They felt like blacks tried to invade our territory. Mexicans looked at them when they walked down the street . . . you know how they do it.

Woman (Los Angeles, E): Yeah, like the blacks look at Mexicans. Or even Mexicans at whites.

Another man in this Los Angeles English-language group said: "Everyone does it. I hear from my little nephew and sister that they do it. We don't like it when it is done to us, but we do it to other people." Note that in their comments about whites, Latino participants talk about discrimination as coming *from* whites; however, in their comments on black-Latino relations, participants are at least as likely to talk about discrimination originating from Latinos *toward* blacks. The relations with whites and blacks are seen quite differently.

To conclude this section on intergroup relations, we would like to make two closing comments: Along with the commentaries in this section concerning perceptions of discrimination, there are other allusions that are relevant to Latinos' sense of community. In a number of instances participants referred to other Latinos as "we" and "us"; similarly, the participants often spoke of "Latinos" or "Hispanics" as part of a group to which they themselves (the participants) implicitly belonged. These references connote some notion of Latino "community" that occurs alongside the various complexities in the level, types, and sources of perceived discrimination. This is discussed in greater detail in our chapter on Latino identity (Chapter 7). Second, issues of relations with or discrimination from representatives of "the state" (that is, governmental officials, which may include the police) did not appear in the focus group discussions. Survey data might help explain the absence of this topic, though not completely; only 14% of respondents in the LNS (2006) said yes when asked if they (personally) had been "unfairly treated by the police" (see Table 4-2), and in the LNPS (see de la Garza et al. 1992: 92, 171–172) the vast majority of Latinos felt they were treated well by "public officials." On the other hand, when asked if the "police treat Latinos fairly in your community," a substantial portion of LNS respondents, 38%, said "No" (see Table 4-5). It could well be that the questions posed by the moderator did not evoke such concerns. Or it may simply be that the issues are simply not salient to or on the minds of the participants, which would be consistent with the low levels of perceived personal discrimination reported in the survey data, though not necessarily as consistent with the evidence on perceptions of discrimination against Latinos as a group.

Intragroup (Latino-Latino) Relations

Our analysis of the growing Latino community indicates that Latinos largely live, work, and socialize with other Latinos (see Chapter 7 in this volume), though there were over twice as many cases of intergroup discrimination mentioned compared to intragroup discrimination (roughly 49 to 21) in the focus groups. Assertions of intragroup discrimination, though not frequent, are not unusual, either. The group conversations are useful for highlighting participants' perceptions of intragroup discrimination, and the responses in Pew Survey regarding intragroup discrimination also suggest this is an important issue to consider. Also, among those who perceived some type of discrimination, about 13% of LNS respondents said it was from a Latino (refer back to Table 4-4).

Differences or disagreements about language, nativity, and national origin seem to be the source of occurrences of perceived discrimination from other Latinos. There is implicit tension about how a Latino should behave, often judged by the ability to speak Spanish, and how a Latino should succeed in the economic sphere, often judged by a Latino's ability to adapt to American demands (for example, the ability to perform well on the job, speak Spanish, or seek education). The discussions imply that a general expectation is that a Latino should be aware and active within their culture (which may explain issues about being able to speak Spanish, or English, or both), as well as able to adapt to the United States, with the main goal of advancing economically, which may explain the perceptions that American-born Latinos think of themselves as superior to non-Latinos. Accordingly, Latinos who are seen as achieving social and economic advancement at the expense of their cultural awareness and participation are seen as being less authentic. This tension is summed up by one of the participants who stresses: "That's the thing, while we are American, born here, we can't forget our heritage. . . . We are American, and we do have to speak English well, but don't forget where you came from." A woman in the Washington, DC, English-language focus group noted as well that: "Sometimes there is [discrimination] within the Latinos. . . . In my dad's store we have a lot of people from El Salvador and my husband is from El Salvador. My own Bolivian family has this prejudice against people from Central America, especially from El Salvador.

Because they're coming from the pueblos and they're not as educated, and so there is this mentality that you have to treat them in a different way, and it's been very difficult for me."

When considering intragroup relations, intergroup relations may also be relevant because Latinos sometimes feel "caught in the middle" between Latinos and whites in the society, as illustrated in the following:

> *Woman (Houston, E):* I get it both from the people that come from Mexico and I get it from the people that come from other Spanish [countries]. And I get it from the white people because people that come from Mexico from other land countries, they ask, "Do you know how to speak Spanish?" and I say "Yes" and they turn around and say, well, like being criticized because I speak English and I don't speak enough Spanish. And then from the white people I am criticized because I don't speak enough English and I speak Spanish. So I am right there in the middle and I hear it from both sides when they come and you know . . . the Hispanic people sometimes they can be cruel.
>
> *Woman (Washington, DC, E):* Well, you get that [discrimination] in the reverse, too. . . . [W]hen we came over here, very few Hispanic families were in this area, so all my friends, growing up, they were all white. But then, when the Hispanics started moving in the communities, in school, I would get dirty looks from the Latin kids that would come in. Because all my friends were white growing up and that's who I hung out with, those were the people I grew up with. *But they [Latino kids] kind of looked at me like I was selling out or "Why are you hanging out with them and not hanging out with us . . ." With me, they spoke Spanish and I answered in English and they felt like, "Oh, you're too good for us?"* and some things like that and "No, that's just what I'm used to. I don't live in Guatemala, I live in the U.S."

The frustration about Latino-Latino treatment was evident in this lengthy exchange among the Spanish-language focus group in Houston. Also, note that a reason suggested for why there may sometimes be less discrimination from whites is due simply to the lack of contact with them.

> Woman A (Houston, S): [O]n discrimination, well, *from white towards Hispanics I have not had any because I don't work, right?* But when I was pregnant my doctor sent me to WIC; well, I didn't speak English and didn't ask for anything, my sister in-law presented her pay stub and a Hispanic woman that was helping us said to me, "You don't qualify" and I said "OK." Then, there was an African American woman and she asked me, "What happened?" I told her, "She said that I don't qualify." She went and asked the Hispanic, "Why she didn't qualify?" The Hispanic said, "She makes too much money" and "Who is making the money, her sister-in-law or she that is pregnant?" The Hispanic said, "Well, her sister-in-law" and "Who is pregnant?" She said "her" do you see, you didn't wanted to help her. *You see, that was the first time I faced somebody here, and for me a Hispanic woman didn't help me.*
>
> Moderator: And that was because she was a Hispanic from here and you were an immigrant just arriving?
>
> Woman A: I think so; I just had arrived and I thought that a Hispanic (woman) could give a hand, but the hand came from an African American.
>
> Man A: Just as happened to me.
>
> Woman B: Yes, she represents the "power," the power that she has from this side.
>
> Woman A: But I think this one was a Hispanic born and raised here.
>
> Man B: [W]e experienced something similar. Once, I was helping one of my cousins to buy a car. . . . We went to the dealership in the same clothes we came from work because we didn't have a chance to change it, so we're dirty. When we got there we saw a Hispanic guy; we said to ourselves, we are lucky; he is going to give us a hand, we felt supported. We came close, he saw us and ignored us; he didn't help us, I think because of the way we were dressed and maybe

because he thought we were Hispanics and we might not have money, or he thought we didn't have enough to put down about $500, or who knows, but he did not want to help us. Then, an African American came and asked, "How may I help you?" So, we told him that we would like to buy a car, he said okay. He helped us very well, much better that we expected, and on top of that he gave us a discount on the car. My cousin gave the money to pay for the car in full and, in cash, as appreciation for his help my cousin gave him $500. He went in front of the Hispanic that was working there and told him, "For you not wanting to help him, see what he gave me." *Just because of the appearances, he didn't want to give us a hand.*

Woman B: Being from the same race doesn't mean that they are going to help each other.

Woman C: I think is because . . . we are Hispanics right? But some Hispanics are better prepared than others, right? I studied nursing, and for 10 years I worked to support myself as a voluntary, over there [in Mexico] we're all Hispanics. When I came here I felt comfortable when I saw a Hispanic, but I have seen that because they are better prepared with English and all, is like they treat us with inferiority.

This discussion in the Dalton, GA, Spanish-language focus group also captures views about workplace relationships among Latinos, suggesting that Latino supervisors' place and status in the workplace encourages certain behaviors of trying to "look good" by sometimes being hard on Latinos.

Moderator: Are your coworkers Hispanic?

Woman A: They are Hispanic, but supervisors are white.

Man: There are blacks, Hispanics, but the hard jobs they give to Latinos and Latinas.

Moderator: Are there any Latino supervisors?

Woman B: There are a few, but sometimes they are worse than white supervisors.

Woman C: I would rather have a white supervisor.

Woman B: When there are Mexican supervisors they want to look good and they treat people bad sometimes.

From the Spanish-speaking group held in Houston, we hear irritation expressed when they discuss prejudice experienced from fellow Latinos:

> *Woman (Houston, S):* I remember one time my daughter went to eat at a Mexican restaurant and when she was paying she told the cashier, "I have these three coins and I'm going to give it to you," and the Latina at the cashier said to someone else [in Spanish], "Look at these Americans— they come to eat rice and beans although it's with pennies." Then, my daughter—that knew Spanish and understood what she was saying—told her in Spanish to keep her beans and rice and "I don't need come to eat here" and left.

Additional evidence of intragroup tensions was expressed during the English-language focus group in Los Angeles:

> *Woman (Los Angeles, E):* I personally feel that Latinos don't support each other. We have Hispanics out there with a lot of talent and the Hispanics don't support them. The whole world is about money.
> *Woman (Los Angeles, E):* Not all. Some support.
> *Moderator:* Is it a problem?
> *All:* Yes, it is a problem.
> *Another woman:* That's because *we have too much competition.*

However, comments by other participants implied that intra-Latino relationships were not necessarily discriminatory or "a problem" as such, but that Latinos may not help each other as much as do other groups.

> *Woman (Los Angeles, E):* I don't think that Hispanics discriminate against Hispanics as they did at one time. We've accepted each other a little better—a bit more solidarity— but not enough to get us ahead.

Woman West Liberty, IA, S): I work as a manager in a restaurant, and when I began working there, there were a variety of people. My manager is Lebanese. All of his bosses are also Lebanese, and they help them out a lot. I think they do what we don't. *Once we start to excel, we stop helping our friends, but they [the Lebanese] don't stop; they continue to help each other out no matter what.*

Discrimination or Something Else?

Separation/Indifference/Isolation/Detachment?

Apart from intergroup relations directly, we hear a number of comments from participants indicating that they perceived as much (or more) distance or indifference from non-Latinos, and it appeared others were too isolated or detached for discrimination to be an issue. A heterogeneous neighborhood does not necessarily imply interactions and contact. Here are illustrative examples from Latinos living in predominantly non-Latino neighborhoods or employed at places with large numbers of non-Latino workers but having limited contact with non-Latinos:

> *Man (Washington, DC, E):* It's pretty much been good, the neighborhood where I've been living right now, I've just moved about three months ago. . . . It's just basically that I know my two next-door neighbors and the rest it's just pretty much a "hi" when they're coming by, but that's it. . . . It's not that close of a community. Everybody lives their own lives.
>
> *Woman (Dalton, GA, S):* All my neighbors are white, but I work third shift so I don't have time to meet them.
>
> *Moderator:* How are the people you work with? Is there collaboration, acceptance with the people you work with?
>
> *Man (Los Angeles, S):* In this place, there is a lot of separation. The whites separate themselves even though they say "hi," they still separate themselves into groups.
>
> *Man (Los Angeles, S):* I have been working at Walt Disney Studios for 15 years, and have seen that the Americans

do separate themselves from the Hispanics. They say that my people are stealing. They segregate themselves. One does feel separated from them even because of the way we speak English.

Along with Latino/non-Latino separation, some participants also reported Latino separation from each other by national origin groups:

> *Woman (Los Angeles, S):* Not only whites [separate], but Latinos as well. The Mexicans or Salvadorians do. I have a sister-in-law who is Salvadorian, but I don't know why they still separate themselves [at work].
>
> *Man (Los Angeles, S):* I see that we as Latinos are the same as well. It is not only Americans or Asians [who separate]. A lot of times it is done because of work. A lot of times it is also because of the country.

Several times we heard expressions of Latinos feeling caught in-between their "own" and non-Latinos. Some of those expressions are noted elsewhere, as parts of other comments, but here is one specific example:

> *Man (Washington, DC, E):* My first neighborhood was predominantly white and as I got older more Latinos moved in. But I definitely noticed more prejudice as the time went on. I was the only Latino hanging out with like five or six white kids. There were a lot of Latinos who came straight from their countries. And at the same time they would look at you like, like I was kind of in-between. I mean the whites don't accept you and the Latinos don't accept you.

Conclusion

This chapter has provided an extensive set of narratives concerning Latinos' perceptions of intergroup and intragroup discrimination and, indeed, concerning intergroup and intragroup relations more broadly. The evidence from our focus groups, along with the existing survey research, demonstrates a range of views by Latinos on these issues.

After reviewing the focus group comments, we can better appreciate how and why survey research produces both the broadly similar yet also somewhat disparate findings that we noted.

The extent to which the assorted dimensions of intergroup and intragroup relations were discussed varied considerably across the focus groups. The participants highlighted a difference between intergroup relations and discrimination. The latter primarily discussed white discrimination toward Latinos, but also touched on intragroup discrimination, by Latinos toward other Latinos. Intergroup relations did not necessarily involve discrimination per se. In numerous instances in the focus group discussions, there are mentions of white indifference to or isolation from Latinos. At other times, the discussion of intergroup relations is suggestive of the "contact hypothesis," meaning that people of different race/ethnicity are initially hesitant or even dislike interaction with others (in this case, Latinos), but after some level and frequency of contact, barriers are lessened and discrimination appears to diminish. Other participants imply that they believe the decline of dislike from Anglos/whites is more apparent than real, feeling that the dislike is just more subtle or suppressed, or suggesting that it manifests itself through economic forms of inequality, but has not really ended. There are also comments suggesting that participants may not necessarily perceive personal discrimination per se, but that they feel they are disliked, and have fewer opportunities because of their location in the social and economic structure of society. There is a sense expressed by some participants that whites do not wish or want Latinos to do well. Yet, just about as often, we also hear clearly positive attitudes and hopes for improvement and advancement in the political, social, and economic lives of Latinos in the United States. We see evidence suggesting the emergence of and obstacles to a sense of place and community between Latinos and whites and even among Latinos more broadly.

We also hear different speculation and assessments of the reasons for how much change in these relations has occurred over time, and how, and why, the relationships could change in the future. Along with numerous allusions to discrimination, participants perceive substantial improvements in intergroup relations. Relatively modest levels of perceptions of individual experiences with discrimination stand in some contrast to assertions of discrimination against Latinos in general. Intragroup discrimination concerns are articulated more clearly and explicitly than in some of the early survey research. Finally, comments about black-Latino interactions suggest cases of better treatment of Latinos by blacks but sometimes negative treatment of blacks by Latinos. While the findings are complicated, the groups' comments elaborate on the nature of this complexity.

In addition to illustrating the breadth and depth of perceptions, the comments by participants suggest some hypotheses offered in other research, which can perhaps be analyzed further in future studies. One of those propositions is that Latinos are more accepted where Latinos comprise a larger portion of the population or where there are more diverse populations overall. And while a number make those claims, the *reasons* they offer differ. Some indicate contact and familiarity of Latinos and others eases the way toward less discrimination. Others suggest the acceptance of Latinos by non-Latinos may occur grudgingly; that is, they imply that non-Latinos come to grips with Latinos' presence almost out of a necessity stemming from large (and growing) Latino populations in their neighborhoods and cities. We also heard that variations in intragroup relations may occur based on the socioeconomic backgrounds of Latinos in their home country or within the United States, the amount of time the newcomers have been in the United States compared to those already present, language ability, as well as nationality differences; these seem to shape such relationships, and competition may also be a source of intragroup discrimination.

The evidence discussed in this chapter helps us better understand the nature of perceived discrimination and, in turn, may help explain how and why such sentiments occur and what circumstances may make them more or less common or intense. There appears to be both continuity and change in those views, at least as best as we can tell, comparing the narratives to past and recent surveys and based on observations offered by focus group participants. As difficult as it may be to fully identify and explain perceptions of discrimination, it is worth the effort because such perceptions have a variety of implications for Latinos in society and politics (Schildkraut 2007) and for their prospects for making America home.

5 New Homes in New Communities

Living in Rural America

A significant change in the fabric of Latino life in the United States has been the substantial spread of Latino populations to states where they have heretofore been largely unknown. Latinos have emerged as meaningful population shares in many states and exceed the African American population in about half of them. The emergence of large, rapidly growing minority populations, competing for jobs and triggering significant economic and social changes, is sure to raise a variety of interesting political questions.

The growth of Latino populations in the Deep South and Midwestern Farm Belt presents new challenges for the study of Latino life in the United States. Scholarly examination of Latinos outside of urban areas, such as in the suburbs (Alba, Logan, et al. 1999), is comparatively recent, and for these new and primarily rural communities has only just begun (Baker 2004; Cantú 1995; Michelson 2003; Williams, Alvarez, and Andrade Hauck 2002). It is not clear whether the new emerging communities will experience a repeat of the circumstances and conflicts that characterized the development of earlier Latino populations in California, Texas, and elsewhere, thereby illustrating substantial continuity in Latino experience in America.

Alternatively, Latinos in these communities may break from past experiences and chart a new path to political and social incorporation, one that will undoubtedly present new and different obstacles even as some previous pitfalls are avoided. It is clear from events so far, however, that whatever process emerges will not be free of contestation and social conflict.

These new locations clearly differ from some of the earlier locations in their predominantly rural or small-city character. Large-scale urban settlement of foreign-born Latinos in Los Angeles, Miami, New York, Chicago, and Houston has been studied at length and is more or less well understood by sociologists and political scientists with these foci. But social patterns in smaller cities and small towns, particularly in environments with long histories of racial contestation—such as the deep South—or little experience of racial diversity of any sort—as in the Midwest—represent a largely unexamined set of processes. This is not to say that there is no history of Latino rural settlement or migration. Much of the early points of contact between Latino and Anglo Americans took place in small, predominantly agricultural or rural communities in Texas and New Mexico. These were predominantly native born rather than immigrant Hispanic populations. In fact, in many of these instances, it was the non-Hispanic whites who were the newly arriving population. Latino immigrants, of course, have been a key component of Latino agricultural labor and were present in significant numbers in the central valley of California, the Coachella Valley, and elsewhere. Immigrant laborers were also used in places such as Fort Madison, IA, to work on railroads and in other industrial efforts. Much of these experiences, however, pre-date a substantial scholarly focus on Latinos in general and immigrant Latinos in particular and, thus, are unexamined with the tools of contemporary social science.

In this chapter, we explore three principal questions regarding the growth and experiences of newly emerging Latino communities. First, we outline the size and geography of these new communities and explore the source of geographic dispersion of the Latino population across the states. Second, we draw on extensive focus group data to explore the character of these communities, their life experiences, and social interactions. Do Latinos in these newer settlement areas feel welcomed, excluded, or somewhere in between? What is the nature of interethnic contact in these environments—conflictual, cooperative, or conditioned on immediate circumstances? Finally, we examine whether there is any evidence of successful political incorporation of these new population into policy-making institutions. We bolster these claims with data drawn from the Latino National Survey (LNS) and other sources and conclude with a variety of thoughts regarding what we have learned regarding newly forming Latino communities in the American heartland and, perhaps more importantly, what we have yet to learn.

Demographic Change and Its Causes

That the national Latino population has grown is obvious to any but the least observant Americans living in the Southwest and in other major metropolitan centers. The largest share of the Latino population growth continues to be seen in California, Florida, and Texas; however, a close examination of the 2000 census data, reported in Table 5-1, suggests that the most rapid Latino population growth (as a percentage) was in states not usually associated with Latino politics.

Table 5-1 reports the top 12 states in terms of growth in the Latino population percentage across the past two decennial censuses. In each case, the level of increase exceeds doubling; in a couple of instances, the Latino population increased almost fourfold in a single decade. Nearly all of these states—with the exception of Nevada—are in regions of the country not usually associated with Latino settlement. The

TABLE 5-1   STATES WITH THE LARGEST PERCENTAGE LATINO
POPULATION INCREASE, 1990–2000

State	% Change	Total Latino Population
North Carolina	394	378,963
Arkansas	337	86,666
Georgia	300	435,227
Tennessee	278	123,838
Nevada	217	393,970
South Carolina	211	95,067
Alabama	208	75,830
Kentucky	173	59,939
Minnesota	166	143,382
Nebraska	155	94,425
Iowa	153	82,473
Mississippi	148	39,569

rural Midwest, the Great Plains, and the Deep South account for most of the states with unusually rapid growth.

Of course, the total population numbers are not large, but neither are they inconsequential. Just as is the case nationally, the Latino population in these more rural environments where the Latino community is very new is unevenly distributed, suggesting that this population growth, while small in statewide terms, might be significantly changing the complexion of the communities where concentrated. This appears to be the case, as we illustrate in Table 5-2.

Table 5-2 illustrates the uneven impact of Latino population growth across counties in states with newly emerging Latino subpopulations. We report the statewide population percentage and then identify example counties where the Latino population percentage is significantly larger than in the state as a whole. As is readily apparent, the impact of growing Latino populations can be profound on specific communities, even in states where the overall percentage remains modest. For example, in Georgia, while the overall state population percentage for Latinos was 5.3 in the 2000 census, several counties had Latino populations approaching 20% and one—Whitfield—has a Latino population in excess of 20%. Similarly, while Nebraska's statewide population percentage for Latinos was 5.5, in Dawson and Colfax counties, more than a quarter of the population were self-identified Latinos. And in Washington State, whose overall population is about 7.5% Latino, Yakima County is over one-third Latino, and both Adams and Franklin counties are rapidly approaching the 50% mark. So while Latinos remain a small share of these states' populations, it is clear that the nature of entire communities has been profoundly altered by these demographic trends.

What has fueled this sizable growth in new areas? In large measure, the answer is jobs. Rapidly growing employment needs in agriculture, food processing, and low-skilled manufacturing—coming, as much of it did, in the 1990s when national unemployment was consistently below the full-employment target of 5%—created powerful incentives to in-migration to these areas. Of these industries, perhaps the biggest effects have come from large-scale food processing. Processed food manufacturers such as Cargill and Tyson employ tens of thousands of workers in agricultural areas. For example, Cargill's website estimates it employs more than 7,000 people in Nebraska and Iowa

TABLE 5-2　STATE LATINO POPULATION SHARES AND COUNTIES
　　　　　　WITH HIGH CONCENTRATIONS

State/County	Latino %	Geography	County Seat	Political Representation, County and Other
Arkansas	3.2			
Benton	8.8	NW, Fayetteville-Springdale-Rogers, AR-MO Metro area	Bentonville	0
Bradley	8.3	S, rural	Warren	0
Carroll	9.7	NW, rural	Berryville	0
Hempstead	8.3	SW, Hope Micro area	Hope	0
Sevier	19.7	SW, rural	De Queen	0
Yell	12.7	W, Russellville Micro area	Danville	0
Georgia	5.3			
Atkinson	17.0	S, Douglas Micro area	Pearson	0
Echols	19.7	S, Valdosta Metro area	Statenville	0
Hall	19.6	N, Gainesville Metro area	Gainesville	0
Whitfield	22.1	NW, Dalton Metro area	Dalton	0
Iowa	2.8			
Buena Vista	12.5	NW, Storm Lake Micro area	Storm Lake	0
Louisa	12.6	SE, Muscatine Micro area	Wapello	0
Marshall	9.0	Central, Marshalltown Micro area	Marshalltown	0
Muscatine	11.9	E, Muscatine Micro area	Muscatine	0
Woodbury	9.1	W, Sioux City, IA-NE-SD Metro area	Sioux City	0
Nebraska	5.5			
Colfax	26.2	E central, rural	Schuyler	0
Dakota	22.6	NE, Sioux City Metro area	Dakota City	0
Dawson	25.4	Central, Lexington Micro area	Lexington	0
Hall	14.0	Central, Grand Island Micro area	Grand Island	0
Morrill	10.1	W central, rural	Bridgeport	0
Scotts Bluff	17.2	W central, Scotts Bluff Micro area	Gering	0

(continued on next page)

TABLE 5-2   *Continued*

State/County	Latino %	Geography	County Seat	Political Representation, County and Other
North Carolina	17.2			
Duplin	15.1	Central, rural	Kenansville	0
Lee	11.7	Central, Sanford Micro area	Sanford	0
Montgomery	10.4	Central, rural	Troy	0
Sampson	10.8	Central, rural	Clinton	0
Washington	7.5			
Adams	47.1	SE, rural	Ritzville	0
Chelan	19.3	Central, Wenatchee Metro area	Wenatchee	0
Douglas	19.7	Central, Wenatchee Metro area	Waterville	0
Franklin	46.7	SE, Kennewick-Richland-Pasco Metro area	Pasco	Pasco School Board, 3 of 6 members*
Grant	30.1	Central, Moses Lake Micro area	Ephrata	0
Okanogan	14.4	N central, rural	Okanogan	0
Walla Walla	15.7	SE, Walla Walla Micro area	Walla Walla	0
Yakima	35.9	S central, Yakima Metro area, 8 cities or towns	Yakima	1 of 3 county commissioners, 0 on Yakima city council, 2 of 6 on Yakima School Board, plus several small-town successes†

Source: U.S. Census Bureau (2001) and National Association of Counties (www.naco.org).
* Includes president, one elected member, and one student representative.
† Yakima School Board numbers include superintendent and one elected member. Additional elected officials include 2 of 8 on Grandview city council, 2 of 7 on Wapato city council, 2 of 5 on Wapato School Board (1 is chair), 1 of 7 on Toppenish city council, 1 of 5 on Toppenish School Board, 1 assistant superintendent of Toppenish school district, 2 of 5 on Sunnyside School Board.

at 20 different plants. Tyson has 32 facilities in Arkansas alone, with about a dozen each in Iowa, North Carolina, and Georgia; eight in Nebraska; and nearly a hundred more across the Farm Belt in other states.

Exactly what share of the workers at these plants are Latinos is hard to estimate. However, the Associated Press reported during the May 1, 2006, immigrant economic boycott that Tyson had to completely shut down production at more than a dozen plants and curtail activities at others, while chicken processor Perdue Farms closed eight of its fourteen plants (Flaccus 2006). Similarly, Cargill announced that it was closing its meat-packing operations for the day, since production would be so severely compromised by Latino absenteeism as part of the boycott (Burgdorfer 2006). It is safe to say that Latinos, many of whom are immigrants—legal and undocumented—comprise a significant share of the workforce in this industry.

The evidence is compelling that Latino migration to these agricultural and manufacturing environments has been encouraged by the employers in question. For example, Schlosser (2004) has documented the economics of the labor market in meat-packing, contending that large-scale producers such as Tyson have aggressively driven down wages in the industry—and enlarged its capacity—through the active recruiting of undocumented labor and a coordinated assault on labor unions. Working conditions are bad, and the low-paying industry is described as having the highest "rate of serious injury" of any occupational category. Schlosser contends that, adjusted for inflation, real wages in the meat-packing industry "have declined by more than 50%" in the past 25 years.

These dynamics are further exacerbated by the U.S. Supreme Court's decision in *Hoffman Plastic Compounds, Inc. v. NLRB*.[1] In this case, decided in spring 2002, the Supreme Court relied on the undocumented status of a worker to nullify a finding of the National Labor Relations Board (NLRB) that the worker had been mistreated (in this case, laid off for supporting a union organization effort) and was thus entitled to back pay. The Court took issue, not with the justification of the NLRB in making the decision, but essentially with the legal status of the worker in question. As a consequence, current case law essentially excludes undocumented aliens from any of the various federal worker protections, likely making them a much more desirable class of employee for corporations seeking to reduce labor costs and avoid unionization struggles.

Not surprisingly, Latino migration into these new areas, then, has produced more than a little economic conflict and resentment. For example, non-Hispanic workers at the Mohawk Carpet facility in Dalton, GA—another industry with a rapidly growing Latino workforce—have filed a class action lawsuit under RICO [Racketeer Influenced and

Corrupt Organizations] Act statutes, seeking to punish manufacturers who drive down labor costs through knowingly employing undocumented workers. Similar actions have been considered against Tyson, Iowa Beef Packing (a division of Tyson), and others, though additional suits are on hold pending the Supreme Court's review of whether RICO statutes can be applied to a single manufacturer (*Mohawk Industries, Inc. v. Williams*, 05-465).[2]

Patterns of migration are interesting and reflect long-established understanding of the chainlike nature of migration (Alba and Nee 2003). Specifically, the movement of migrants to specific destinations in the United States has clustering patterns driven, first, by information networks regarding the existence and availability of employment in those locations and, second, by the resources presented by early arrivals to facilitate the migration of newer immigrants, often family members, neighbors, and friends from the country of origin. Chain migration patterns are best visible at the community level since, often, individual towns will be the locus of collective settlement. Still, statewide data can help us illustrate how settlement patterns may vary. Figure 5-1 reports the Mexican states of origin for immigrants living in these emerging communities, as captured by the 2006 LNS.

Of course, we should not overstate the degree of clustering. Latin American immigrants come from every nation in the region and every state within Mexico. Not surprisingly, then, the category "other" is the modal category in Figure 5-1 for all states. Also, states with large migrant populations in the United States are represented in nearly all of the U.S. states listed below. Still, the differences between the states are visible. Arkansas, for example, has a large number of immigrants from Guanajuato, while Washington's immigrant population is dominated by immigrants from Michoacán. Jalisco is a prominent donor of immigrants to Arkansas, Georgia, Iowa, and Washington but is not among the top five sources of immigrants to North Carolina.

Although the level of heterogeneity in place of origin remains generally high, we can speculate about potential implications of the different migration patterns to political attitudes and actions. Latin American nations and Mexican states vary considerably in political cultures and in specific experiences of electoral competition as opposed to one-party dominance. We would expect national and state origin differences may come to play a significant role in the political socialization

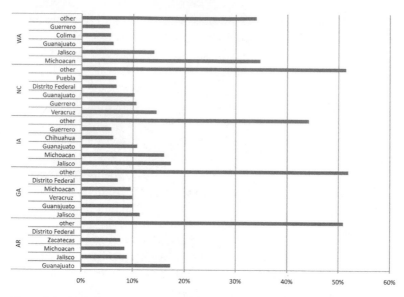

Figure 5-1 Variation across new receiving states by Mexican state of origin

of these immigrants to the American political system. To the extent that settlement patterns reflect these geographic patterns, Latino communities in one state—and more likely in individual towns and counties, where the effects of chain migration are better observed—may come to exhibit political characteristics that are distinct and driven at least in part by circumstances in their home communities.

Of course, many of these workers come to the new receiving areas not directly from Mexico but from other U.S. states. Figure 5-2 illustrates the scope of this second-stop migration phenomenon. Looking again at data from the LNS, we see that more than half (52%) of all immigrant respondents in Iowa came there from a "first stop"; that is, another state. In Arkansas, almost half (46%) fall into this category, while in Georgia, North Carolina, and Washington, the numbers hover around 35%.

Two-stop migratory patterns raise interesting implications of their own. First, the movement of Latinos from high-density established states into newer receiving states suggests that significant economic or quality of life factors have created a push-pull dynamic that has facilitated the geographic dispersion of the Latino population across the United States. That is, Latino immigrants leave places like California and Texas for the newly emerging communities in Arkansas and Georgia for a reason, and the lure of employment opportunities just discussed is an obvious factor. In the LNS, we asked Californians if they had ever considered leaving. About one in six indicated an interest in living elsewhere, and when asked why, over a quarter indicated the cost of housing while another 15% stated job opportunities were greater elsewhere.

Second, two-stop migratory patterns may shape how Latinos in new areas understand American society, form political views, or orient themselves in other ways to life in the United States. This pattern suggests that these newer communities may still enjoy the benefits of experience had by fellow Latinos in other environs and comprehend the political environment, organize, and mobilize more effectively than we would otherwise expect from communities that are entirely new.

Of course, the patterns of two-stop migration are not identical across the new receiving states and are clearly driven by geographic proximity, as is clearly illustrated in Figure 5-3. This variation is sure to shape the Latino politics in these new states as they emerge. Washington State's new Latino population is overwhelmingly Californian in origin, as over 74% of Washington second-stop immigrants previously lived there. By contrast, only 19% of Georgia's immigrant community has a past in California. Many second-stop migrants in Georgia came to the state either from Florida or, ironically, from another new receiving state, North Carolina, around 15% from each, in fact. In Iowa,

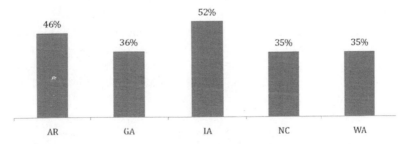

Figure 5-2 Percentage of immigrant respondents who report having lived in another U.S. state

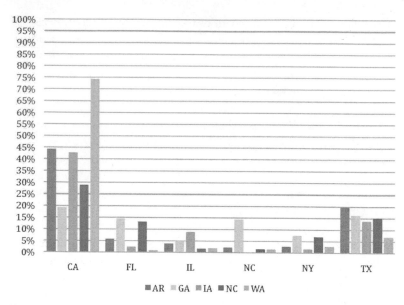

Figure 5-3 First-stop locations for second-stop migrants in new receiving states

43% of respondents had lived in California, and another 9% had lived in Illinois. New York and Florida make their greatest contributions of new Latino immigrants to North Carolina and Georgia, while Texas sends more to Arkansas.

In summary, the expansion of the Latino population into new areas is the inevitable result of job opportunities created by labor shortages and corporate preferences for reducing labor costs, as well as quality of life challenges in Los Angeles, New York, and Chicago that make rural relocation more attractive. Moreover, the very forces driving up Latino population shares in these areas are the same as those likely to create resentment, conflict, and competition between and among racial and ethnic groups once Latino communities are established.

Another critical element contributing to the potential for tension and conflict is the change to existing racial dynamics that is posed by large-scale growth in Latino populations. The southern and border states are places where the dynamic of racial and ethnic politics has generally conformed to the more traditional black-white paradigm. Moving from dichotomous to trichotomous racial politics is very likely to disrupt existing political patterns and coalitions, create economic competition between groups near the bottom of the economic ladder, and result in tension or even conflict (Rodrigues and Segura 2007). African American workers, finding themselves still mired in unskilled and low-income populations, are very likely to resent the presence of economic competitors, a resentment that may be fueled by the behavior of employers who, as we mentioned above, have incentives to hire undocumented aliens.

The rural Midwest represents, perhaps, an even more radical departure since Iowa, Nebraska, and Minnesota (outside of the Twin Cities) have historically been overwhelmingly white. In many instances, the migration of Latinos into small Midwestern towns represents the local residents' first experience with racial or ethnic diversity in their immediate environment. The literature in political science has emphasized for many years the important effect proximity has on racial attitudes (Giles and Hertz 1994; Gilliam et al. 2002; Hajnal 2001; Soss, Langbein, and Metelko 2003), and if those effects are replicated in these environments, we could see the policy environment for new Latino communities become indifferent to their concerns or, as the earlier work suggests, hostile.

The data are consistent with these expectations. In general, Latinos in these newer receiving areas perceive some resistance to their presence, and the degree varies across states. Figure 5-4 reports respondent perceptions in the LNS to popular attitudes toward the

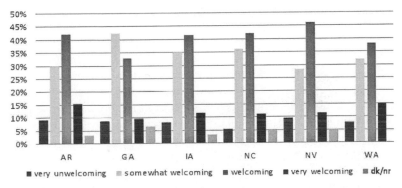

Figure 5-4   Latino assessments of public attitudes in new receiving states: welcoming or unwelcoming? (dk/nr = don't know/no response.)

Latino communities in these new environments. In general, the news is mixed. A slim majority of respondents in all but one of the new receiving states found the environment somewhat or very welcoming. On the other hand, about 40% of the respondents perceive their environments as somewhat or very *unwelcoming*. In terms of between-state variation, both Nevada and Arkansas err slightly on the positive side, while respondents in Georgia err significantly on the negative side. A majority of the Latino respondents in Georgia (51.1%) found the environment somewhat or very unwelcoming, almost 8 percentage points more than the next highest level of perceived hostility, in Iowa (43.4%).

Case Studies of Social Incorporation

To explore the social and economic experiences of members of these new communities, we conducted three focus groups in areas where the Latino populations were a comparatively recent phenomenon—Dalton, GA, Muscatine, IA, and West Liberty, IA. Within these three groups, however, there was variation in the percentage of immigrants, length of residence, and establishment of the community. The groups in Dalton and West Liberty were conducted in Spanish, as a consequence of a largely immigrant population. The Muscatine group was conducted in English.

Dalton, GA, is pleased to call itself the "Carpet Capital of the World," in reference to the large textile and carpet-manufacturing center there. Dalton is a city of approximately 28,000 people and the county seat of Whitfield County (pop. 83,525) in far northwest Georgia, in close proximity to Chattanooga, TN. About 22% of the county's population is self-identified as Latino or Hispanic, and an impressive 40.2% of Dalton's population identifies as Latino. Comparable numbers for the 1990 U.S. Census are astonishingly lower. For example, the 1990 census showed just 1,846 foreign-born persons in the entire county, just 2.5% of the population. Of the eight focus group participants, only two had been in Dalton for more than ten years. In short, this is a very new Latino community.

Both West Liberty and Muscatine, IA, are in Muscatine County, in the southeast section of the state and bordering on the Mississippi

River. The county population of approximately 42,000 is about 11.2% Latino—up from just over 7% ten years ago. The City of Muscatine is the county seat and represents more than half of the county population. The city is 12.3% Latino (up from 8% in 1990). The length of residence in Muscatine varies considerably. Southeast Iowa has a long-standing Latino population as a consequence of railroad workers brought to Fort Madison nearly 100 years ago. A quarter of the Muscatine focus group represented these lifelong residents, but as the population growth figures suggest, new arrivals represent a substantial and growing portion of the population and the remaining group informants.

In contrast with Muscatine, the Latino population of West Liberty is made up almost exclusively of foreign born and recently arrived in the area. The town's primary, indeed only, industry is poultry processing, though it was once an important rail junction and remains a bedroom community for Iowa City. The principal Latino employer in West Liberty is West Liberty Foods, a cooperative independent food processor created after Louis Rich, Co. announced plans to close the plant. Some residents of West Liberty also commute to an IBP plant in Columbus Junction, approximately 20 miles south. Unlike the situation in Dalton, the movement of Mexican Americans to West Liberty began as far back as the late 1960s (including one of the group informants). Nevertheless, the vast majority of the population and focus group arrived within the last decade, many from the Mexican State of Durango. In the 1990 U.S. Census, the town had just under 3,000 residents and was 23% Latino. In the 2000 U.S. Census, the town showed a net population growth of 13.5%—in a state where population growth is nearly flat. But Latinos now represent 40.5% of the city's 2000 population (3,332), signifying that there has been a net *decrease* in the non-Latino population, a subject of considerable concern given evidence of white flight from the local schools.

All three locales demonstrate significant "second-stop" migration. Among the foreign-born informants in our focus groups, half of the Dalton group, a majority (seven of twelve) in Muscatine, and five of eleven in West Liberty report having lived elsewhere in the United States before moving to their current cities of residence—usually California, Texas, New York, or Chicago.

Muscatine

The residents of Muscatine, IA, had, by far, the most positive assessment of their quality of life, perhaps owing to the larger share of informants (and the underlying population) that was native born, as well as to the substantially longer history of Mexican Americans living in the various river towns of Southeast Iowa. "People in Muscatine are nice people," reported one man, who moved there from Texas 20 years earlier. Another, an immigrant in his mid-thirties who had only been in Muscatine for a year, reported "loving it here." He reported his plans to relocate his family, who have been waiting for him to establish a place to live. "[A]fter this meeting I am going to pick up my family from Texas to bring them back here." When probed about why he liked it so well, he went on. "The people here are more innocent. For example, if I ask for directions and they don't know where it is, they'll do anything to try to help me—get the telephone book. In Texas, they would send you to the other side of town knowing all along that it wasn't the right way to go."

There was, however, an honest recognition in the group that some tensions with non-Latinos—the presence of stereotypical expectations and cultural differences—remain, even in a generally pleasant environment. One woman—a mother and grandmother born in Texas who has spent the majority of her life in Iowa—indicated that some aspects of interethnic relationships just won't work in her experience. "Yeah, we had a *tamalada* with all Latinos—just for fun. I can't see myself doing this with Anglos. I had an Anglo friend tell me, 'Don't wake me up at 6:00 A.M. to go do anything,' and that is when we all meet to do this. I guess also because of age, it's either take me or leave me." One middle-aged man, born in the area, reported, "Muscatine isn't perfect. . . . When I moved here, a neighbor stereotyped me because I was Hispanic and young. But he found out later I wasn't what he thought I was, so he still says 'hi.'" The woman with the *tamalada* also reported a racial slur being used against her son seven years earlier. Even when social relations are good, there are pockets of resistance and discomfiture (Williams, Alvarez, and Andrade Hauck 2002).

The perception of prejudice persists, and the group largely reported maintaining friendships primarily within the ethnic group. Nevertheless, several informants perceived that the climate had im-

proved, making specific references to the growth of interethnic amo-
rous relationships. The man from Texas, among the oldest in the group,
offered, "I think people can understand we are all the same. [You see]
Anglo women with Latino babies, you ask their names and they say,
'Panchito.'" A younger female informant agreed, but with a caveat:
"True, you see a lot of interracial relationships, but not at the high-
society level. Abortions come into play at that level. You don't see little
Heather having a baby with Juanito." Still, the sense of the group was
that prejudice had declined a bit.

When queried about recent changes, nearly everyone pointed to
the spillover effects of the recent population growth. A female immigrant and parent in her late thirties said, "You can find Mexican prod-
ucts at Hy-Vee[3] and other stores that you couldn't find before. Also,
newspapers advertise Latino celebrations like Cinco de Mayo." The
older woman said she was "proud to see more Hispanic students on
honor rolls and to see more Hispanic young adults attending college."
The group indicated that there was a lack of "Spanish leaders" in town,
which they thought caused the demise of the aforementioned local
Cinco de Mayo celebration. Nevertheless, the comments about the
quality of life were positive overall, citing quality schools, secure jobs,
and cheaper rent. When asked about what the most important issues
remaining to be faced included, the overwhelming consensus was education and legal/immigration status.

West Liberty

Though a mere 18 miles away, the tone and attitude in the group in
West Liberty, IA, was a world apart from those of Muscatine. This was
a very dissatisfied collection of informants, and though the tone was
set by one particularly bitter male informant, the concrete examples of
incidents that served as causes of concern are sufficiently detailed to
suggest a community that is, at the very least, feeling troubled.

As the population numbers suggest, Latino population growth has
come with an accompanying white flight, which has not gone unnoticed
by the Latino population. "The Americans are leaving town," reported
one man in his early 40s who has lived in West Liberty, off and on, for
more than 20 years. A middle-aged mother of five who has been in
town ten years claimed that "when the Latinos started to buy houses,

the American people started to sell theirs." Another middle-aged man very recently arrived from Mexico had a relatively clear picture of what the perceptions of white residents were: "There are Americans who think that their properties are going to be worth less because it's [sic] located in a Mexican neighborhood." A recently arrived woman said simply, "Americans don't want to be around Mexicans."

The experiences at the schools appear to be problematic as well. The local school district has already had to implement a desegregation plan, essentially curbing the number of families who are given permission for an out-of-district transfer. In addition, a bond issue necessary to replace a seriously aging high school failed on multiple occasions before finally passing in a pared-down version by the slimmest of margins.

But problems with the education establishment have also clearly filtered down to the individual level and have generated considerable resentment among the local Latino population, reflected in the stories and perceptions of our informants. Two comments are specifically worth noting. One woman described her son's perception of school treatment: "My son at school never went to write on the board up front, only the American kids went." Another described what appears to be classroom-by-classroom segregation of her children:

> My daughter is in the seventh grade and she tells me that the teacher separates them, the Mexicans in one side of the room and the Americans in the other side. And my son that is in the fourth grade tells me that his teacher also separates the Mexicans and Americans. I say that the kids see how they get separated and learn from this, and they want to separate themselves by being less.

The sense of powerlessness—political and otherwise—was also quite clear. "I have seen a lot of discrimination at my workplace. It seems like the Americans do not want to see us do better." A younger man recently arrived, after spending a significant time in New York, characterized white attitudes, particularly in the workplace, as follows: "They see us as a human machine. We feel more pressure."

In terms of a sense of belonging, there appeared to be something of a conflict both within the group and within individual respondents. For some, the feelings were best reflected in this comment by one of the male informants: "I believe we always are going to be foreigners, even if we are established here. People always say they miss their country." Others, however, consistent with earlier work (Hurtado, Gurin, and Peng 1994; Rumbaut 1997), report being changed by life in the United States, conflicted, and in some instances, expressed a desire to remain in the United States, citing a variety of reasons. An older woman, who had been in the United States for a long period of time, said plainly, "I already feel like I belong here. I no longer want to go back." The role of women is particularly at issue, though earlier research suggests that the pressures and conflicts of assimilation are greater for women (Baker 2004). One of the younger women, however, pointed to a more specific difference. "In Mexico, I lived with domestic violence, and there wasn't any protection for me. Here, I have that protection from domestic violence." The role of children in this sense of place was palpable. For one young woman who had been in Iowa for less than a year, children were a significant impediment to return. "For those who have children here, it is very difficult to expose their children to the Mexican culture." And the unhappy middle-aged man expressed his loss of place bitterly, "I am not from here or there. You miss your town, but your family . . . kids . . . are here and they won't follow you back there if you want to return."

Friendship networks were reported to be primarily within the ethnicity. But despite what appear to be polarizing circumstances, there does appear to be growing contact between whites and Latinos. The oldest male, a long-time resident, reported befriending Americans through his church. He and another informant, the older woman, announced that they each had multiple Anglo sons-in-law, while a third had an American brother-in-law; "You have to coexist," she said. In an amusing twist, the older woman (with two Anglo sons-in-law) waxed poetic. "It's the same with everyone—you have good and bad people."

Dalton

Dalton's Latino population is large, like Muscatine's, but is more akin to West Liberty's in terms of length of residence and date of migration. The informants reported a clearly more positive take on their experiences than those in West Liberty, specifically with respect to neighborhood and friendship patterns. These findings, then, are somewhat at odds with the survey results regarding perceptions of community attitudes toward Latinos. Some informants reported generally positive social interactions with Americans of other ethnicities. One woman who had been in Dalton seven years reported cordial—if distant—interaction. "All my neighbors are white. We do know each other and we say 'Hi' all the time. They bring us presents at Christmas, and I cook tamales for them, but we do not know each other well." A male, in Dalton about a decade, had another positive interaction, this time with an African American neighbor. "I had a black neighbor and he liked to come around. We used to drink sometimes, he was good, and our children were friends."

Many of the comments portrayed a reality that was more mixed, however. For example, a woman who has been here about ten years reported, "I like my neighbors. They like us also, but we do not understand each other." A male college student echoed those sentiments. "Our neighborhood is 50/50. All Hispanics know each other but the whites are not close." One school teacher indicated the emergence of white-flight. "We used to know all the neighbors when I grew up, but now everyone is moving out of that neighborhood." Another woman agreed, and commented, "They have stereotypes and they think we are all bad. So, they all sell their houses and move out of that neighborhood."

There is some disagreement about the evolution of white attitudes. While some informants saw things improving, others did not, a difference best captured by an exchange between two informants, one male, and one female. In response to the facilitator's question about changing white perceptions, the man said, "Their attitude is better. They used to look at us differently. I think it is better now," to which the woman replied, "I do not see them changed that much. They only got used to seeing us."

Almost everyone in the group agreed that Dalton as a place was getting better. The teacher reported, "There is more money, more people pay more taxes, and more people are buying homes." Another woman agreed. "The economy has improved. We spend and we work hard but we also spend our money here." One of the men added, "We had nothing when we came; we now buy furniture, tools, home improvement material, so we spend." The oldest in the group and a ten-year resident of Dalton went on:

> I have noticed that most Hispanics fix their houses. There were very old houses and now Hispanics have bought them and fix them. I have three houses, and we put concrete in the driveways. Even a white neighbor came and helped us fix one of the houses, so old houses look better.

There is less positive to say about how the community's contribution is seen by the town's other residents. When asked by the facilitator if the community credited Hispanics for the city's growth, a woman who had been in Dalton the longest at 13 years said flatly, "NO!"(emphasis in the original). A young man, who had been in Dalton since he was 14, went on: "They never have and never will. They know it, but they won't accept it."

Most informants clearly indicated that they still felt more "Mexican" than "American," though often with a caveat. And they do recognize personal and social changes as a consequence of living in the states. A comparison of social conditions again raised the issue of domestic violence, this time from a 56-year-old man. "I think here women have more protection. The environment in Mexico for women is more aggressive. It is better here. I am against domestic violence." To this, the teacher replied, "Men are changing, a little bit."

Political Incorporation

All three locations in which we conducted focus groups have significant populations with little measurable political power. The Dalton City Council is 100% white, as is the Whitfield County (GA) Commission and Whitfield County School Board. A quick examination of the various boards and appointed commissions at both the municipal and county level reveal very few Hispanic surnames. This story is essentially the same in both Muscatine and West Liberty, IA. There are no Latinos on the Muscatine County Board of Supervisors, nor the Muscatine City Council, or the West Liberty City Council, nor do any serve on either school board. Though the population percentages vary from 11% to over 40%, political power customarily lags behind population growth, and these cases are consistent with that trend. With sufficient time for naturalization or native births to swell the ranks of the citizen population, sustainable claims for local, school, and state legislative representation are likely only a single redistricting cycle away, and perhaps even a congressional district in North Carolina or Georgia, but Latino political power in these locales is far more a story of potential than actual power.

Referring again to Table 5-2, this pattern is not confined to the three locales discussed in detail here. Looking across six states with quickly growing, nonmetropolitan Latino populations, we see that the complete lack of political representation is the norm, rather than the exception. Several of the counties represented have population percentages clearly sufficient to win elections in single-member districts, but the results suggest that a variety of obstacles—which may be electoral, geographic, or citizenship status-based—serve to severely limit Latino access to elected office.

One notable exception is in metropolitan Yakima, WA, where Latinos hold a seat on the county commission and two seats on the school board for the city of Yakima, as well as a variety of council and school board seats for smaller municipalities. The Latino community in the Yakima Valley is somewhat more established and contains a higher percentage of U.S. citizens, which is likely responsible for a level of electoral success that is somewhat unusual in comparison to the other counties presented here. More importantly, the U.S. Department of Justice has intervened in Yakima pursuant to Section 3 of the Voting Rights Act of 1965, resulting in both a July 2004 consent decree[4] and subsequent election monitoring, which may well have played an important role in Latino empowerment. The Justice Department has also monitored elections in Franklin County (WA),[5] the only other jurisdiction listed in Table 5-2 where Latinos have secured some electoral success. As such, it is not at all clear that success in Franklin or Yakima counties necessarily foreshadows a more general pattern of Latino incorporation in rural environments.

As a consequence, then, it is less surprising that not a single group informant in any of the three rural groups made any mention of elected officials. Even though the discussions frequently included education, crime, and other quality of life issues in which government

plays a leading role, politicians and office holders were never referenced. There were, however, several comments regarding the need for
"leadership," identified by one participant in Dalton, GA, as Latinos'
most pressing problem. Said one 36-year-old immigrant male, "We
need more Latino representation—leaders who fight for our rights,"
but it was not clear from the context of his statement that he was referring to elected officials.

Conclusions about New Latino Communities

The specific experiences of Latinos moving into rural, "heartland"
communities vary and suggest the need for substantial research focused on their evolving circumstances. In some instances, these experiences of white flight, alienation, and residential segregation clearly
echo the experiences of generations past in places where we are more
accustomed to studying Latino politics. Disturbing conflicts in the
schools, the maintenance of largely ethnically distinct friendship patterns, and the sense of resentment clearly do not bode well for the
prospect that political and social relations in these communities will
develop differently than they have elsewhere. Moreover, patterns of
political exclusion and the utter lack of representation echo historical
circumstances of earlier communities and suggest that old conflicts—
over ballot access, polarized voting, and political incorporation—will
need to be reenacted in new settings.

On the other hand, there are specific differences in these cases that
might serve to suggest an alternative set of expectations for the future.
First, in at least two of the three cases (and perhaps all three), the influx
of Latinos—largely Mexican immigrants—has meant the survival and
even revival of towns that had fallen on harder times. Rural America
has continually lost population share (and in some instances, absolute
numbers) for much of the last century. This is particularly problematic in the Great Plains, where entire towns have disappeared or, at
the very least, local schools have been closed and consolidated, remov-
ing a central institution from community life. While the new arrivals
represent changes for which long-term residents may be ill-prepared,
they have also represented community growth, the introduction of
new businesses, and a future for these communities. The exact economic impact of Latino migration to the new receiving communities

is of critical importance to the lives of the residents, Latino and non-Latino alike, and deserves closer examination.

Second, the nature and quality of life for those living in these more isolated communities is, in many respects, incomparably better than many urban circumstances. Though several of our informants expressed the same concerns about crime and other hardships, many made specific reference to the safety of their communities and their fondness for the small-town environment. Quality schools, the relative absence of large-scale gang activity and violent crime, low costs of living and particularly of housing, and plentiful job opportunities compare favorably to urban environments in Southern California and elsewhere. And, as we have already suggested, many of these rural-dwellers are second-stop immigrants with firsthand experience of other environments in the United States, having lived in urban Latino enclaves in Texas and California, Chicago and New York, before coming to these smaller communities. At least one obvious future line of comparative inquiry would focus on outcome differences—educational, economic, and political—between urban and rural Latino communities.

Third, the comments in two of the three communities (West Liberty, IA, is the possible exception here) suggest patterns of interethnic social and economic contact that are *not* uniformly difficult but rather vary across individuals. For sure, moments of cultural misunderstanding and initial distrust were reported by informants who saw them as both distressing and driven by stereotype. But informants also reported frequent positive interaction with other racial and ethnic communities, intermarriage, and diverse classrooms. The experiences of social integration in these small towns are multifaceted and not easily characterized as good or bad, and additional work is required to assess conditions under which these interactions are likely to take on more positive and more negative tones.

6 Transnationalism and the Language of Belonging

The dramatic increase in immigration to the United States since 1965, particularly immigration from Latin America, has sparked debates about how attached immigrants really are to the United States. Two sets of factors lend these questions some credence: The first is the sheer numbers of immigrants, now making up more than 12% of the U.S. population, more than half from Latin America, with perhaps more than twelve million having entered the country illegally, occupying a precarious perch in this country's social, economic, and political space. The second are the issues highlighted in the previous chapters: the desire to achieve a modicum of success and stability (the American dream) through education, home, and work, which is deterred by a series of barriers expressed through discrimination and difficult interaction in new hometowns. Together these two factors might well lead to conclusions that immigrants are choosing to keep their ties to their countries of origin, to entertain thoughts of return when possible, and to minimize both their material and psychic investment in their new country of residence.

A good deal of the recent literature in the immigration field, particularly in sociology and anthropology, has focused on "transnationalism," or the ways in which immigrants maintain sociopolitical and economic ties and create new social arenas across the borders of nation-states. From this perspective, migrants' identities are increasingly characterized by fluid, multiple attachments that stretch across frontiers in a "single field of social relations" (Basch, Glick-Schiller, and Szanton-Blanc 1994: 5; Smith and Guarnizo 1998; for a recent collection in this vein, see International Migration Review, special issue, 2003). As two leading researchers in this field describe it:

> Over time and with extensive movement back and forth, communities of origin and destination increasingly comprise transnational circuits—social and geographic spaces that arise through the circulation of people, money, goods, and information. . . . Over time, migrant communities become culturally "transnationalized," incorporating ideologies, practices, expectations, and political claims from both societies to create a "culture of migration" that is distinct from the culture of both the sending and receiving nation (Massey and Durand 1992: 8).

The key here is that immigrants are described as living their lives simultaneously within two or more nation-states (Basch, Glick-Schiller, and Szanton-Blanc 1994: 28), but at the same time, to some extent, *apart* from those nation-states. In this view, territorial boundaries are seen as increasingly less relevant as an organizing principle of social interaction (Basch, Glick-Schiller, and Szanton-Blanc 1994: 52; Glick-Schiller 1999); this change is facilitated by the ease of travel and communication in an era of email and internet cafes, video conferencing parlors in which immigrants can see and talk to the family they have left behind, instant money transfers, and cheap airfare. Scholars point to the existence of organizational networks, such as hometown associations, or immigrant attitudes and behaviors, such as engagement in remittance practices (immigrants sending money back to relatives in their countries of origin), travel back to immigrants' countries of origin, and the desire to return to live there, as evidence of these transnational ties (Alarcón 2002; Conway and Cohen 1998; Guarnizo 2000; Orozco 2000). Recent public opinion surveys among Latinos have highlighted some of this same evidence (Waldinger 2007). Inevitably, the evidence of "eroding borders" has been picked up by conservative commentators to suggest that immigrants are failing to assimilate into American society and that immigrants, particularly Latino immigrants, are threatening American interests (Huntington 1997, 2004a).

These conclusions belie the much more complex portrait that emerges from contemporary research on transnational immigration, which suggests that for many immigrants there is not a stark trad-eoff between "assimilation" into their new receiving society and continued ties to their country of origin. Despite the dramatic increase in immigration to the United States, and the apparent ease of travel and communication with kith and kin in immigrants' sending countries, immigrants are not maintaining ties with their countries of origin over their ties to the United States. As some recent scholarship points out, assimilation—understood as the strength of identification with immigrants' new country of residence, the adoption of the dominant language, the creation of new civic and social ties, and participation in receiving country politics (Alba and Nee 2003; Gordon 1964)—continues alongside transnationalism (Levitt 2001; Morowska 2001; Segura 2007; Waldinger 2006).

This chapter reinforces the findings of this more complex view of transnationalism, presenting evidence from the focus group discussions that suggests that Latinos do indeed maintain affective ties to their countries of origin, but that these ties are conflicted. The focus groups reveal that immigrants feel increasingly "American" even as they retain other ethnic identities. The conversations in the focus groups indicate as well that immigrants and their children indeed continue to travel back to their countries of origin but often with mixed feelings: They no longer feel "at home" when visiting the countries in which they were born. Despite any ties they have to their countries of origin, overwhelmingly Latino immigrants plan on remaining in the United States. The complexity of immigrants' social ties is reflected by the fact that although many have strong social ties with co-national or co-ethnic compatriots, they share a great many ties (including marriage) with members of other ethnic and racial groups as well. Their children are more acculturated, for good and ill, into American society than their parents. Overall, the results point to a process of immigrant settlement in the United States. This is a process full of complexity and ambivalence, rather than stark, clear-cut choices. Drawing from the focus groups as well as the 2006 Latino National Survey (LNS), this chapter highlights these complexities through several key themes that appear in these conversation and in survey results: identification with "being American," immigrants' ambivalence about ties with and travel back to their countries of origin, and transnationalism and assimilation among immigrants' children.

Feeling American

Do Latino immigrants shy away from identifying with "being American"? The fear that loyalties to immigrants' countries of origin will overshadow their attachments to the United States accounts for at least some of the disquiet expressed by commentators observing immigrants' transnational ties. Do Latino immigrants feel they belong in the United States? One way to answer this question is to look at how Latinos choose among different identity labels. Figure 6-1 illustrates the choices immigrant respondents make if forced to choose—that is, they could *only* choose one—among three identity options: Latino/Hispanic, their country of origin, and "American."

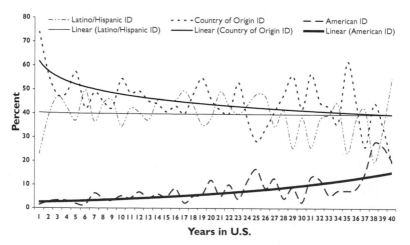

Figure 6-1   Forced-choice identity options among first-generation Latino immigrants arriving in the United States as adults

Figure 6-1 clearly illustrates two trends: One is the relative rise of "Latino" or "Hispanic" as an identity choice, gradually replacing a preference for a narrower country of origin identifier among adult immigrants. Among immigrants in their first year in the United States, more than 70% prefer the use of a country of origin identifier (for example, as Mexican, Salvadoran, or Dominican), and less than 30% prefer the pan-ethnic labels Latino or Hispanic. By year 3 in the United States, pan-ethnic labels vie with country of origin labels as respondents' preferred identity option—between 40% and 50% of respondents choose one or the other. However, the second story the chart tells is that there is a steady rise in the number of respondents opting for "American" as their primary identity, accelerating rapidly by year 35 in the United States.

Among those who migrated to the United States as adults, American is rarely their primary ethnic identifier. But their attachment to the label increases noticeably over time. Figure 6-2 illustrates this trend by tracking the percentage of respondents who identify "very strongly" as American by their year in the United States, without making them choose between this and other identities they might hold. In year 1, about 15% of adult Latin American migrants answer they feel very strongly American, and this percentage rises steadily with time

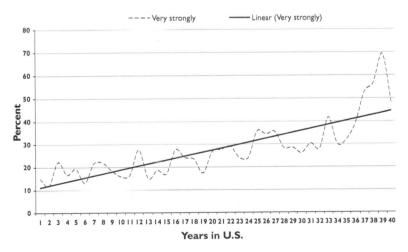

Figure 6-2 Identification as American, among first-generation Latino immigrants arriving in the United States as adults

spent in the United States. By year 37 a majority of respondents feels "strongly American."

These two graphs—on forced choice among identity options and the measure of feeling "strongly American"—indicate, on the one hand, immigrants' growing attachment to the idea of being American and, on the other, the continued pull between American and other ethnic attachments among first-generation immigrants, particularly those migrating as adults. However, it is not really the case that immigrants are choosing one identity at the expense of the other, but rather that immigrants hold these identities simultaneously—becoming more "American" even as they keep strong attachments to both their country of origin and a larger sense of being Latino or Hispanic. Table 6-1 illustrates immigrants' multiple attachments more clearly. Among first-generation Latino immigrants, the modal response in the figure is an indication of a "very strong" attachment to "being American" as well as a very strong attachment to respondents' countries of origin. Immigrants prefer to retain both identities, not having to make the choice (as in the "forced choice" question illustrated in Figure 6-1) of one at the expense of others.

The focus groups further illustrate the complexities of immigrants' identity choices. One of the questions asked in the course of the focus groups meetings was "How do you feel here in this country? Do you feel like strangers or that you are an American?" This question elicited a complicated range of responses. Policy and scholarly debates focus most often on two end points: either feeling fully American or identifying solely with one's country of origin. But there is a gradation of responses in between these two end points that illustrates the subtleties of Latinos' feelings about membership and belonging, with individuals feeling strong attachments to, and some alienation from,

TABLE 6-1   FEELING "AMERICAN" VERSUS FEELINGS TOWARD
            COUNTRY OF ORIGIN IDENTITY

Strength of Feelings toward Being American	Strength of Feelings toward Country of Origin			
	Not at All	Not Very	Somewhat	Very Strong
Not at all	27.2	60.4	16.8	78.3
Not very	33.4	42.1	18.0	75.7
Somewhat	36.9	37.7	20.3	74.2
Very strong	37.5	34.0	26.0	66.0

both their country of birth and the country they now live in, the United States.

Focus group responses to the question, "How do you feel here in this country?" illustrate the full range of people's complex feelings about belonging. A substantial segment of focus group participants—both native and foreign born—clearly indicated they felt more at home in the United States. They felt they were from here, and therefore that they were American. This response appeared in focus groups across the country, including those both in English (E) and Spanish (S):

Woman (Miami, S): I'm from here, I'm an American.

Ivan (New York, S): I don't have family in Colombia; they all passed away when I was young. I don't miss Colombia. To me this is my home.

George (Washington, DC, E): Oh, I feel really comfortable here. I feel at home.

Claudia (Washington, DC, E): I feel like an American. I haven't been to Guatemala since we came, and I really want to go back and see it, but all my family is here and I can't even imagine what it's like.

Rachel (Muscatine, IA, E): This is the land of the free. . . . Down in Mexico I live wealthier than here, but here I have my freedom. I don't want money; I want to be free in my religion. My goal is to become an American citizen.

Maria (West Liberty, IA, S): I already feel like I belong here. I no longer want to go back.

George (Houston, E): I feel I am an American. . . . I like living here. I wouldn't go anywhere else.

Soraida (Los Angeles, S): I think I am more from here. . . . My mother likes to watch television in Spanish, and I like to watch it in English. I think I am more from here.

These quotations all signal a sense of belonging in the United States. These focus group participants emphasized the positive pull of an American identity—a place of opportunity and freedom, of comfort and home, of family ties. They indicated they had made a choice—reflected in their choice of identity labels—to "be American."

The focus groups also included participants who clearly had made a decision to stay in the United States but still had some feelings of ambivalence. These respondents spoke of being split between their attachments to the United States and to their countries of origin. They were, they said, "half and half" or "neither from here nor there":

> *Norberto (Miami, S):* I feel accepted, not an outsider, but I'm not sure I feel American.
>
> *Patricia (New York, S):* I am not from here nor there. I have my family here. . . . I do like it here, but I spent my happiest years in Guatemala. . . . You can make the same food here, but the food in your country tastes different. But I live here and this is where I am going to stay.
>
> *Eliseo (West Liberty, IA, S):* I feel like I don't belong to this country . . . [but] I have been here half of my life and half over there. I feel I am part from here. Everything I have done, regarding work experience, is here.
>
> *Maria (Miami, (S):* I feel both. I feel American but still keep ties with people in Colombia. I feel both.
>
> *Woman (Washington, DC, E):* I feel comfortable here, but home is Puerto Rico.
>
> *Javier (Muscatine, IA, E):* I was raised in Mexico, but also in the U.S., so I feel half and half.
>
> *Jose (West Liberty, IA, S):* I am not from here or there. You miss your town but your family is here and they won't follow you back there if you wanted to return.

The views of these respondents are those least likely to be represented in black and white debates on transnationalism—in which people must definitively choose one identity or one country over another. These conversations indicate a recognition of the investment immigrants have made in the United States and of the ties and loyalties that keep them here, while at the same time acknowledging other identities and loyalties—to kin, experiences, and personal histories in immigrants' countries of origin.

A third, smaller group of participants noted that, despite living in the United States, they still felt they did not belong. They felt like foreigners or outsiders in American society:

Man (Washington, DC, E): I feel like an outsider.

Luis (West Liberty, IA, S): I believe we are always going to be foreigners, even if we are established here. People always say they miss their country.

These individuals still felt a strong attachment to their country of origin:

Roberto, Pablo, Maria, and Rosa (Dalton, GA, S): "100% Mexican." "I dream in Mexican." "My heart is in Mexico."

The perspective that they, as immigrants, were permanent foreigners, strongly attached to their countries of origin, was very much a minority view within the focus groups, one that appeared most commonly among respondents in focus groups, like the ones in Iowa or Georgia quoted above, that had high percentages of very recent Latino immigrants.

A significant number of respondents, clearly, felt entirely at ease in the United States and, on the whole, identified as American. Not surprisingly, most of those giving this response were from the English-language focus groups—still largely first-generation, but having spent more time in the United States and, as indicated by the choice of language, having a greater degree of social incorporation in the broader receiving society. However, professions of identity with and attachment to the United States were far from absent in the Spanish-language focus groups. A smaller group of respondents felt they were not comfortable in the United States at all and did not feel they belonged in the United States. Again, it was not surprising that these views tended to be from the most recent arrivals, particularly from respondents from the Spanish-language focus groups held in Iowa and Georgia. The plurality of responses, however, was in between, expressing an ambivalent attachment to the United States that on the one hand acknowledged an abiding commitment to this country, while on the other hand recognizing deep emotional ties to their countries of origin.

Not all identity choices confronting Latinos are between competing *national* identities. The focus group with Puerto Rican New Yorkers brought out a different theme. That set of conversations brought out *another* alternative between identifying as American and identifying with migrants' countries of origin: an attachment to a local, rather than a national, identity. The modal response for the New York focus group in English, almost all of whom were of Puerto Rican descent (and among the Puerto Ricans in the New York Spanish-language focus group) was to identify first and foremost as "New Yorkers" rather than as "American" *or* "Latino":

> *Shirley (New York, E):* I feel like a New Yorker. I don't think I can relate to places like Utah or Texas. I just feel like I belong in New York. Being Puerto Rican is accepted in New York. I never say I'm from the U.S. I say I'm from New York. I feel like this is where I belong.
>
> *Damaris (New York, E):* I feel like a New Yorker. This is where I grew up. The Bronx, Queens, and Brooklyn: that's all I know.
>
> *Carlo (New York, S):* You can be an Hispanic, but you are as much of a New Yorker as the person next to you. . . . If something happens, you are suddenly thinking like a New Yorker—the attitude.

The moderator followed up their initial responses to ask, "Do you think in terms of New Yorker, American, Puerto Rican, in what order?" That question elicited these responses:

> *Eric (New York, E):* New Yorker, Puerto Rican, American.
>
> *Shirley (New York, E):* We are used to that, but even in Buffalo, New York, you are an outsider. They still look at you like you are someone else. You are different.
>
> *Rosedaline (New York, E):* More New Yorker. I went to Atlanta and everyone else was black. At the clubs and restaurants, people were looking at me because there you are either black or white.
>
> *Man (New York, E):* We went down to Florida and I felt like a foreigner in some of those states. I would go into a McDonald's and people would stare at us. You can feel like a foreigner.
>
> *Haydee (New York, E):* I'm an American. [But] we too drove to Florida and were looked at not as foreigners, but as New Yorkers.

The comments of Puerto Rican respondents indicate their attachment to a *local* identity, more than a national one, or even a strictly ethnic identity. Respondents identified as New Yorkers above all and emphasized that this identity did not travel well elsewhere in the country. Only in New York was their Puerto Rican-ness, their potential foreignness, taken for granted: They were simply New Yorkers, like everybody else. As several respondents pointed out, in other parts of the United States they felt not necessarily like Americans, but like foreigners. This loyalty to a locality was not as clearly expressed in other focus groups (although many respondents expressed attachments to their neighborhoods and cities). At the very least, these responses suggest the possibility that assimilation and incorporation in the United States may have local, regional, and state dimensions that may not be fully captured by simply focusing attention on the adoption of *national* identities. The response of our Puerto Rican respondents in New York suggests that the local context of assimilation matters quite a bit in how Latinos identify as American and how they see themselves (as, for example, Puerto Rican or as Latino).

The focus group participants' views of their attachments to the United States or their choice of identities seem to reflect a rejection of either/or alternatives. Both the LNS and the focus group results indicate that Latino immigrants express a strong and growing sense of belonging in the United States while also expressing loyalties and attachments—both transnational and local. If these immigrants experience transnationalism, it is not either/or.

Diminishing Returns

If immigrants seem to avoid either/or identity choices, perhaps other measures capture transnationalism more starkly. Common measures for transnationalism are indicators of immigrants' contact with and travel to their countries of origin and their desire to return to live there permanently. The implication is that frequent travel back to one's country of origin, remittances, and regular communication indicate continuing ties with individuals, networks, and places there, whereas the desire to return indicates a weakness of ties and lack of commitment to the receiving country. The strength of ties to the immigrants' countries of origin, then, is a proxy for transnationalism. However, as with identity, the survey and focus group results indicate a mixed picture: Immigrants have ties to their countries of origin, but their "home" country is, despite real ties to family and friends left behind, the United States.

Figure 6-3 shows the response of Latino immigrants who migrated to the United States as adults when asked a question about whether they had plans to ever go back to their countries of origin to live permanently. What is striking about this graph is that it indicates that on arrival to the United States a majority of Latino migrants say they would like to return to their countries of origin, but by the time they have spent fewer than five years residing in the United States, more Latino migrants indicate they plan on remaining than say they have plans to return. By year 15 fewer than 20% of first-generation adults say they would like to return to their countries of origin. Some of these voices appear in our focus groups, particularly among more recent arrivals:

> *Fernando (Miami, S):* I would like to return [to Cuba]. There's something missing. . . . I have a hungry feeling. I miss the land.

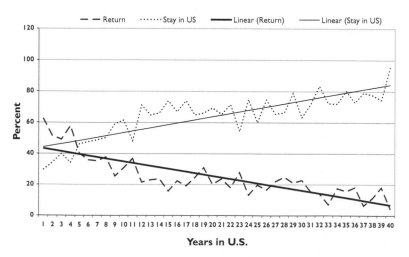

Figure 6-3 Plans to return permanently to country of origin, among first-generation Latino immigrants arriving in the United States as adults

Rosa (Dalton, GA, S): When we can't work anymore we'll go, maybe. *[But note the "maybe."]*

The focus groups indicate, as with the trend illustrated in Figure 6-3, that the desire to return drops off quickly for those residing in the United States. Plans to return do not seem to provide evidence of transnationalism. However, the patterns for travel back to immigrants' countries of origin are quite different from those for plans to return permanently.

Reported frequency of travel back to the country of origin varied widely among the focus group respondents. For instance, among the Puerto Rican focus group in New York City, responses to questions about travel back to Puerto Rico ranged from yearly visits to travel fifteen years previously. The responses among first-generation immigrants in the Spanish-language New York City focus group indicated travel to their countries of origin ranging from twice a year (to Puerto Rico) to travel more than ten years prior. One Puerto Rican respondent noted that he rarely traveled, "But," he said, "I telephone every week!" In general, the pattern seemed to be that respondents living in communities of more recent arrivals (for example, those in focus groups like those in Dalton, GA, and West Liberty, IA) traveled back to their home countries more frequently. However, wherever they were held, each focus group had at least one respondent who traveled at least once a year to their country of origin. At the same time, there were a few participants in the focus groups who indicated they had *never* traveled back to their country of origin.

The evidence from the focus groups is reflected in the more general LNS data. Figure 6-4 graphs the answers first-generation respondents (among those who arrived to the United States as adults) gave to the question of how often they visited their country of origin. Note that, as with the focus group responses, most Latino immigrants have traveled to their countries of origin. By year 14, a majority of Latino migrants to the United States have traveled at least once to their country of origin, and in year 21 in the United States that figure is close to 90%. Travel actually *increases* with time in the United States; the relatively low travel in the first years of residence likely reflects the time it takes for immigrants to establish permanent residency and acquire U.S. citizenship, after which it is easier for them to travel back to Latin

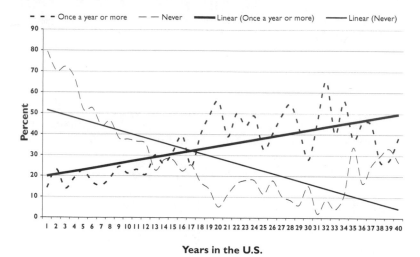

Figure 6-4 Frequency of travel to country of origin, among first-generation Latino immigrants arriving in the United States as adults

America. However, again echoing the focus groups, only a minority of respondents traveled once a year or more.

Travel is a reflection of continuing contact with family in immigrants' countries of origin. Upon arrival to the United States, more than 70% of Latin American migrants say they keep in frequent touch with family they left behind, contacting them once a week or more (Figure 6-5). Family and friends left behind are the basic reason for transnational contact of all kinds—communication, remittances, and travel. However, as Figure 6-5 indicates, these ties do weaken over time. The frequency of contact diminishes steadily over time spent in the United States. The frequency of remittances—money sent to family and others in immigrants' countries of origin—also declines with time in the United States (see also DeSipio 2000). The percentage of immigrants who *never* send money increases steadily over time, and by year 20 in the United States, more first-generation Latinos *never* send money home than send money once a month or more (see Figure 6-6).

Overall, these figures show that close ties to family and friend in immigrants' countries of origin drop steadily, even as immigrants' travel increases. The survey evidence seems mixed: Immigrants quickly indicate they do not intend to return, and regular contact and

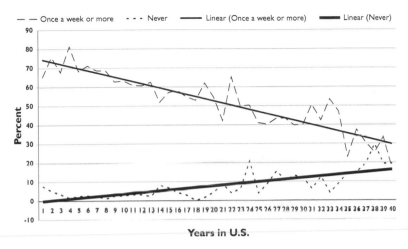

Figure 6-5 Frequency of contact with friends and family in country of origin, among first-generation Latino immigrants arriving in the United States as adults

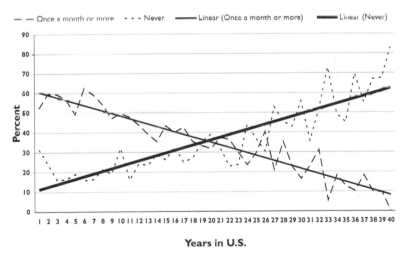

Years in U.S.

Figure 6-6 Frequency of remittances to friends and family in country of origin, among first-generation Latino immigrants arriving in the United States as adults

remittances decrease over time, but travel actually seems to increase with time in the United States. So does travel indicate the strength of ties to immigrants' countries of origin? The answer, seen through the focus group responses, is mixed: Immigrants certainly travel, but that travel, paradoxically, seems to reinforce their decision to remain in the United States.

Despite the fact that almost all the focus group participants who talked about travel had apparently made at least one trip back to their countries of origin, for many, their view toward these countries could be summed up by the sentiment "nice place to visit, but wouldn't want to live there":

> Olga (Miami, E): Even though I love my country [Colombia] so much . . . I wouldn't live there.
>
> Della (Miami, E), in response to query about feeling like an outsider: Here? No, not in the United States. Never. In Puerto Rico I did. Totally lost. It's beautiful but I'm totally at a loss.
>
> Tony (Washington, DC, S): I . . . dreamed of going back to Puerto Rico to retire, and after one month I told my mom I had to go back. It is beautiful, but it was not the same. Here everything is easier.
>
> Man (Washington, DC, E): I might feel like going back to my country, but to visit. I mean, I wouldn't move there.
>
> Walter (Los Angeles, S): I love my country [Guatemala], but I can't stand it too much over there.
>
> Woman (Los Angeles, S): I agree. I love my country, and go back every four years, but I cannot live or work there. I go for a week and I am ready to come back.
>
> Woman 2 (Los Angeles, S): My parents have been here for five years, and the first year they went back about four times. The second [year] they went back about three times. Now they had not been there for two years, but they went back about two weeks ago and now they can't stand being there.

A significant portion of the respondents in these focus groups indicated that when they *had* traveled, they didn't enjoy the experience of return to their country of origin. Note this was true for participants in both Spanish-language and English-language focus groups (participants in Spanish-language focus groups, on the whole, had been in the United States for a shorter time). When asked to elaborate on why they did not enjoy travel to their countries of origin, the responses participants gave touched on three themes: a sense of social disconnection, the lack of economic opportunity, and sheer physical discomfort.

Many respondents in the focus groups described a sense of social disconnection on going to visit their countries of origin. What focus group participants found on going back to visit is that, echoing the title of Thomas Wolfe's novel, "You can't go home again."

> Woman (New York, S): When you go to your country you feel as if you don't fit in anymore.
> Moderator (New York, S), summing up the group's discussion: Returning is like immigrating again.

Travel "home," as described by focus group participants, led to feelings of dislocation, of being an outsider in one's "own" country:

> Sergio (Miami, E): Every time I'm in Puerto Rico, I'm like, "Damn, I gotta leave tomorrow!"
> Omar (Miami, E): I went to visit my country: it was the first time in 13 years. . . . When I went [to Nicaragua], I felt like an outsider there, because everybody kept looking at me. "Where are you from?" . . . They look at you like you're weird. . . . I felt accepted with my family okay, but with the rest of the people not really.
> Man (Washington, DC, S): I felt like a foreigner. I went back to my country and my family felt foreign. After two years I came back.
> George (Washington, DC, E): I feel comfortable in Mexico, but I don't feel like it's home.
> Julio (Los Angeles, E): When you go to Mexico and speak English, they target you as being different.
> Beatrice (Los Angeles, E): I've visited my family in Mexico, but I feel like an outsider there.

The irony of immigration is that Latino migrants to the United States might not feel entirely comfortable in the United States, but on returning to their countries of origin to visit, found they were no longer comfortable there either.

Those who experimented with going back to live or visiting in their countries of origin found that going back made them appreciate economic opportunity in the United States, and of being relieved of worries about corruption and crime.

> *Shirley (New York, E):* I lived in Puerto Rico a few months, with my mother, but it didn't work out, so we came back. *(In response to a follow-up query: why?)* It was not the lifestyle that my mother wanted, it was hard for her to get a job; she would stay at home.
>
> *Norberto (Muscatine, IA, E):* I've never gone hungry here [in the United States]. . . . They take your money down there at the border when crossing into Mexico—they call it *la mordida*. They are money-hungry in Mexico.
>
> *Horacio (Muscatine, IA, E):* In Guatemala you can't walk without being robbed. I feel safer here and there are better jobs.
>
> *Man (Los Angeles, S):* [T]here are no opportunities there. Even though someone says they have plans to pay their debts and go back, they don't.

The subtext in these comments is that while life in immigrants' home countries might sound good in the abstract, the practicalities of making a living—having a job, not worrying about the loss of livelihood—favored remaining in the United States.

The final theme that came up in conversations about travel home was simply the sheer physical ignominy of travel outside the United States. Latino immigrants described going back and finding a lack of what they had come to expect as basic services—water, electricity—and safety.

> *Dina (New York, S):* After five years of being here, I arrived [in El Salvador] . . . and I wanted to come back the next day. . . . There was no water, no electricity. . . . My daughter had an intestinal infection and almost died. . . . After two years I went back and the same thing happened. Every time I go the same thing happens. . . . I don't ever want to go back.

> *Guillermo (Washington, DC, S):* I go to Mexico, and it is still pretty, but I still like it here. The opportunity, security here is better. You go to Mexico, and they will rob you as soon as you get off the plane.

Again, the subtext to these comments is that the benefits of day-to-day living in the United States, whatever its costs, outweigh the discomforts of returning.

Overall, the prevailing sentiment among respondents was against ever returning permanently to their country of origin. As the LNS data shows, a majority of even recent immigrants indicate they plan on staying in the United States, and this sentiment steadily increases the longer immigrants remain in the United States.

> *Armando (Miami, E):* I would not go back. My only remaining child lives here. My four grandchildren are here. I left the day I got married. The last day I was there was the same day I got married. I may go after a few years to visit . . . [but] the school I went to is no longer a school. The church I was married in is now a dance hall. What am I going to see? Destruction? No, I have no interest in going.
>
> *Gaby (Muscatine, IA, E), in response to a query about ever going back:* No!
>
> *Monica (Dalton, GA, S):* I do not want to go back.
>
> *Multiple respondents (Los Angeles, E), answering question about returning to Mexico and becoming a Mexican citizen:* No!
>
> *Soraida (Los Angeles, S), in response to a question asking if she will stay in the United States for the rest of her life:* Yes, God willing, yes.

The longer immigrants stay, the less likely they are to have the social ties that would draw them back: Their families and friends are increasingly in the United States. Even some of those expressing a desire to go back recognized the ties that might keep them in the United States.

> *Pablo (Dalton, GA, S):* I wish we could go back to stay, but it gets harder every time. It is confusing because my children are here. We had plans to go back, but maybe not.
>
> *Brenda (Houston, E):* If all my family moved to [Argentina] I would do it, but that's not going to happen.

Latino immigrants travel back to their countries of origin but want to remain in the United States. Travel is a sign of transnationalism, in the sense of ties linking immigrants to their countries of birth, but paradoxically, what emerged from the focus group conversations was that travel also reaffirmed immigrants' decision to migrate to the United States in the first place.

If this is true for all Latino immigrants, it is particularly true for women. The LNS shows a significant difference in the desire to return between male and female respondents. In answer to the question about plans to return to live permanently in their countries of origin, 26% of all first-generation women who had immigrated to the United States as adults said that yes, they planned on returning permanently to their country of origin, whereas 39% of men gave a similar response—a 13-point difference (Figure 6-7). The focus groups give some insight into why these gender differences might exist.

> *Laura (West Liberty, IA, S):* In Mexico I lived with domestic violence, and there wasn't any protection for me. Here, I have that protection.
>
> *Alma (Dalton, GA, S):* When I go back [to Mexico] I see that men are *machos*. I do not like the atmosphere there.
>
> *Soraida (Los Angeles, S):* I have been very independent and have worked since I was 17. . . . Everything I want, I get; but I know if I went there [to Mexico] it would be different.

Staying in the United States allows immigrant women to pursue possibilities they would not have experienced in their countries of origin. These women are not all feminists, but they appreciate the independence and freedom from coercion they have living in the United States.

On the face of it, respondents' travel patterns and related patterns of contact and remittances seem to confirm the transnational argument of strong ties to immigrants' countries of origin and weak ties

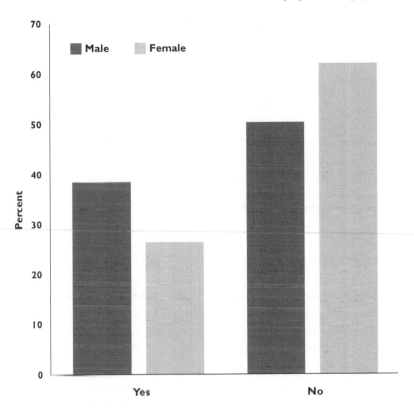

Figure 6-7   Plans to return to country of origin, for men and women, among first-generation Latino immigrants arriving in the United States as adults

to the United States. That is, almost all respondents had traveled to their countries of origin, some of them quite often. However, delving more deeply, it appears that many had quite negative or mixed opinions about their experiences returning to their home countries. Across almost all the focus groups, both those conducted in English and those in Spanish, respondents offered unsolicited opinions indicating that they felt out of place when going back to visit, and that they were unlikely to stay for good. Implicitly or explicitly, they signaled they were likely to remain in the United States. Even those expressing a desire to return often couched their responses in terms of unlikely possibilities. Those saying they would stay in the United States, on the other hand, were much more adamant—they were here to stay, and they knew it.

The Second Generation

An ancillary question is whether transnational ties—ties to immigrants' countries of origin—is present in the second generation. If the first-generation narrative is a story of gradually diminishing ties to the country of their birth, the story for the succeeding generations is one of both diminishing ties and, for a small percentage, of continued interest in their parents' countries of origin. Figure 6-8, for example, graphs data from the 2006 LNS showing the frequency of contact with friends and family in respondents' countries of origin. In the first generation, more than half of foreign-born Latinos have weekly contact with their family and friends they left behind. With each succeeding generation the percentage having frequent contact declines. A little over 30% of second-generation immigrants have weekly contact with family abroad, and only 15% of the third generation do. The percentage having no contact at all rises steadily across generations, from under 10% in the first generation to over 20% in the second generation to over half in the third generation. Additional evidence of declining ties among later generations is evident in the trend line of LNS respondents reporting they sent remittances home, by generation (data not

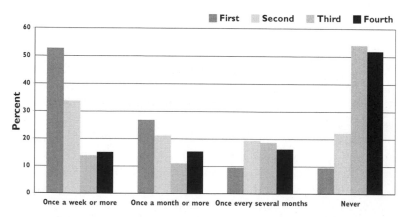

Figure 6-8 Frequency of contact with friends and family in respondent's country of origin among Latinos, by generation in the United States

shown). The percentage never sending any money back to their countries of origin rises from 36% in the first generation to over half in the second generation and over 80% in the third generation.

These patterns are echoed in the focus group findings. Almost all respondents across the thirteen focus groups acknowledged that they did not expect their children would ever want to return to their country of origin. When asked if their children would want to go back to live in their parents' place of birth, the responses were often emphatic:

> *Elba (Miami, S):* No! . . . When I arrived from Puerto Rico, I didn't change. [But] my little girl changed more when she got here. She wanted to be American. It was hard.
>
> *Maria (Dalton, GA, S):* My kids think they belong here. We [their parents] are happy but we know we belong there. My children are happy when we go to Mexico, but they stay there for three weeks and they start getting ready to come back. They think they belong here.
>
> *Man (Los Angeles, S), speaking about taking his young cousins to Mexico:* They didn't even want to shower because the hot water went out; we had to heat up some water. . . . [Once back in the United States] they didn't want to go back. . . . They never accepted it there.

The sentiment among the first generation that their children were "American" and were in the United States to stay was reinforced in some focus groups, particularly in Miami, in which the moderator also asked about the social contacts their children had. The Miami responses universally suggested that children had friends across ethnic groups and that these children, whatever their origin, were "American."

> *Man (Miami, S):* My kid has 100% American friends.
>
> *Maria (Miami, S):* My kids don't have any preference on the nationality or race of their friends. To them they are all equal.
>
> *Rosa (Miami, E):* My son's best friend's mother is from Haiti. . . . My daughter's best friend is from the islands, Jamaica. They are from Cuba, Colombia, from everywhere.

On the whole, the pattern is toward greater social acculturation in the second generation. Although parents may remain ambivalent about their ties, identity, and commitment to the United States, their children for the most part are not.

There were some exceptions to this general rule in the focus group discussions, but they were very much exceptions:

> *Martin (Los Angeles, S), speaking of his daughter:* I have all of her papers for her, she can go to school and everything. She is very comfortable there. She goes on vacation and she loves it there. . . . I tell her she is Mexican, and she says "yes."

This pattern emerges from the broader survey data too. Overwhelmingly second-generation immigrants in the survey were more disinterested in the politics of their parents' countries of origin and shied away from participating in organizations like hometown associations that had explicit links to their parents' hometown concerns (contrary to Glick-Schiller and Fouron 1999; and Smith 1998). But in these instances there is a minority of the second generation that still retains its ties to their parents' countries of origin. Figure 6-9, for instance, graphs levels of interest in country of origin politics by generation. What is striking is first, that few respondents express a strong interest in country of origin politics, and second, that while this interest declines somewhat in succeeding generations, about 10% of second-generation respondents indicate they have "a lot" of interest in country of origin politics.

Likewise, Figure 6-10, which illustrates participation in country of origin-related clubs, associations, or federations among immigrants, by generation, shows, on the one hand, that very few individuals in any generation participate in hometown associations or the like. But the graph also indicates that participation in country of origin organizations, while still under 10% for the second generation, is as high or higher as participation among first-generation immigrants. The overall story is one of increasing attachment to the United States across generations, but with persistent ties to the country of origin among a small minority of second-generation respondents—once again complicating the story of strong attachments to the United States versus strong attachments to immigrants' countries of origin.

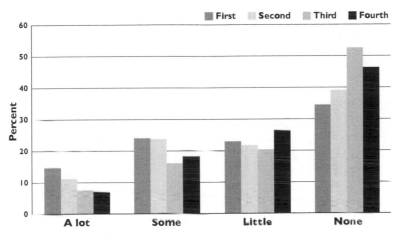

Figure 6-9 Attention paid to country of origin politics, among Latinos in the United States, by generation

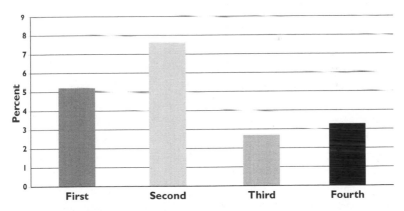

Figure 6-10 Participation in the activities of a club, association, or federation connected to the town or province family came from, among Latinos in the United States, by generation

Conclusion

Our conversations with focus group participants and the results of the LNS both suggest that the stark contrast between "assimilation" and "transnationalism" painted in some of the social science literature and by some commentators is dramatically overstated. As the results from the focus groups indicate, Latino immigrants identify themselves as

"American," and see themselves as remaining in this country. However, there is also some ambivalence, particularly among first-generation immigrants, about their sense of belonging—made to choose among their identification with the United States and their country of origin their American identity is not their first preference; this is not translated, however, into a desire to return. Latinos' travel and remittance of money to relatives in their countries of origin are an indication of transnational ties, but the focus groups show that those who travel often have profoundly ambivalent reactions to their visits, which only reaffirms their decision to immigrate to the United States. These commitments are even more noticeable in their children, who, even more than their parents, seem certain to stay in the United States. It is worth noting, however, that a small minority among the second generation continues to have a strong interest in participating in the politics and affairs of their countries of origin, further confounding attempts to draw tidy distinctions between attachments to the United States and attachments to sending countries. Ties to countries of origin (discussed in the focus groups only in terms of identity, travel, and desire for return, rather than remittances) are apparent, but these are tempered by what appear to be stronger ties to the country of residence. Transnationalism exists, but appears subordinate to the concerns of Latinos as they make their way in the United States. To put it more strongly: transnational ties may in fact *reinforce* immigrants' attachments to the United States. There is plenty of room for further research on Latino transnationalism. But if the findings here suggest anything at all, it is that further exploration into these issues is only likely to highlight additional complexities in Latino behavior and attitudes, challenging the either/or dichotomies of assimilation versus transnationalism.

7 The Evolving Latino Community and Pan-ethnicity

Explorations into the Confluence of Interactions, Networks, and Identity

I f this book is an attempt to capture important facets of life that characterize the Latino community in the United States, we begin with the presumption that such a "community" does, in fact, exist. For more than a decade, the mass media, political officials, activists, and academics have examined the evolving "Latino" community on the presumption that the term had meaning. This community has resisted precise definition but is generally understood to include persons whose origins/ancestry are connected to Latin America and the Iberian Peninsula. The open question, however, is whether this group has a sense of itself as a community. That is, do members of this group perceive commonalities with others in the group, feel a sense of attachment, and perceive the value or necessity of collective political and social action?

Such has not been the scholarly consensus. The Latino community has been previously characterized as a subpopulation of distinct national-origin groups with a limited attachment to one another (de la Garza et al. 1992). Early work on pan-ethnic terminology has generally found little usage or self-identification with these overarching identities. In the absence of significant identification by group membership, speaking in terms of community interests and actions might be premature or even entirely off base.

The focus of this chapter, then, is an exploration of the presence, extent, and bases for a sense of community among Latinos in the United States. Specifically, we explore the concept of pan-ethnicity, examine the circumstances under which such identities might come to the fore and gain political importance, and search for evidence regarding the level and importance of pan-ethnic identities among America's Latino minority. Both our own data and the work of others offer growing evidence of substantial change on this dimension, that the use and identification with pan-ethnic terminology is increasing, that bridging beyond national-origin "boundaries" is more prevalent than in the past and is present in many different aspects of community life. Recognition of shared interests—in terms of class background, shared values, customs, language, interactions, social networks, and similar daily circumstances—has served to broaden and deepen the sense of pan-ethnic identity among the Latino residents of the United States. Whether and how these factors affect the nature and strength of community, to a significant extent remains both a theoretical and measurement challenge.

Our analysis of pan-ethnicity and community is organized around a number of queries. First, how is community constructed and understood in the daily lives of our Latino focus group participants? Second, to what extent does a sense of ethnicity and/or pan-ethnicity (along with the concomitant dimensions of language and culture) serve to connect persons and help create and sustain a community? What are the dimensions for this pan-ethnic aggregation in terms of nativity, language use, generation status in the United States, and the social diversity of one's networks? Finally, how does national origin, as a phenomenal reality and a set of salient identities, interact with or relate to the emerging pan-ethnic consciousness? That is, how are they integrated in various aspects of Latinos' lives?

Integrating Pan-ethnicity within the Field of Minority Politics

The growing racial and ethnic diversity of the American population, and the phenomenon of large-scale immigration to the United States, have driven the field of minority politics to move from a purely "black-white" paradigm to one that incorporates a broader range of racial/ ethnic groups and between-group interactions (McClain and Stewart 2002; Segura and Rodrigues 2006). This broader scope of research has included more attention and examination of Native Americans (Nagel 1994; Wilkins 2007), Asian Americans (Espiritu 1992; Lien 2001; Omni and Winant 1994), and Latinos (Fraga et al. 2006b; F. Garcia and Sanchez 2007; J. Garcia 2003), often in comparison with—or in contrast to—patterns and issues found in the better-studied African American community.

There are, of course, fundamental differences between African Americans, on the one hand, and several of the other racial and ethnic groups identified on the other. Specifically, the phenomenon of slavery and its aftermath in American history largely wiped away ethnic and linguistic distinctions among blacks already living in the United States while creating a lengthy shared history of resistance and political action. By contrast, both Latinos and Asian Americans confront the American political system with a host of divisions and distinctions within each group and a much shorter historical experience available to transcend these distinctions. While Latinos largely share a common language and religion—both important cultural markers that might facilitate identification and cooperation—they remain divided by national origin, generation, immigration history and status, and even by their formal relation to the U.S. polity.[1] Moreover, racial identifications in Latin America are, themselves, quite complex, incorporating elements of European, African, and indigenous cultures, languages, identities, and appearances in racial and cultural blends that vary significantly across the nations of Latin America and even within them. There are good reasons, then, for Latinos to be understood as distinct national-origin groups and not as a single racial/ethnic minority. For Asian populations, lacking a shared language and faith and, in some instances, sharing a history of between-group conflict in the nations of origin, the difficulties of shared identification and cooperation are even more daunting.

One of the central queries of the Latino National Survey (LNS)[2] was to examine whether the Latino population is sufficiently and effectively self-identified as a racialized or ethnic minority community for us to envision this identity as the basis for their interface with the U.S. political system. With the myriad distinctions between and among national-origin groups, generations, and the like, the aggregation of Latinos requires a sense of ethnicity or race that can be extended beyond tribal and national-origin parameters. That is, the "construction" of such a community involves not just the presence of common circumstances, but also the perception and/or recognition of the same.

Ironically, one impetus for this collective identity may, in fact, come from the very political institutions on which the group wishes to press claims. For Latinos, umbrella or pan-ethnic label(s) emerged as a way in which political institutions would deal with the policy and political concerns of the different Latino subgroups as a single entity. In 1977, a bill sponsored by then-Congressman Edward Roybal (D-CA) required that federal agencies collect "statistical" data on the Spanish-origin population. As a result, a broader group category of Hispanic, Spanish origin, or Latinos became the official mode to talk about the twenty-plus Hispanic national-origin groups in the United States. Subsequently, group concerns and status would be categorized as Latino or Hispanic (Hayes-Bautista and Chapa 1987), a practice mimicked in the mass media's reporting. Treatment of various national-origin populations as a single group was also evident in the output of public policies regarding the distribution of economic and political resources.

One of the consequences and parallel developments was the construction of broader group "boundaries" among these Latino subgroups (that is, beyond national origin and culturally based affiliations). Padilla's work on the development of Latino consciousness (1986) discussed how previously disparate Latino subgroups (primarily Mexican and Puerto Rican) living within a single political environment made conscientious efforts to transcend traditional national-origin boundaries to form a more expansive group configuration. Demands and political activism took the form of advancing Latino interests and pan-ethnic associations. The idea of a pan-ethnic Latino community was facilitated by institutional responses to an apparently similar set of Spanish-speaking and Spanish-origin groups, and—more importantly—by Latino activists who consciously promoted a broader group identity to maximize group size, presence, and political resources (J. Garcia 2003; Jones-Correa and Leal 1996).

Research on pan-ethnicity, then, must consider not only the use of a pan-ethnic label, but also the perceptions of commonalities, interactive social networks, and a broader social identity that give that label meaning—and ultimately political importance. Previous research on identity (J. Garcia 1982) has distinguished between ethnic identification, identity, and labeling. The choice of specific labels represents the product of the identification process. That is, there are factors and experiences that influence an individual to internalize or incorporate a sense of group attachment and affinity. A sense of ethnic identification is affected by one's national origin, experiences, behaviors, and interactions. Pan-ethnicity captures both a sense of belonging to a group and the organizational-based activities to advance Latino (as opposed to a specific Latino subgroup) group interests and concerns. As a result, the concept of pan-ethnicity closely parallels group consciousness in that a political linkage is associated with the presence of a politicized individual.

The construction of a pan-ethnic community, then, is not built on a single impetus but rather has two distinct motivations: attitudinal and instrumental. By "attitudinal," we refer to the orientations among Latino subgroup members and their predispositions toward a sense of pan-ethnicity, attitudes that are invariably linked to political involvement. The relevant set of political attitudes would generally include political efficacy, political and personal trust, interests and attention to things political, all understood through the lens of personal and collective experiences and perceptions of group distress, disadvantage, and discrimination.

By "instrumental," we mean the creation of group boundaries broader than the traditional boundaries constructed for the purpose(s) of expanding the group's resource base and enhancing its presence in larger sociopolitical arenas. That is, the very recognition that pan-ethnic identity creates a larger cadre that is likely to be more successful in pressing demands on the political system serves as an impetus to such an identity. And, of course, to the extent that resulting policy reflects these demands, writing the pan-ethnic identity into statute, the impetus is reinforced and the identity institutionalized.

Since we are examining the behaviors and beliefs of individuals, for our purposes, it is the underlying disposition to locate oneself in a broader community that is critical. The attitudinal nature suggests an important affective component to the identity, sentiments capturing in-group attachment, and the perception of commonality in many life dimensions. The instrumental nature of pan-ethnicity suggests that the use of any Latino identifier might reflect more than internalization of one's personal identity, but rather a selective use to facilitate a political agenda and means to organize one's political world. Pan-ethnic identity, then, includes the basis for group affiliation and affinity, a specific label(s) or descriptor(s), and an evaluative process of assessing the group's status vis-à-vis American society (Oboler 1992).

The remainder of this chapter is an exploration of some of the major bases of a community among Latinos from many different national origins, varied experiences and exposures in the United States, linguistic skills, class status, and different communities of residence. We recognize that a sense of community is affected by cognitive, affective, and behavioral elements. Both the LNS and the focus group sessions afford us the opportunity to develop a comprehensive "portrait" of the daily lives of our Latino participants and how their sense of self and patterns of interactions are affected by notions of identity and connectedness with other persons. It is within this context that pan-ethnicity functions as a community builder among Latinos and has behavioral consequences that extend much beyond acquiring broader group identification.

Predecessors to the LNS: Benchmark Indicators of Pan-ethnicity

We begin this section with basic population figures for the wide range of national-origin groups usually subsumed under the pan-ethnic umbrella. In Table 7-1, we present the breakdown of the Latino subgroups derived from the 2004 American Community Survey. While the Mexican-origin population continues to be the largest Latino subgroup (63% of all Latinos), significant demographic change has occurred. Among the notable developments have been the continuing gains among Central and South Americans, as well as Dominicans, as shares of the overall Latino mix. The population increase for Dominicans is so large that they are rivaling Cubans as the third largest Latino subgroup. In addition, the Dominican concentration in the New York metropolitan area is almost equal to the size of the Puerto Rican community, representing a sizable and politically important shift. Among the growing Central American population, persons from El Salvador and Guatemala are the most numerous. Similarly, Colombians, Peru-

TABLE 7-1   U.S. LATINO POPULATION IN 2004 WITH
             SUBGROUP TOTALS

	Estimate	Lower Bound	Upper Bound
Total	285,691,501	—	—
Not Hispanic or Latino	245,232,305	245,208,228	245,256,382
Hispanic or Latino	40,459,196	40,435,119	40,483,273
Mexican	25,894,763	25,734,311	26,055,215
Puerto Rican	3,874,322	3,783,673	3,964,971
Cuban	1,437,828	1,384,398	1,491,258
Dominican	1,051,032	990,557	1,111,507
(Dominican Republic)			
Central American	2,901,679	2,786,152	3,017,206
Costa Rican	120,316	98,938	141,694
Guatemalan	698,745	642,315	755,175
Honduran	407,994	365,775	450,213
Nicaraguan	248,725	215,824	281,626
Panamanian	113,053	95,257	130,849
Salvadoran	1,201,002	1,134,595	1,267,409
Other Central American	111,844	89,257	134,431
South American	2,215,503	2,140,054	2,290,952
Argentinean	189,190	164,563	213,817
Bolivian	90,401	74,674	106,128
Chilean	106,458	92,566	120,350
Colombian	686,185	641,807	730,563
Ecuadorian	453,360	407,540	499,180
Paraguayan	14,123	7,998	20,248
Peruvian	399,240	359,869	438,611
Uruguayan	41,577	31,084	52,070
Venezuelan	164,699	144,561	184,837
Other South American	70,270	58,231	82,309
Other Hispanic or Latino	3,084,069	2,974,061	3,194,077
Spaniard	358,570	323,770	393,370
Spanish	656,169	616,552	695,786
Spanish American	57,417	45,769	69,065
All other Hispanic or Latino	2,011,913	1,928,636	2,095,190

Source: U.S. Census Bureau, 2007 American Community Survey

vians, and Venezuelans are the largest South American groups. Overall, the gains from the Caribbean and Central and South America have had the effect of altering the mix of Latino subgroups, both in more traditionally settled areas as well as in emerging ones.

Pan-ethnic label usage has been examined extensively since the expansive Latino National Political Survey (LNPS), conducted in 1989–1990 among the three largest groups at that time—Mexicans, Cubans, and Puerto Ricans. Since then, the Pew Hispanic Center (and its predecessor partners with the *Washington Post*) has been conducting national polls of Latinos since 1999. Focusing first on the LNPS, their in-depth interviews with the respondents indicated a very limited sense of pan-ethnic Latino community across a variety of measures. For example, examine Table 7-2, which reports respondents' preferred self-identification label. Most LNPS respondents identified and described themselves primarily in national-origin terms (that is, as Mexicanos, Puerto Ricans, or Cubanos). Only one-third said they perceived a high degree of cultural and political commonalities across the three Latino subgroups. While the level of reported interactions and contact with members of their own national-origin group was high, there was only a modest level of reported contact with Latinos from other subgroups. Thus, at that time, the perception of a Latino community was largely confined to one's own national-origin group.

In terms of pan-ethnically based labels, only a small percentage of the LNPS respondents selected the pan-ethnic identifiers "Hispanic" or "Latino" as part of their social identity. Interestingly, among those respondents who indicated a Latino or Hispanic label, one-half defined the term as a surrogate for their respective national-origin group, while the other half used the term to be inclusive of all Latino subgroups, further undermining the notion that the pan-ethnic label signified pan-ethnic sentiment. Respondents who perceived a high

TABLE 7-2   PREFERRED ETHNIC IDENTIFICATION BY NATIONAL ORIGIN AND NATIVITY (LNPS)

	Mexican Origin		Puerto Rican		Cuban	
Ethnic Identification	Foreign-Born	Native-Born	Foreign-Born	Native-Born	Foreign-Born	Native-Born
National-origin group	659 (85.6%)	461 (61.8%)	324 (84.1%)	113 (56.7%)	476 (83.0%)	36 (40.6%)
Pan-ethnic	106 (13.7%)	212 (28.4%)	49 (12.7%)	39 (19.4%)	68 (11.9%)	18 (20.1%)
American	3 (0.3%)	73 (9.7%)	11 (11.8%)	43 (21.3%)	26 (4.5%)	34 (39.3%)
Total	770 (100.0%)	746 (100.0%)	386 (100.0%)	199 (100.0%)	573 (100.0%)	86 (100.0%)

Source: Adapted from Table 2-27 in R. de la Garza, L. Desipio, F. Chris Garcia, J. Garcia, and A. Falcon, *Latino Voices: Mexican, Puerto Rican and Cuban Perspectives on American Politics* (Boulder, CO: Westview Press, 1993), p. 40.
LNPS = Latino National Political Survey

degree of cultural and political commonalities across the Latino sub-groups represented less than one-third of all of the respondents. Questions were asked in a manner that assessed the extent of commonality of pairs of Latino subgroups (that is, Puerto Rican and Cuban; Mexican origin and Cuban). The degree of perceived commonality did vary by the specific paired combinations of Latino subgroups, with the closest pairing being Puerto Ricans and Cubans.

One contributing factor to the lower levels of perceived common identity was the very modest level of inter-Latino subgroup interactions and contact. In an historical sense, this is hardly surprising. At the time of the LNPS, the Latino world was confined largely to interacting within one's own national-origin group, reflecting the extreme geographic segregation of Latino subgroups in different corners of the country. The concentration of the three largest Latino subgroups (that is, Mexican origin, Puerto Rican, and Cuban) during the early 1990s was largely regionally defined.[3] That is, Puerto Ricans were found primarily in the Northeast, Cubans were located in Florida, and persons of Mexican origin were living in the Southwest. Pan-ethnic sentiment and identity are neither necessary nor likely when one is never in the position to interact with Latinos of other national origin groups.

The sole exception to this geographic isolation at that time was metropolitan Chicago, which had significant Puerto Rican and Mexican populations. This co-location and the political circumstances of the time provided both the opportunity for cross-group interaction and subsequent identification, as well as the instrumental impetus to amalgamation for political gain. Not surprisingly, then, the earliest inklings of emerging pan-ethnic identification were in Chicago, where two national origin groups resided within the same political boundaries (Padilla 1986).

Of course, a central motivation for this study has been the rapid demographic change in the Latino population in the United States over the past two decades, and it is our expectation that these changes will have significant implications for the emergence of pan-ethnic sentiments. To the extent possible using between-survey comparisons, we want to look for evidence that the frequency and importance of pan-ethnic labeling might have changed with the circumstances. In Table 7-3, we use the Pew Hispanic Center survey of 2002 to explore

TABLE 7-3   TERMS LATINOS *EVER* USE TO DESCRIBE THEMSELVES,
            BY NATIVITY AND GENERATION IN THE UNITED STATES*

Background Characteristics	Total Latinos	Foreign- Born Latinos	Native- Born Latinos	Generation in the United States		
				1st	2nd	3rd +
Respondent's/ respondent's parents' country of origin						
Yes	88%	95%	74%	95%	82%	66%
No	12%	4%	25%	4%	18%	34%
"Latino" or "Hispanic"						
Yes	81%	85%	74%	85%	77%	72%
No	19%	15%	25%	15%	23%	28%
American						
Yes	53%	32%	90%	32%	85%	97%
No	46%	67%	9%	67%	15%	3%

Source: Pew Hispanic Center/Kaiser Family Foundation, 2002 National Survey of Latinos (Washington, DC: Pew Hispanic Center).

* Question: People choose different terms to describe themselves. I'm going to read you a few different descriptions. Please tell me whether you have ever described yourself as any of the following . . .

label preferences. The respondents were asked whether either of the terms "Latino" or "Hispanic" were ever part of how the respondent described himself or herself. The responses are noted for all of the Latino respondents as well as by nativity and generational status.

The results in 2002 pretty clearly indicate an emerging multidimensional identification. A significant percentage of all Latinos in the Pew survey identified themselves both in terms of their national origin *and* using a pan-ethnic label. Though the use of national origin descriptors remains slightly higher, this pattern is more than evident for the pan-ethnic identifiers. Perhaps most importantly, because of the proximity of these questions, respondents were in a clear position to understand that the pan-ethnic term was not merely a synonym for their national-origin group but was intended to signify the broader and more inclusive supra-ethnic identity.

The survey option also included the identity choice of "American." In this case, the generational status of the respondent is more closely associated with identification as an American. This survey was conducted almost thirteen years after the LNPS, and one can see a movement toward the presence and acceptance of a pan-ethnic identity along with a maintained national-origin identity.

But what of forced choice? That is, if respondents had to choose a single identity for themselves (admittedly an artifice), which would it be? In Table 7-4, the respondents to the Pew study are asked to select the term that they would use *first* to describe themselves. Similar to the results of the LNPS, national-origin preference prevails such that 54% of all Latinos prefer that reference. However, almost one-fourth of the Latinos prefer Latino/Hispanic as their first choice. The preference for national-origin label is most evident among the first generation of foreign-born Latinos, and drops noticeably among the third generation.

Finally, in Table 7-5, we break down responses to the question posed in Table 7-3 by the respondent's national-origin group. Recall that this was not the forced-choice question, and respondents were free to report multiple identities. Again, reference to one's country of origin or ancestry is the dominant response across national-origin subgroups (ranging from 62% to 93%). The only major outlier is the "other Hispanics," a relatively ill-defined group. Similarly, these respondents also "embrace" the pan-ethnic terms at high levels. Three-fourths or greater indicate the use of Latino/Hispanic as a way to describe themselves. Finally, the variation of responses is more noticeable in terms of identification with the term "American." A majority of Puerto Ricans, Cubans, and other Hispanics responded with American identity as part of the way to describe themselves. This was much less the case for the other Latino national-origin groups, a difference most likely driven by a combination of citizenship status and immigration experiences, as well as generation in the United States.

TABLE 7-4 TERMS LATINOS CHOOSE *FIRST* OR *ONLY* TO IDENTIFY THEMSELVES, BY GENERATION IN THE UNITED STATES*

| | Total Latinos | Generation in the United States | | |
		1st	2nd	3rd +
Respondent's/ parents' country of origin	54%	68%	38%	21%
Latino/Hispanic	24%	24%	24%	20%
American	21%	6%	35%	57%
Don't describe themselves as any of these	1%	1%	1%	1%

Source: Pew Hispanic Center/Kaiser Family Foundation, 2002 National Survey of Latinos (Washington, DC: Pew Hispanic Center).

*Among those who describe themselves as more than one term, the first or only term they use . . .

TABLE 7-5   TERMS LATINOS *EVER* USE TO DESCRIBE THEMSELVES,
BY COUNTRY OF ORIGIN*

National Origin	National Origin Group		"Latino" or "Hispanic"		American	
	Yes	*No*	*Yes*	*No*	*Yes*	*No*
Mexican	88%	11%	82%	18%	50%	50%
Puerto Rican	91%	9%	81%	19%	77%	23%
Cuban	89%	11%	73%	26%	62%	38%
Total Central American	93%	7%	86%	14%	35%	65%
Total South American	87%	13%	83%	17%	40%	59%
Salvadoran	92%	8%	83%	17%	35%	65%
Dominican	92%	7%	90%	10%	42%	58%
Colombian	89%	11%	85%	15%	42%	58%
All others	62%	35%	66%	34%	93%	7%

Source: Pew Hispanic Center/Kaiser Family Foundation, 2002 National Survey of Latinos
(Washington, DC: Pew Hispanic Center).

*Question: People choose different terms to describe themselves. I'm going to read you a few
different descriptions. Please tell me whether you have ever described yourself as any of the
following . . .

The Pew studies generally demonstrate a level of pan-ethnic identification higher than what was observed in the LNPS. Though it still
trails national origin as the preferred identifier, it is clear that pan-
ethnic concepts are frequently used by the Latino population of the
United States to refer to themselves, at levels that rival national origin
descriptors. Now, almost two decades after the LNPS, the question
remains as to whether this pan-ethnic terminology and identification
serves as a marker for more deeply held senses of community among
Latinos. That is, has the sense of community—understood as shared
political, social, and economic circumstances and linked futures—
transcended national-origin subgroup isolation and extended to other
Latino subgroups?

In our focus groups, we were able to probe how broadly or nar-
rowly our informants define their community, whether they do so in
specifically ethnic and/or pan-ethnic terms, and whether this community sentiment extended to a perception of collective futures. In
the next sections, we examine both the focus group data and the relevant LNS survey data. We look to the focus groups to ascertain, first,
whether a Latino community persists as an accurate descriptor of the
social networks and interactions that characterize the lives of Latinos, and second, whether there is evidence of a pan-ethnic identity,

as illustrated by the use of pan-ethnic terminology and conceptions of "community" clearly encapsulating a broader identity. Moving beyond these structured conversations to the survey data, we document the evidence for a Latino "linked fate," akin to that of African Americans (Dawson 1994), and the perception of shared circumstances between and among Latinos and Latino national-origin groups. In general, the picture that emerges from these two modes of inquiry is one in which Latinos appear to have developed a clearer recognition of their "group-ness" and a conception of community that extends beyond their immediate familiars to include others—from their own and other national-origin groups—whose circumstances are similar.

Observing Community and Pan-ethnicity in the LNS Focus Groups

We examined the frequency and context in which our Latino focus group respondents use any terms to describe their friends, co-workers, and geographical communities. We have already noted the diversity among the Latino populations at each of our focus group sites. The structure of each focus group was to explore themes of adaptation, experiences in their respective communities, self-perceptions of their own group, and the role of associations and identities. For the most part, the moderator explored these themes with minimal cues as to "appropriate" labels or descriptors in the questions about interpersonal networks and a sense of attachment.

There was considerable variation among the participants and between the focus group locations. The groups reflected the range of locales visited, as well as the diverse range of Latino subgroups present. We held groups in areas with long-standing Latino populations that are now becoming more mixed in terms of Latino subgroups. We also visited emerging Latino communities in other parts of the country, regions previously "unsettled" by significant numbers of Latinos (J. Garcia 2003). This diversity in national-origin group was immediately evident during the process of participant recruitment at all focus group sites. For example, the New York participants were Dominican, Puerto Rican, Peruvian, Colombian, Salvadoran, and Guatemalan. It appears that the Washington, DC, area (two focus groups were drawn from the suburbs and another from the District proper) had the widest diversity of Latino subgroups. Virtually all of the Latino subgroups were represented over the three focus groups in metropolitan Washington, DC. The national-origin mix among the participants in the more rural areas (that is, the focus groups in Iowa and Georgia) was less diverse, but still demonstrated some aspects of diversity in terms of state of origin and nativity status. For example, in Muscatine, IA, respondents were from three different states in Mexico (Coahuila, Zacatecas, and Jalisco), Chicago, El Salvador, South Texas, and Guatemala.

Another indicator of the new diversity within the Latino community is evident in the participants' descriptions of family, friends, neighbors, and co-workers. In most cases, participants' social networks were comprised of Latinos from many different countries of origin, as well as non-Hispanic whites, African Americans, and Asian Americans. For some, intermarriage was the engine of subgroup diversification in their social networks. For example, in Houston, Barbara had "whites," a Brazilian, and Mexican nationals in her family. Also, in Houston, Brenda had a Romanian uncle and cousins who were Argentinean and Brazilian.

Friendships extended primarily to other Latinos. Many participants reported social connections to non-Hispanic whites, African Americans, and Asian Americans, but for the majority of our informants, both immigrant and U.S.-born Latinos comprised the most prominent part of their social network, though we saw some evidence of segmentation by nativity.

The social distance between Latinos—particularly immigrant Latinos—and other groups was evident in myriad ways. In many instances, the informants would refer to their non-Latino friends or neighbors (that is, those not of minority background) as "Americans." This distinction carries with it, we think, considerable meaning and reflects our overall take in this effort. That is, foreign-born Latinos do not perceive themselves as a fully incorporated segment of this society, even as they recognize that this is, for the foreseeable future, their home.

Here are three examples:

Maria (Miami, S): I like the people (in my neighborhood) the most. I have lived here for twenty-four years—it's my

house. Most are Cubans, but there are some Mexicans and
Puerto Ricans. There are Americans [sic: whites] too. We
often think, why are they here? But they mix well.

Omar (Miami, E): In my neighborhood, there are lots of Latin
people. We are talking about Cubans, Puerto Ricans,
Colombians, everything.

Woman (Washington, DC, E): My best friend is white, but I
have a lot of black friends who I can relate with because of
the whole minority thing, even though not culturally. Of
course, being Latina, I have lots of friends from different
Latino backgrounds.

Language also played a significant role in defining the makeup of
one's social networks. Among the Spanish-speaking focus group participants, there was a greater tendency to have other Latino friends,
while the bilingual or English-speaking participants had a wider mix
of Latino and non-Latino friends. Obviously, the racial and ethnic
composition of their neighborhoods impacted their social networks.
For the most part, the Latino respondents tended to live in primarily
Latino areas. On the other hand, those Latinos in more racially/ethni-
cally mixed neighborhoods not only interacted with a more diverse set
of persons, but also noted their perceptions of their "American" neighbors. For example:

Lisa (Los Angeles, E): It depends where you live. If there is
diversity, they get along better. With one race, it is harder.
Where I live, there are a bunch of Mexicans. When a black
person comes into the neighborhood, or a white person,
people ask, what are they doing here?

Josefa, fifteen-year resident (New York City, E): I live in a
quiet area. It is mostly immigrants, but they have been
here a long time. They have their own homes. . . . They are
Croatians, Jews, and Italians. The majority is immigrants,
but they have work in the city for a long time.

Participants in Dalton, GA (an emerging area of Latino migration, especially of Mexican origin), commented on the virtues of small-
town life (less crowding, single-family residences) while critiquing the

negative stereotypes held by "natives" regarding the cleanliness and trustworthiness of Latino people. In Dalton, Latino informants reported being very conscious of Anglo neighbors' perceptions of Latinos. The potential judgment by out-group members appears to have had an effect on the informants' behavior. In hopes of greater acceptance, they reported, among other things, being more conscientious about the upkeep of their property, making efforts to speak some English, and having a pleasant demeanor. Similar accounts were conveyed in the focus groups in the two Iowa rural communities. For example:

> *Janice (Muscatine, IA, bilingual):* [T]he south end of Muscatine is mostly Hispanic. They pretty much keep to themselves. They stay out of other people's business. They always have their own music going (usually Spanish music) while cleaning house or doing yard work.
>
> *Raquel (Muscatine, IA, S):* I live in a neighborhood of a variety of people from El Salvador, a lot of teenagers, but the Anglos are very difficult with their neighbors that are Mexican, especially the workers or laborers. There is not much communication between Anglos and Mexicans. I am very friendly. I enjoy living here, but it is very challenging.

Groups included participants living in primarily Latino and in non-Latino neighborhoods. Not surprisingly, this varied by generation and nativity, as second-generation participants had a greater likelihood of living in more racially and ethnically diverse neighborhoods. The dynamics of changing neighborhood composition sometimes exacerbated intergroup tensions, but eventually a critical mass of Latinos served to dispel some of the prevailing stereotypes, along with increased intergroup interactions and dating.

The increased familiarity occasionally paid dividends. On some occasions (in New York, Miami, and Los Angeles) the participants mentioned "other cultures trying to get with the Latinos"; that is, Latinos were viewed by out-group members as desirable friends, neighbors, or even love interests. Informants referenced things such as values, hard work, strong family ties, or cultural manifestations, including food and music, that were seen as desirable and served to bridge intergroup distance. From this perspective, participants' experiences reflect the inclusion and visibility of Latinos in the larger American consciousness (that is, as artists, actors, in mass media, and in food) and suggest that this inclusion has—at least in some instances—served to create a more receptive climate. For example:

> *Nolberto (Muscatine, IA, bilingual):* When you have more Latinos, people are not as prejudiced because a majority is overruling and also there are a lot of interracial couples due to this. I think people can understand that we are all the same. Anglo women with Latino babies—you ask their names and they will say "Panchito."

Beyond neighborhood interactions, the role of the workplace as a primary source of friendship networks appears pivotal in the creation of a larger sense of community. For our participants, the overwhelming preponderance worked in environments where other Latinos comprised the majority of the workers.

> *Carlos (Houston, S):* [A]lmost all of my co-workers are Latinos.
> *Fernando (Houston, S):* [A]lmost all of them. Spanish is the predominant language spoken here.

Most participants identified the workplace as the source of most of their friends and as a locus for connecting to Latinos from their own and other national-origin groups. For example, Francisco (Mexican American) refers to his Chilean friends he met at work.

Among those participants who work in more ethnically diverse workplaces, the inclusion of non-Latinos was more prevalent, but not to the exclusion of Latino friends. For example, Betty (also Mexican American) says she has both white and Hispanic friends from work. Another woman reported:

> *Patricia (New York City, S):* I work for the city. There are a lot of Hispanics and Americans. It is very quiet. The Americans are very nice; they speak Spanish.

It is clear that in some instances, the workplace was able to connect participants to non-Latinos. In others, however, the outcome was less successful. For example, in Miami, one participant indicated that he had non-Latinos friends from work, but his closest friends are always Latinos. Another explained the situation in these words:

> *Fernando (Miami, S):* [W]here I work I am more comfortable with the Cubans and other Latinos. Americans are not really friends; they are more like acquaintances.
> *Monica (Los Angeles, S):* Most of my co-workers are Hispanics. While they are Hispanic, the supervisors are all white.

Also, for those having both Latino and non-Latino friends, the context of social activities tended to vary. In Miami, an informant commented that going dancing and "night clubbing" was more common with Latino friends than non-Latinos. Elsa from Muscatine, IA, mentioned a specific activity that she could not see herself doing with her non-Latino friends:

> *Elsa (Muscatine, IA, S):* Yeah, we had a *tamalada*[4] with all of the Latinos—just for fun. I can't see myself doing this with Anglos. I had an Anglo friend tell me—don't wake me at 6:00 A.M. to do anything; yet that is when we all do this.

Even Latino-dense social networks include interactions with other minority group members and Anglos. As a result of such contacts, we noted possible attitudinal change induced by growing awareness and actions on the part of non-Latinos. As Latino social networks and familial ties become more racially/ethnically diverse, these contacts interact with Latino self-images and seemingly have the combined effect of accentuating our focus group participants' sense of pan-ethnic self-awareness. This pattern of perceptions has pan-ethnic identity consequences. For example:

> *Barbara (Houston, E):* [T]hey knew the type of family we were; there wasn't going to be a problem with us so, like, they accepted us. As the years had gone by, they are letting more Hispanics in because I think they are realizing we're always going to pay the rent on time; we're always going

to pay our bills early, because that is the type of Hispanic Americans we are.

Man (Los Angeles, S): I think it is the character of each person. I get along well with my neighbors. One of them is American and I just had an experience with him, where I helped him out. We have a cluster box, and they put someone else's mail in my box, and I just give it to them because they are close by. I think it depends on how you are with other people. I have Mexican neighbors as well, and we talk and everything.

Rigo (Dalton, GA, E): [O]ur neighborhood is 50/50. All Hispanics know each other, but whites are not close. Our white neighbors would put cat litter at the end of his yard, but close to ours. We don't even know their names.

Maria (Dalton, GA, bilingual): All of my neighbors are white. We do not know each other and we say hi all of the time. They bring us presents at Christmas, and I cook tamales for them, but we do not know each other well.

Perhaps most extreme in this observation was a participant in New York:

Ivan (New York City, S): My neighborhood is like the UN, because the homes are lined up; first are the Colombians, the Jews, Chinese. But no one interacts with each other. One knows they are there because you see them working in their gardens, and that is how you know they exist. I don't know their names, faces, if they are married, have children, or nothing.

On the one hand, it is noteworthy from our focus group members' experiences that the Latino everyday world can be more racially and ethnically diverse than is usually characterized in popular accounts. On the other, however, social networks, workplaces, and neighborhoods clearly remain highly segregated. And even when there is proximity between Latinos and non-Latinos, relationships can remain cool or polite, as Maria and Rigo both noted. There tends to be a social and affective distance between Latinos and non-Latinos, especially Anglos, as evidenced in these comments.

That Latinos continue to live lives among social networks dominated by other Latinos from their own and other national-origin groups seems clear, even as exposure and social connections with outgroup members increases. Latinos are a community. But this is a far cry from saying that Latino identity is self-conscious, crosses nationalities, and is politically relevant. Do our focus groups provide evidence in this regard? We think that they do.

For starters, several participants took pains to illustrate the pan-ethnic nature of their identities and social networks. For example, in the case of identifying friends, it was not unusual that an informant would say, "I have five Hispanics and one white close friend," and then go on to specify the origin or background of each friend identified.

Perhaps more importantly, the use of pan-ethnic terminology was consciously an attempt to transcend the boundaries of national-origin groups:

> *Claudia (Washington, DC, E):* It's more like all of us together. It's not I'm Guatemalan or you're Bolivian or they're Nicaraguan; it's we're Latinos and we all know, we can relate. We know how we are. We can all feel comfortable about being around other people from other countries.
>
> *Man (Los Angeles, E):* [T]he type of change carries over to Latino politics. People get together and help each other out. We get ideas from other races. Politically wise, some politicians are making a difference . . . like the new chief of police. He's making a difference. We have to support them.
>
> *Joy (Washington, DC, E):* [Y]ou know in my dad's neighborhood, we have a lot of people from El Salvador and my husband is from El Salvador. My own Bolivian family had this prejudice against people from Central America, especially from El Salvador. It was because they were coming from pueblos and they were not well educated, and so there is this mentality that you have to treat them in a different way. It has been difficult for me, but I am changing.

Armando (Miami, E): [S]o the lower class groups that Marisol pointed out, primarily the South American poor people coming in. (What countries are they from?) They come from Nicaragua, Costa Rica, Honduras, and Guatemala. Not many from Colombia, because they don't live in this part of town. Anyway, we know all kinds of Latinos.

The weight of evidence among the focus group participants did indicate that the primary use of pan-ethnic identifiers was substantial. Terms such as "Latino" and "Hispanic" have clearly penetrated the national consciousness, as the subjects of this study have indicated. When the person identified friends or co-workers or the makeup of the communities in which they were living, the social categories used were Hispanics/Latinos, Americans, blacks, or Asians. The focus group moderator would have to probe further to get the participant to "delineate" the specific national origin or provide other, more detailed information. In those situations, the individual would say I have some Mexican co-workers/friends or Brazilians, Peruvians, and so on. Consistently, the intergroup distinction would be between Latinos and non-Latinos. As Latino subgroups are more mixed in a wider range of communities, the pervasiveness of a Latino/Hispanic referent is more evident.

Moreover, it appears clear in this evidence that the meaning attached to pan-ethnic labels is exactly how we would understand them; that is, transcending national-origin groups. This is clearly the case in multinationality Latino environments, such as the two groups conducted in metropolitan Washington, DC. That is, when in the presence of a group of Latinos of mixed national origin, we should not be surprised if the terms "Latino" and "Hispanic" appear, even if they otherwise might not occur in a single-subgroup environment. At the same time, our focus groups in all seven sites indicate that "single-subgroup" environments are now rarer. From a comparative perspective, the only location from the LNPS sites in which the frequent use of "Latino" was evident was in Chicago, an early location where Latinos of different national origins were co-located. As we have already noted, Chicago at that point had an extensive history of subgroup diversity as well as the instrumental use of pan-ethnic terms by activists and political advocates hoping to create a broader Latino consciousness and, by extension, greater political impact.

Is that the story here? Have these informants in other parts of the country now experienced the same level of conscious pan-ethnic identity construction that was present in Chicago? Possibly, but other factors certainly played an important role. Obviously, the public discourse has significantly facilitated the adoption of these pan-ethnic labels. The media especially has taken to systematically describing this population as Hispanic or Latino, and has therefore played a major part in this broader awareness and usage of Hispanic or Latino identifiers. The degree of incorporation into the "regular" language of these focus group participants reveals a level of awareness and language integration more visible than that in the period in which the LNPS was conducted.

Part of the focus group protocol involved asking each participant how he or she identifies himself or herself. The more common responses were those of parental roles, familial roles, work-related position or occupation and, occasionally, class. These responses are consistent with social identity research. At the same time, the inclusion of Latino or Hispanic or a national-origin identifier provides a glimpse into a person's social identity "constellation." While use of a Latino or Hispanic identifier remains less prevalent than some others, it was quite common and not at all the rare event it was during the LNPS in 1989. Most persons listed or identified either a national origin or pan-ethnic term—Latino or Hispanic—in their group identity clusters, sometimes both. For example:

> *Carla (Washington, DC, E):* Nicaraguan and a woman.
> *Moderator:* Which one is first?
> *Carla:* I would say Nicaraguan, then woman.
> *Marco (Washington, DC, E):* Latino, son, grandson, nephew. Occupation is not really a part of whom I am. *(He is a purchasing manager for a computer company.)* So I would say the order would be—son, husband, Latino.
> *George (Washington, DC, E):* I would say Latino, Hispanic in addition to being a husband and a father. I do not know why I feel more comfortable with the word Hispanic.
> *Javier (Muscatine, IA, bilingual):* Mexican, because I feel more comfortable with that.

Mauricio (Los Angeles, S), in a discussion of citizenship and identity: My wife gave me all of the forms because I did not want to get them. I always said I was Mexican and I would stay Mexican. One time when I went back to Mexico and I did not understand one of the words and they asked if I was Mexican, and I said yes; but I left when I was five years old.

Sergio (Miami, E): I would say musician, worker, and I would say Latino, too.

In summary, the evidence from the focus groups is overwhelming. Pan-ethnic consciousness appears to have taken root in individual self-identity, the definition and understanding of community, and the intentional expression of political and social commonality. The prevalence of Latino communities nationwide where multiple national-origin groups live and work together, compounded by the media's relentless definition of these populations as a single entity, have redefined the boundaries of community and facilitated the emergence of a strong all-encompassing identity where scarcely any existed just two decades ago.

We do need to offer one important caution. The meaning of pan-ethnic references and terminology is not automatically clear in social environments where a single national origin group dominates the social landscape. For example, if a Mexican American from the Rio Grande Valley in South Texas were to use the term "Latino," can we say for sure that she meant to imply all peoples of Latin American ancestry? Or is Latino, at least in her social setting, a synonym for Mexican American? More than likely, the answer here is both. When listening to a radio station whose format is "rock en Español," she may refer to the music as Latino because it includes Cuban, Puerto Rican, Colombian, and Mexican performers and mean it in the pan-ethnic sense we conventionally assume. Yet, when discussing representation on the local city council, her use of Latino clearly means "Mexican," since the Latino community to which she might refer is, in fact, exclusively of Mexican ancestry.

The point we wish to make here is that the use of pan-ethnic terminology reflects a variety of distinctive forces. It may be an indication of identity, but might also reflect the experiences of an individual living where the Latino population is more diverse in terms of national origin,or even merely the evolution of colloquial expression prompted largely, if not completely, by the adoption of the term in the media, by government, and by academicians.

We conducted mirror focus group protocols in most of the focus group sites. That is, Spanish-speaking and bilingual/English-dominant groups were organized. The language of the focus group participants did not seem to affect the use of and identification of Latinos in the more pan-ethnic terminology. That is, the reference to co-workers, friends, and neighbors was, again, distinguished by Latino and non-Latino referents. The distinctiveness of Latinos and "Americans" (or Anglos) was noted with some frequency. In most cases, it dealt with stereotypes that each had about the other or differences regarding the centrality of family or social celebrations. In this manner, the lessened internal differentiation among the various Latino subgroups and heightened differences between themselves and non-Latinos, especially Anglos, could be working as a pan-ethnic mechanism. The Latino world as experienced through all of these focus groups clearly indicates a sense of identification as Latinos and the persistence of national-origin demarcations.

Pan-ethnicity and the Spanish Language

One element that we feel should be highlighted is an empirical regularity that the reader may have already taken note of. While the use of pan-ethnic terminology was common, language was often identified as the most salient aspect of this identity. There was some variation, of course, but the cultural marker of Spanish-language fluency repeatedly appears as an important aspect of identity and commonality.

> *Barbara (Houston, E):* [I]n reality, we're all Hispanics; we speak Spanish, even though it is a different kind of Spanish. Society is more accepting of Hispanics. We are getting more educated, more civil. We are realizing what is important for our race and our culture, for our children.
>
> *Woman (Washington, DC, S):* I have seen a lot of Hispanics moving into this area. . . . I never say Latino; I say Hispanic. To me everyone here is Hispanic. We all speak

Spanish. . . . When people speak Spanish, it does not matter where you are from. It seems familiar to me.

We were surprised to see the connection drawn by these informants between the linguistic basis of pan-ethnicity and the preferred pan-ethnic terminology. That is, on the "Hispanic" versus "Latino" question, these speakers clearly felt the label "Hispanic" specifically referenced language, which they felt was important. Naturally, there was significant variation on this response as well. It was evident in Miami and Los Angeles that Latinos more frequently used the label "Latino" as the descriptor to place persons of different Latino national origins, whereas in the case of Washington, DC, one of the participants explicitly stated that he preferred the term "Hispanic" instead of Latino. In fact, in two different focus groups held in Washington, DC, several participants reiterated their preference for "Hispanic." Nevertheless, while the protocol of the focus groups did not concentrate on the meaning of labels or differences in their use, the word choices among the participants appeared quite deliberate.

The role of language as the salient marker of identity and a key element of pan-ethnicity should not be underestimated. Moreover, we found a number of informants who—specifically referencing language as the root of pan-ethnic culture and identity—mourned the loss of the language for themselves and their children and, occasionally, took steps to restore Spanish language skills.

> *Mario (Los Angeles, E):* I'm learning Spanish now because I want to associate with my own people.
>
> *Pedro (Los Angele, E):* When I was younger, I did not want to speak Spanish. My family spoke Spanish to me and I would only answer in English.
>
> *Eric (New York, E):* That's the thing, while we are American, born here, we can't forget our heritage. My daughters, I try to teach them Spanish. I bought DVDs to teach them Spanish. They only speak English, and I am trying to tell their mother as well, because you can never forget your heritage. We are American and we have to speak English well, but don't forget where you came from.

Of course, this reliance on language as an engine of pan-ethnic unity is also potentially double-edged. On the one hand, the salience of language in defining the "group" helps to overcome national origin, racial, and cultural differences in defining who is actually Latino or Hispanic, contributing to both the strength of this identity and the breadth of community that it encompasses. On the other hand, as language proficiency declines across generations, we wonder if the reliance on language (or indeed any cultural marker) to provide the defining limits of community thereby dooms that community to dissipation and political irrelevance with the passage of time and generations. When fewer Latinos speak Spanish, hold *tamaladas*, or live apart from non-Latinos, will the pan-ethnic identity mean as much?

Reinforcing Focus Group Members' Insights: Preliminary Results from the LNS

Our previous discussion extracting the insights and comments from the LNS focus group participants does portray a very noticeable degree of community building across Latino national-origin groupings. The forms of community are reflected by the inclusion of a "Latino" identity in informants' portfolios of roles, extensive social networks with a diversity of Latinos, and an awareness of their "distinctive" practices and customs. At the same time, our Latino participants have regular interactions with non-Latinos, including closer personal relationships, but the nature of these contacts is mediated by a sense of ethnicity, national origin, or being Latino.

Are our focus groups reflective of patterns exhibited in the broader community? That is, did the discussions we witnessed and reported here capture the dynamics taking place in the larger Latino population? We think so. In this section, we briefly present some preliminary results from the LNS that complement—and reinforce—our previous data, findings, and discussion.

In the LNS, the respondents were asked if they had a preference for the terms "Hispanic" or "Latino," or if either was acceptable. Additional questions asked the respondents how strongly they identified themselves as Latino, with their national-origin group, and as American. Earlier in this chapter, we presented results showing the substantial growth in pan-ethnic identification, even under the artificial conditions of forced choice. We reported results on these questions by nativity, generation, and national-origin group in Tables 7-3, 7-4, and 7-5.

Table 7-6 reports association between strength of pan-ethnic identification and preferred pan-ethnic terminology. The results in Table 7-6 represent the bivariate analysis of these two items. Regardless of the pan-ethnic term they preferred, a supermajority of respondents felt that they strongly identified with the pan-ethnic label. Moreover, the percentages for strong pan-ethnic sentiment among those identifying as "Hispanic" and those preferring "Latino" are nearly identical. We earlier speculated that the centrality of language to pan-ethnic solidarity and identity might bias pan-ethnic sentiment in favor of "Hispanic" as the preferred term, but no evidence of this appears in the large-scale LNS survey results.

In Table 7-7, we explore further the extent of Latino identification by introducing the respondent's birthplace or nativity. Again, willingness to express pan-ethnic identification is compared across native and foreign-born and Puerto Rican island-born Latinos. When we combine those whose identification is somewhat or very strong, there is little differentiation across this dimension; 85.9% of the native-born identify as

TABLE 7-6   LATINO NATIONAL SURVEY: RESPONSES ON STRENGTH
OF PAN-ETHNIC IDENTITY, BY RESPONDENT'S
PREFERRED LABEL*

	Hispanic	Latino	Either Is Acceptable	Don't Care	Total
Not at all	93 (8.7%)	30 (2.7%)	80 (3.6%)	101 (6.3%)	304
Not very strongly	183 (6.1%)	67 (6.0%)	160 (5.8%)	160 (10.0%)	470
Somewhat strongly	707 (24.0%)	246 (22.2%)	690 (24.9%)	433 (27.0%)	2,076
Very strongly	1,938 (64.1%)	746 (67.2%)	1,811 (65.4%)	879 (54.8%)	5,374
DK/NA	88 (2.9%)	21 (1.9%)	30 (1.1%)	30 (1.9%)	169
Total	3,009	1,110	2,771	1,603	8,441

*Question: How strongly do you think of yourself as . . . Latino/Hispanic?
† The percentage totals sum to 100% for each column.
DK/NA = Don't know/No answer; $\chi^2 = 142.60$; $p \leq 0.0$.

TABLE 7-7 LATINO NATIONAL SURVEY: RESPONSES ON STRENGTH
OF PAN-ETHNIC IDENTITY, BY RESPONDENT'S PLACE
OF BIRTH*

	Mainland United States	Puerto Rico	Some Other Country	Total
Not at all	113 (4.6%)	11 (2.4%)	188 (3.3%)	312
Not very strongly	179 (7.3%)	19 (4.1%)	326 (5.7%)	524
Somewhat strongly	625 (25.7%)	79 (16.9%)	1,402 (24.5%)	2,106
Very strongly	1,477 (60.6%)	346 (74.6%)	3,600 (63.0%)	5,423
DK/NA	42 (1.7%)	9 (1.9%)	164 (3.5%)	215
Total	2,436	464	5,680	8,580

*Question: How strongly do you think of yourself as . . . Latino/Hispanic?
DK/NA = Don't know/No answer; $\chi^2 = 51.14$; $p \le 0.0$.

Latinos in comparison to 91.5% Puerto Rican island-born and 88.1%
foreign-born. Again, the extensive presence of Latino-ness was evident
in both the focus groups as well as respondents in the LNS.

The next two tables explore the possible bases for this group affinity and attachment. In Table 7-8, the respondents were asked some
questions as possible bases for Latino commonalities. The first one presented deals with respondent perceptions of commonality on political
issues such as representation and power, again looking for differences
across strength of pan-ethnic identifications. There is a higher level of
perceived common political interests among stronger Latino identifiers. A preponderance of all respondents reported strong pan-ethnic
identification, and it does not appear that this identification is heavily
influenced by perceived political commonality. Even respondents who
perceive little in common with the political circumstances of other
Latinos report strong pan-ethnic identification (58.9%), though it is the
case that the perception of having a great deal in common yielded a
somewhat higher percentage of strong identifiers (70.2%). In Table 7-9,
a question is posed, but the basis for community is a sense of a group
"linked fate" between the respondent's national-origin group and
other Latinos. Again, stronger Latino identification is associated with a
greater degree of group-linked fate. Among those perceiving a strong

TABLE 7-8   LATINO NATIONAL SURVEY: RESPONSES ON STRENGTH
OF PAN-ETHNIC IDENTITY, BY RESPONDENT'S
PERCEPTION OF POLITICAL COMMONALITY*

	Nothing	Little	Some	A Lot	Total
Not at all	47	67	85	65	264
	(8.0%)	(3.8%)	(2.9%)	(2.5%)	
Not very strongly	49	134	154	139	476
	(8.4%)	(7.7%)	(5.3%)	(5.3%)	
Somewhat strongly	129	442	849	543	1,963
	(22.1%)	(25.3%)	(29.0%)	(20.7%)	
Very strongly	347	1,069	1,794	1,845	5,055
	(58.3%)	(61.2%)	(63.0%)	(70.2%)	
DK/NA	13	34	45	31	123
	(2.2%)	(1.9%)	(1.5%)	(1.2%)	
Total	585	1,746	2,927	2,623	7,881

*Question: Thinking about politics, representation, and power, how much in common do you
have with other Latinos?
DK/NA = Don't know/No answer, $\chi^2 = 660.5$; $p < 0.0$.

TABLE 7-9   LATINO NATIONAL SURVEY: RESPONSES ON STRENGTH
OF PAN-ETHNIC IDENTITY, BY RESPONDENT'S
PERCEPTION OF INTRA-LATINO "LINKED FATE"*

	Nothing	Little	Some	A Lot	Total
Not at all	54	42	67	96	259
	(7.8%)	(3.7%)	(3.1%)	(2.4%)	
Not very strongly	57	102	129	193	481
	(8.2%)	(9.1%)	(6.0%)	(4.8%)	
Somewhat strongly	161	306	652	867	1,986
	(23.3%)	(27.3%)	(30.2%)	(21.7%)	
Very strongly	395	651	1,271	2,767	5,084
	(57.1%)	(58.1%)	(58.8%)	(69.4%)	
DK/NA	19	16	36	58	129
	(2.7%)	(1.4%)	(1.7%)	(1.5%)	
Total	686	1,117	2,155	3,981	7,939

*Question: How much does your national-origin group doing well depend on other Hispanics/
Latinos also doing well?
DK/NA = Don't know/No answer; $\chi^2 = 461.995$; $p \leq 0.0$.

connection between their group and other Latinos, 69.4% strongly
identify with the pan-ethnic term. However, even among those with
little perception of linked fate, a majority (57.1%) strongly associate
themselves with the pan-ethnic identity.

This additional data from the LNS reinforces the overall patterns evidenced by our focus group participants. The reinforcement lies with a prevailing sense of being Latino in conjunction with the maintenance of national-origin identity. Though a sense of group commonality of circumstances contributes to this pan-ethnic sentiment, the associations are not sufficiently strong to conclude that pan-ethnicity is instrumental. The strength of pan-ethnic identification, even among those with little perception of common interests and futures with other Latinos, suggests that there are other factors making important contributions to this developing important political and social identity.

Community, Change, and Continuity

The vehicle of fourteen focus groups provided us with an insightful view of how contemporary Latinos, in a variety of American communities, live and relate among themselves and with other "Americans." We focused our analysis on the "building blocks" of an ongoing community—that is, shared values, cultural practices, language, social networks, and similar circumstances. One could differentiate segments of the Latino population by nativity, by English or Spanish language use, or by generational status in the United States. Analytically, these dimensions are being considered more systematically in a variety of research endeavors examining the public life of Latinos. For our purposes, an essential aspect of that public life is how connected Latinos are to each other, and whether the personal experiences and circumstances drawing them together are sufficient to engage collectively in political action. The crux of this type of inquiry goes beyond the depth and scope of the LNS focus group project, but valuable perceptions were derived from our "conversations" with Latinos in many settings. The subsequent LNS of more than 9,800 respondents can build on our understanding of the experiences of these Latino focus group participants.

Through the use of focus group discussions, we tried to establish the changes and continuity for Latinos in the United States, as well as the complexities of such a diverse community. We can comment on several distinct patterns. The continuity for Latinos has centered on the maintenance of national origin-based affinities and interactions, and the relative social (and in some cases physical) distance between Latinos and their non-Latino fellow citizens and residents of the United States. Latino national-origin status continues to affect where persons reside and with whom they interact. Other migration-related research reinforces the use of individuals' social networks as bases for information about residential or community destinations, employment, neighborhoods, and retail services. From our focus group participants, we know that these interactions are quite common. One could describe this continuity as the persistence of ethnically dense social networks, manifested where Latinos both live and work. If we overlay the previously mentioned segments within the Latino community (that is, Cuban, Puerto Rican, and Mexican origin), these dense networks are even more prevalent among the more recent Latino immigrants in the United States. At the same time, second-generation Latinos who live in more racially and ethnically diverse neighborhoods/work settings clearly develop extensive interactions with non-Latinos, even as they maintain the majority of their social and economic interactions with other Latinos.

The other elements of continuity lie with the importance and diligence of cultural and linguistic traditions. That is, cultural traditions, practices, and continuation of Spanish language use are prevalent across most communities. Even those Latinos who are further removed from the immigration experience either acknowledge these cultural elements or attempt to maintain or even recover them. This has implications for building a collective community than can transcend variations within the Latino community. Spanish language can certainly influence who the primary members of a social network are likely to be. From the Spanish-speaking participants, it was evident that language could limit the extent and participation in broader networks, but could also serve to facilitate cooperation and cross-nationality community building.

Our theme of continuity and change also enables us to document some changes as well. Part of the selection process of identifying focus group sites was capturing some communities that were less traditional areas of settlement. The experience of Latinos in "emerging areas" does provide some contrasts with those Latinos in more traditional areas. The dynamics of intergroup relations (that is, between Latino and non-Latino) is much more visible and can be intense. Awareness of intergroup differences and suspicions about the degree of acceptance (or resistance) by Anglos is found in the focus group members' comments. At the same time, there is a diversity of contacts across racial and ethnic lines. Ethnically dense Latino social networks do not appear to preclude the presence of "secondary" networks with non-Latinos.

A broad characterization of Latinos as socially isolated is not supported by our focus group results. In many regards, our participants' social networks are quite diverse, but stratified. That is, for many, other Latinos (either from one's own national-origin group or other Latinos) serve as the primary or most personal network, even as extensive contacts with other groups, in workplaces, diverse neighborhoods, and even families, emerge. As a result, these interactions serve to inform Latinos about the "external world" and how they fit into the larger society. Our examination of Latinos and evolving community would suggest strongly that change and continuity have had complementary effects in the further establishment of an active and viable community in the United States.

The dimension of complexity centers on the breadth of interactions for these Latinos and how they learn both to navigate through their own societal understandings of their places of residence, as well as sustain connections with their communities of origin. As evidenced by Chapter 6, on transnationalism (Jones-Correa 1998), Latinos negotiate social stratification systems, primary and secondary familial relationships, and intergroup relations and stereotypes and attempt to adapt to present-day needs and future aspirations for themselves and their families. Our examination of pan-ethnicity reflects the inclusion of a wider identity in addition to their own national-origin references. It is an evolving community in which adaptation to changes as well as the familiar "benchmarks" of a community, common circumstances and cultural traditions, produce real challenges to define and place oneself within the larger society. Change, continuity, and complexities are a "regular part" of living as a Latino in the United States.

8 Conclusions

Paradoxes along the Way to Making America Home

As we reflect back on what we have learned from this study, let us start by reconsidering ideas set out at the very beginning of this endeavor. The first word of our book's subtitle, *"Making,"* was intentionally meant to imply something ongoing, in the works, even "in progress," and connoting a process as much as or more than an outcome, because our subject matter seemed to require that. It is inherently difficult, yet very important, to try to explain this moving target and to capture the temporal essence of phenomena as socially intricate as the past and present situation of Latinos in American society, a group that can be thought of variously, and more or less correctly, as an ethnic/minority/immigrant/transnational or "just American" group and all or some combination of these terms simultaneously (cf. Jones-Correa 2007; Hero 1992; Skerry 1993). When something is "in the making," it contains both enduring and evolving features; our analysis begins—from the subtitle onward—by acknowledging this and, in turn, striving to do the best of incorporating it into the analysis.

Further, our book's subtitle employs the metaphor of making it *"home."* Again, that word choice was meant to convey important ideas.

The notion of a home goes beyond just the idea of a house, meaning shelter provided by a physical structure comprised of walls, a roof, and so on. "A home" has connotations of well-being, belongingness, and the like; as we use it here it also implies having a legitimate and secure "place" within a larger social and political structure. The notion of a home also carries with it various presuppositions. These include expectations and aspirations of what a home will provide beyond basic shelter—the blueprints that indicate how it will be configured, the building of a foundation, and so forth. "Home" implies social stability, comfort, groundedness, involvement in and commitment to a place. Indeed, considerable social science research finds that areas with higher home ownership (versus renters) experience better social well-being on a variety of indicators (Rohe, Van Zandt, and McCarthy 2001; Rossi and Weber 1996). The broader notion of a city or country as a home carries similar though different implications, suggesting a broader scale of social and political memberships, about identity, legitimacy, place, and acceptance. To what extent are Latinos successfully making a home for themselves in the United States? And what does this home look like? We trust that we can now answer these questions based on our analysis and also provide some indication of what the Latino situation might be in the future.

At the outset of our "inside" view of contemporary life of Latinos in America, we identified and developed four central themes or concepts to guide our examination and interpretations of the voices we heard in various sites across the country. Those themes—change, continuity, community, and complexity—we argue are indicative of dynamic processes that are integral parts of Latinos' lives in America as they seek to make a home or a place in the society. Furthermore, concepts such as these are often intertwined; for instance, much of the increasing *complexity* we described regarding generations, intergroup and intragroup relations, and the like are directly attributable to the vast *changes* in the size and growth, composition, geographic dispersion, and other dimensions of change we identified (see Chapter 1).

The circumstances and array of conditions that frequently emerge from the intersections and simultaneous presence of change, continuity, community, and complexity suggest a series of paradoxes, by which we mean the co-existence of ideas that seem self-contradictory but in reality express a possible truth. Indeed, paradox appears to be a prominent feature of the contemporary lives of Latinos. It has been a central finding of our effort that a comprehensive grasp of the nature of Latino life in the United States today requires coming to grips with a variety of apparent contradictions—beliefs of individuals, assertions of community values, histories, and orientations toward the U.S. polity and society that are often apparently at odds with one another—that are necessary to capture the mixed nature of the Latino experience. That is, Latino-ness cannot be understood without grappling with the nature of an ethnic community deeply rooted in U.S. and North American history and yet vaguely alien to the mainstream of American culture; a community, like preceding generations of new Americans, composed primarily of immigrants and their offspring yet understood as the perpetual "other"; a group of peoples striving for full cultural inclusion in the United States *and* insistent on the retention of the richness of their heritage; a race *and* an ethnicity; a "linguistic minority," most of whom speak English fluently; and as a "community" whose boundaries and self-definition is still evolving.

Historical Descriptions of Latinos and Their Political Development

Before there was much talk about "Latinos" (in general) in the United States, some scholars developed several ways to characterize and summarize the history of Mexican Americans. These approaches to the history of Mexican Americans in the United States (including F. Garcia and de la Garza 1977: 19–33; Barrera 1985; Villareal 1988) illustrate, we think, the long-standing nature of the inherent contradictions of Latino life. With some variation, these scholars identify five distinct historical periods, none of which captures the contemporary experience we describe here. The period between the Mexican War and the Depression (1848–1920s) is alternatively described as one of "forced acquiescence" (F. Garcia and de la Garza), as "communitarian" (Barrera 1985), and as one of "resistance" (Villareal 1988). These descriptors illustrate perfectly how the Latino experience, viewed through different analytical lenses, can take on very different historical complexions, with different levels of agency assigned to Mexican Americans and their Anglo neighbors, and differing interpretations of the primary drivers behind social change. The period from 1920 through the Second World War is understood as one of "adaptation" or "accommodation," while the postwar period is generally seen as a period of "social change" or "politicization." The 1960s and 1970s are understood as the "protest" period, identified largely with the Chicano movement and its surrounding events. Everything since then is characterized as "post-Chicano," a period seen on the one hand as one of "fragmentation" and on the other as "moderation."

This quick overview of the characterization of Mexican-American history highlights two noteworthy points. First, while scholars share similarities in their approaches, there are also important differences in their conceptual characterizations and timelines of the different periods. While "adaptation" in the pre-1920 period, "politicization" in the post-World War II period and the Chicano movement in the 1960s in F. Garcia and de la Garza's typology of Latino history (1977) closely matches Villareal's (1988) characterizations of these periods as ones of "accommodation," "social change" and "protest," it is clear that each scholar, in fact, provides somewhat different emphases and interpretations of history. None, we think, are misplaced but, rather, illustrate the conflicting and shifting currents in Latino life that can operate simultaneously. This is particularly evident in Barrera's interpretation of the Chicano movement as a unique *blend* of communitarian and egalitarian impulses, as well as in his view of the post-Chicano period as having several quite distinct dimensions ("fragmentation, radicalization, and re-traditionalization").

A second point is that neither these nor other political scientists have (to our knowledge) attempted to summarize or characterize the period of the latter years of the 20th and the early years of the 21st century, especially with respect to the various national origin or pan-ethnic groups that have come to be thought of as "Latinos" or "Hispanics." This is natural, of course, because these events postdate their writings, but as we indicated in the introduction to this volume, an awful lot of history has happened in the Latino population of the United States since then. Indeed, the vast majority of that population today is new to the United States since each of those works was published. It is not clear the historical tools scholars of Latinos in the United States have at their disposal have been adapted to contemporary demographic and historical realities.

Before we discuss our findings writ large, it may be useful to first briefly recap our specific findings associated with six topic areas. These findings, as they relate to our thematic framework, are also summarized in Table 8-1.

Recapping Specific Findings

Our analysis focused on six topics of emphasis that emerged somewhat naturally from the focus group narratives. The topics were: (1) the American dream and assimilation, (2) education, (3) discrimination, (4) new settlement in rural towns, (5) transnationalism, and (6) identity. Our findings in almost every instance suggest that in the process of "making it home," that is, as intergroup (and intragroup) social and political ties are formed, paradox is common.

The Americano Dream and Assimilation (Chapter 2)

Latinos have the same long-term goals as other Americans in similar socioeconomic circumstances. They face significant barriers to their success that are largely specific to their immigrant/minority group status, but nonetheless they remain more optimistic about their prospects for achieving their *"Americano* dream" than their American counterparts. Moreover, Latinos are willing to take difficult steps to achieve these goals, including "adapting" so as to better fit into American society. Although Latinos strive to maintain their distinct cultural and language traditions, there is clear evidence, consistent with decades of demographic and sociological work, that Latinos are also assimilating. Even with the considerable growth in size of the Latino population and the continuing importance of immigration from Latin America, we find that their assimilation increases with time spent in the United States and over generations. It is important to note, however, that the process of assimilation is uneven across critical dimensions such as education and income, which suggests that while Latinos may be assimilating, their assimilation may be segmented by class and education.

TABLE 8-1 SUMMARY OF TOPICAL THEMES AND FINDINGS BY ANALYTICAL CONCEPTS

Topical Themes	Continuity (Enduring)	Change (Evolution)	Community (Commonalities)	Complexity (Differences)
The American Dream and Assimilation	Belief in the "dream"; optimism for the future	Growing assimilation; population replenishment	U.S. as "community" reference	Uneven or segmented achievement
Education	Remains high priority; value convergence with societal norms; low achievement	Arguably increased value convergence; possibility of new reforms	Individuals, national-origin groups, and (pan-ethnic) group as a whole having low achievement	Policy preferences, impact of policy reform; implications for educational improvement
Discrimination	Moderate levels perceived; varies by group, place, and social sphere	More recognition of intra-group issues	Latino/non-Latino; English versus Spanish as common bases of community	Intra-Latino; language; nationalities; generational differences
New Settlement in Rural Settings	Previous generation in rural areas; myth of "small-town" inclusion, welcomingness	New presence; economic revival; more nonagricultural employment options	Primarily Mexican; some sense or feeling of being "unwelcomed" or separate from long-term residents	Rural/urban differences; differences across rural areas; intergroup tension
Transnationalism	Abstract "home country" sentiments endure	Actual home country orientation diminishes over time	Connections with home country groups in U.S. and across countries	New assessments of home country's appeal; altered preferences
Social Group Identity	Prominence of national-origin identity and social network	Increased pan-ethnic identification; increased American identity; presence of Latino community; expanding diversity in social networks	Increasing intergroup and intragroup contact and relationships	Factors that contribute to the evolving Latino community; implications of Latinos' multiple identities on their sense of place

Education (Chapter 3)

Education is often thought of as the linchpin of American democracy, particularly for achieving "equal opportunity" for disadvantaged groups and in the society at large. However, conventional wisdom has long held that Latinos do not place the same emphasis or value on education as do others and that Latino parents, for a variety of reasons, are less concerned and less involved in their children's education than other parents. Such claims are nonsense and are unrecognizable in the comments of our focus group informants. Our informants show that Latinos view education in the same way as other Americans, as central to quality of life and social mobility. There is clear value congruence between Latino attitudes and mainstream American views on the critical role that education plays in affecting one's life chances. Moreover, Latino parents do pay close attention to their children's educational experiences and act to intervene or assist—to the extent that they can—when they feel the quality of their children's teachers and schools is lacking. However, our groups also made clear that these parents are often rebuffed in their efforts and that the U.S. educational system to date has not been successful in addressing the particular needs of Latino students. As a consequence, even while Latino parents value education, Latino students continue to underachieve.

Discrimination (Chapter 4)

Latinos' perceptions and personal experiences of discrimination vary greatly by generation, place of residence, occupation, and social sphere. Even as Latinos continue to perceive a moderate level of discrimination from non-Latino individuals and majority institutions, they express hopes for improved intergroup relations and greater equality. There is also increasing recognition of *intra*group discrimination and its negative effects. Our evidence indicates wide differences of opinion among Latinos as to whether discrimination is decreasing (or increasing) and also what might account for that change. Immigrants, overall, tend to perceive less discrimination and are more optimistic about the issue than members of second and later generations. The paradox is that as Latinos become more assimilated, the perception of discriminatory treatment (both given and received) becomes more prominent.

New Settlement in Rural Towns (Chapter 5)

Stereotypic understandings of small-town rural settings usually connote simpler, more accessible, and more welcoming possibilities in a kind of Jeffersonian vision of American democracy.[1] On the whole, the situation for Latinos is mixed in this regard; that is, their sense of feeling welcomed is not necessarily high nor is it uniform across, or within, these rural contexts. While our informants report a lifestyle that is safer and more economically secure than that of their urban-dwelling counterparts, there are substantial challenges facing Latinos in emerging destinations. Moreover, evidence regarding social and economic incorporation suggests the occasional emergence of tension or competition between Latinos and preexisting populations. In fact, we find considerable evidence that these new settlement locations are, in many instances, reenacting the well-established scripts of social exclusion, economic marginalization, and white flight. And, by any measure, political incorporation lags considerably behind other processes of inclusion, as none of the Latinos in these rural communities have managed to secure much political power or influence.

Transnationalism (Chapter 6)

The idea of Latinos in general, and immigrants in particular, maintaining feelings of loyalty or attachment and instrumental connections to their countries of origin is often controversial. Many people presume these transnational ties diminish or even prohibit Latinos' commitment to the United States. To the contrary, we find that continued connections with their countries of origins does not necessarily mean that Latinos still consider those places "home." The focus group conversations indicate our informants have a great deal of ambivalence toward their countries of origin, with return visits actually having the effect of reinforcing their commitment to remain in the United States. Moreover, the extent of transnational ties, even among immigrants, declines fairly quickly, accelerating with the birth of their children in the United States. Our evidence from both the focus groups and the Latino National Surveys (LNS) suggests that the stark contrast often made between "assimilation" and "transnationalism" is dramatically overstated. If anything, transnationalism and assimilation are not only complementary, but in fact are also likely to be mutually reinforcing.

Identity (Chapter 7)

Latinos simultaneously hold multiple identities and also have social networks that are increasingly dense and diverse, but also stratified. Identity and social networking based on country of origin continue to be a prominent feature in the lives of many Latinos. Yet this has not precluded the development of an equally meaningful and vibrant pan-ethnic identity and corresponding social network or the adoption of an identity as Americans, which is also present among most Latinos. Indeed, positive interactions and long-term relationships with non-Latinos are on the rise. However, our informants' relationships with fellow Latinos are still more common and usually primary in comparison with relationships to non-Latinos. The evidence from the focus groups and the LNS indicates the presence of a Latino community that is increasingly self-conscious, crosses nationalities, and is politically relevant. A variety of factors have contributed to this development; some of these include the changing composition of the Latino population, the dispersion of national-origin groups to new areas of settlement or to closer proximity with other subgroups, the desire to retain cultural and language traditions, and both media messages and public policies that encourage pan-ethnic group consciousness.

With these specific findings in mind, we now can elaborate on our overall characterization of the contemporary status of Latinos in the United States.

Our Findings Writ Large

In Chapter 1, we began by describing the ostensibly historic nature of the massive and widespread marches of 2006 and speculated about their larger meaning, suggesting that the marches manifested various elements and impulses in contemporary Latino politics. We also acknowledged that scholarship has not adequately understood the development of Latino politics, and we proffered explanations as to why that might be the case. As noted at the outset, to many observers the marches were "surprising" yet, as we explained, they could just as well be seen as a "culmination" of a series of preceding developments, which we described. Furthermore, we argued that participation in marches demonstrated despair and fear on the one hand, yet, through a form of political participation associated with a "protest" tradition, they also indicated efficacy and trust in the potential responsiveness of the American political system. Hence, acknowledging these juxtaposed and apparently contradictory elements seem essential in making sense of the 2006 marches.

We also noted that the marches, in which Mexican Americans were the largest contingent, also showed signs of an emerging "pan-ethnic" orientation with the participation and visibility of other Latino groups. Additionally, the marchers themselves often said, "Today we march, tomorrow we vote." This suggests a link between different forms of political activity and a connection of current with future political actions, and raises the possibility that the marches will have an enduring impact on Latino unity and activism in American politics, a possibility whose outcome is still undetermined. In any case, the example of the marches began to illustrate the complexity of our subject, serving as an entrée to the more explicitly thematic analyses.

The book's central analytical chapters build on the themes of continuity and change. Our focus group participants' comments offer perspectives familiar from past eras of immigration. We hear them make remarks that reflect a move toward "adaptation" to the United States in, for example, their views about the American dream, assimilation, their educational aspirations, and even in the way they speak about the appeal of the United States compared to their home countries. Participants voice concerns about discrimination as an impediment to social mobility, yet also express hopes for equality. They make observations about their cultural community, though somewhat expanded and increasingly reframed in pan-ethnic terms. Contemporary Latinos, as they appear in our focus groups, present a unique amalgam (though one that is hardly uniform across sites, groups, and other dimensions), owing in large part to the many social changes we have outlined in this book.

One of the consistent and remarkable findings from our focus group (and LNS) evidence is that Latinos frequently hold potentially conflicting sets of values that they themselves feel are simultaneously achievable and desirable. Latinos identify as "American" *and* as

"Latino" *and* in national-origin terms. They emphasize the importance of learning English *and* the maintenance of Spanish. They indicate that Latinos should "change to blend into the larger American society" *and* "maintain their distinct culture." Significant social dynamics within the Latino population (and between Latinos and non-Latinos) revolve around just these sorts of issues.

Furthermore, seeking to accommodate these contrasting sets of values and sentiments is a source of ambivalence or tension (which is directly evident in the focus group narratives), though certainly not unique to Latinos. Studies of American identity as viewed by the Anglo/white population have frequently demonstrated multiple, sometimes contradictory understandings as well (more on this later). The difference, however, is that the multiple understandings that Latinos hold in juxtaposition may differ in their extent and to some degree in kind. Moreover, Latinos are a minority or subordinate immigrant group whose place and behavior in society is frequently questioned by the larger society in a way and to a degree that Anglo/white perspectives are not. For Latinos, a mixed or bifurcated set of identities—feeling strongly Mexican *and* strongly American, for example—invites distrust and a perception of "otherness" that would not logically follow for Anglo/white Americans.

Other lessons from the various chapters elaborate further on the theme of "community" and what that entails. While Latinos mentioned positive interactions with non-Latinos, they do not necessarily equate these with "community" or maybe not with a sense of their core or primary community. Although there are increasing interactions between Latinos and non-Latinos, our focus group participants appear to see much of these as coming out of economic exchanges, or business-type relations, and perhaps out of necessity. They may not be rooted in social connectedness as such. That is, if there is a sense of community it seems often based on a "community of (material) interests" and not on social solidarity or a "community of culture" (J. Garcia 2003). Also, ongoing contact between Latinos and non-Latinos does not necessarily breed familiarity or closeness, nor, on the other hand, does it necessarily lead to conflict or contempt, as the "contact" and "conflict" hypotheses, respectively, would have us believe. Instead, we often heard comments about simply not knowing one's (non-Latino) neighbors, as being separate from them, despite living in physical proximity.

On the whole, and with several qualifications notwithstanding, as we think about views expressed by focus group participants, it seems that it is not a question of whether Latinos see themselves as wishing to or trying to make America their home but rather how and how quickly they are doing so and the impediments they encounter. At the same time, their aspirations are riddled with hindrances based on values in tension and the obstacles posed by the social and political milieus they encounter in the United States. That is, their progress is clearly affected by Latinos' unique situations and their sometimes competing simultaneous aspirations, as well as broader social factors associated with socioeconomic inequality and prevailing norms about what it means to be American.

Situating Our Findings

As helpful as we hope our discussion of various paradoxes "within" the Latino population has been, we want to step back and reemphasize that concepts such as "Latinos" or "Hispanics" are themselves "American" social constructs; that is, they have particular meanings only within the United States. What are the larger normative theoretical benchmarks that Latinos implicitly reference in these identities, and what are the implications for "making a home"? Because making a home is presumably part of as well as linked to "assimilation," we also might think to ask: Assimilation *to* what? Or assimilation *relative to* what or whom (perhaps beyond what we discussed previously)? As we addressed assimilation in our previous chapters, two points, again, suggestive of paradox, stand out. First, Latinos' behavior indicates they seem comfortable with a multiplicity of values and aspirations and think in relative terms. In comparison, dominant, white/Anglo views tend to be more circumscribed or more absolute when it comes to certain issues about identity and national belonging that have consequences for immigrant/minority groups. Second, Latinos do *not* appear to believe in "the wrong ideas" (at least as defined by Anglo Americans), but they are more likely to manifest certain ideas (real or ascribed) that are somewhat novel in the American context and to manifest certain (ascribed) traits that are contested in the public discourse. To demonstrate this, we place our discussion in a yet broader perspective, situating our evidence accordingly.

Scholars have argued that there is not a single tradition, but rather "multiple traditions" in American political thought (Smith 1993, 1997; also see King and Smith 2005). The dominant "liberal" tradition stresses several interrelated beliefs, particularly freedom and liberty, individualism, and equality of opportunity, as defining elements of American culture. Another influential tradition, called "civic republicanism," sees extensive civic engagement emphasizing "community" and "fraternity" as central traits of American society.

There is, however, a third tradition, "ascriptive hierarchy" or inegalitarianism, which focuses on traits such as race/ethnicity and economic class and justifies exclusion or inequality because some individuals and groups are alleged to be more or less worthy of a legitimate place in the polity based on certain traits ascribed to them (Smith 1993). The ascriptive hierarchy tradition is the primary source of ethnocultural or "nativist" conceptions of Americanism. At the core of the ethnocultural conception is the belief in ascriptive criteria for citizenship, the idea that only some races, religions, or cultures are "truly American" (Citrin, Reingold, and Green 1990: 1129). Our focus group (and LNS) evidence suggests that Latinos themselves hold values quite compatible with the two major American traditions (liberal and civic republican), with some additions or modifications, but that on the other hand, Latinos are the targets of attitudes associated with the third set of values revolving around ideas of an ethnocultural or ascriptive hierarchy.

Importantly, scholars claim that these belief systems are often *combined* in the attitudes, practices, and public policies of the dominant population. The application or practice of these belief systems has exerted a deep and longstanding influence on both how the individuals who are formally considered part of the American polity (including "established" racial/minority and immigrant groups), as well as those who might or could become part of it (new immigrants, and ideas about immigration policy), are perceived. Such ideas as democracy (republicanism, popular sovereignty), liberty, equality (of opportunity, in manners), individual achievement (self-reliance), and related notions are seen as part of the "American creed" and are consistent with liberal or civic republican tenets. In contrast, however, "belief in God and *competence in English are particular characteristics that help define a more restrictive, ethnocultural version of American identity*" (Citrin, Reingold, and Green 1990: 1130, emphasis added).

Several studies support the claim that individuals can endorse liberal political ideals and principles as inherently American but *at the same time* (paradoxically?) endorse a nativist or ethnocultural view that only individuals of certain backgrounds possess the moral and intellectual qualities required for democratic citizenship (Smith 1993). Notably, about three-fourths of Californians surveyed in one study "endorsed the idea that competence in English was 'very important' in making one a 'true American,'" and even two-thirds of those who identified as "strong liberals" perceived that "competence in English was 'very important' in making a person a 'true American'" (Citrin, Reingold, and Green 1990).

Schildkraut's research (2007) empirically assesses the extent of "civic republicanism" and "liberalism" in a national survey. She also examines an additional political orientation, "incorporationism," which could be characterized as supportive of multiculturalism in American society. Finally, her research assesses "contested" orientations or beliefs. She focuses on a set of measures to assess liberalism that include "respecting America's political institutions and laws" and "pursuing economic success through hard work," and "letting other people say what they want (no matter how much one disagrees)." To consider civic republicanism, she looks at questions concerning "thinking of oneself as American," "feeling American," and being "informed about" and "involved in" politics. Incorporationism, as Schildkraut develops it, appeals to a tradition of seeing America as a "nation of immigrants" and a tolerant society. Survey questions used to tap this idea asked about the importance of "blending into the large society" and whether one sees "people of all backgrounds as American," but also "carrying on cultural traditions of one's ancestors" and "respecting other people's cultural differences." Especially notable for our purposes, since Latinos are disproportionately non-English speakers and non-citizens, among the beliefs that Schildkraut finds are "contested," or at least about which there are multiple, somewhat conflicting views, are "being able to speak English" and "American citizenship."

Schildkraut ultimately finds that there is wide agreement, essentially a broad consensus, on norms, values, and behaviors that constitute understandings of American identity among whites, but there is *also* solid support for the *multiple* traditions thesis. Taken together, Schildkraut's and other studies generally suggest that there is more than one disposition on Americanism, to the extent the definitions do fall on a single dimension (Citrin, Reingold, and Green 1990). The components of Americanism may also be in tension and do not necessarily match theoretical understandings. Finally, these notions are not always coherent. This being the case among the dominant, white/Anglo group, what did our focus group evidence tell us about Latinos' perspectives about American identity?

While our focus group narratives do not permit a fully systematic analysis, they nonetheless offer powerful commentary on feelings about the sense of identity and "place" in the United States. As we saw, the participants offered some number of enthusiastic comments about economic freedoms and opportunities in America, consistent with "liberal" views, although they also noted that they felt extraordinary demands and hardships, perceived discrimination, and sometimes felt unwelcome. Their sense of identity—as American, as Latino—was hardly simple, but there is also ample evidence of attachments and various "civic republican"-like sentiments among focus group participants. In addition, however, there *are* elements of attachment among many Latinos to "where they came from," to a "heritage," a language, and a "Latino" or national-origin identity that marks Latinos as different. In sum, Latino views are not contradictory or in conflict with those of whites/Anglos, but they are not entirely congruent, and therein lies the problem.

Recall that according to Schildkraut, incorporationism is in fact an "American" identity, though hardly the most prevalent currently, much less historically. That this tertiary understanding of identity may be disproportionately held by a minority/immigrant group, and that this same group *also* has traits that are contested as parts of American identity—namely, having a substantial number speaking a (foreign) language and not born in the United States—evokes an ethnocultural response from the dominant group. Thus, while there is considerable evidence of liberal and civic republican thinking, along with assimilationist views and value convergence, among Latinos, some of their other beliefs and (ascribed) traits function to set them apart from white Americans.

Apparently, not only what is believed, but also who believes it (and how much) matters a great deal. Stated otherwise, Latinos show a considerable mainstream outlook, but they also have an incorporationist bent, which is *not* the majority sentiment in American politics. When such views are held by a minority group that has been partly defined in unfavorable ascriptive terms, making America home becomes more difficult.

Recent events, such as Congress' failure to pass comprehensive immigration reform, U.S. Immigration and Customs Enforcement raids conducted in Latino communities and workplaces, and the passage of anti-immigrant statutes by states and local governments, have also made the climate for Latino "home building" increasingly challenging. Unless there is a significant shift in public policy and attitudes among non-Latinos toward greater tolerance and acceptance of Latinos' contradictions, the process of Latino incorporation could become even more complicated and considerably less robust.

Some Final Thoughts

Assimilation is an important concept and a frequent touchstone in discussions about Latinos, which explains in large part why it appears as a central topic early in our book and is mentioned throughout in various ways. The concept and associated analytical framework(s) was once very prominent (see Chapter 2), then challenged, and to some degree fell out of favor. Recently it has been revitalized and resuscitated as a way to think about immigrant incorporation in contemporary society. It could be said that the concept of assimilation itself has shown change with continuity, evolution with some enduring qualities, and considerable complexity, yet the concept has maintained a core set of ideas. This evolution occurred in part because the earlier renderings of assimilation, most notably the "straight line" or monotonic conceptualizations, could not fully account for the complex phenomena they sought to explain. Additionally, earlier versions of assimilation theory seemed normatively inclined to view any "lack" of assimilation as almost entirely the "fault" of the immigrant group, assigning little agency or responsibility to the actions of the receiving society. Over time, however, scholars came to believe that assimilation is and maybe should be a two-way, interrelated process, involving adjustments by both immigrants and the receiving society and, accordingly, necessitating new conceptualizations of assimilation. Latinos' understandings of American society and their efforts to make their way in American society have evolved in ways that intriguingly parallel the evolving processes associated with the concept of assimilation.

Recent developments in the process of Latinos making their home in America are best understood as a series of paradoxes and tensions. We have sought to not only identify, but to also make sense of, those paradoxes by considering the competing aspirations and realities Latinos confront through the themes of continuity, change, complexity, and the search for community that Latino efforts represent. Part of that has also required the rethinking of central ideas, such as the concept and processes of assimilation.

In trying to make sense of Latinos' contemporary situation, we found that focus groups were especially useful in providing rich and nuanced evidence that complements the numbers-driven, ostensibly rigorous and objective evidence that survey research emphasizes. More qualitative types of analysis (such as focus groups) may be better at revealing everyday life in the making, bringing to light paradoxes that other forms of inquiry do less well. We hope that the combination of our methods, theoretical reformulations, and identification and examination of core themes and topics, with resulting insights on various paradoxes or tensions in Latinos' thinking and lives, will ultimately contribute to improving the status of Latinos in American society and politics.

Notes

Chapter 1

1. Our contacts with community leaders and elected officials were augmented through a series of eight outreach meetings, funded by the Ford Foundation. While not a specific part of the analysis presented here, those meetings provided invaluable insight to local conditions and variations, some of which are reflected in our discussions.

2. However, we have good reason to believe that the ten participants in our last Washington, DC, focus group (primarily recent immigrants from Central American countries), where education and income level are unrecorded, were probably some of the poorest and least educated among participants.

Chapter 2

1. Conducted by the National League of Cities (NLC).

2. Conducted by Lake Research Partners (LRP).

3. More specifically, the respondents were *not* full-time students, retirees, business owners or CEOs, company executives, managers/supervisors, or professionals but they *were* employed at least 20 hours per week or actively looking for work.

4. The use of "S" and "E" denote the language of the focus group participants: English (E) and Spanish (S).

Chapter 3

1. Respondents were allowed to put as many issues they wanted as extremely important.

2. For a fuller discussion of how these reform efforts are likely to affect Latino students, see Martinez-Ebers, Fraga, Lopez, and Vega 2000.

Chapter 5

1. *Hoffman Plastic Compounds, Inc. v. NLRB* (00-1595) 535 U.S. 137 (2002) 237 F.3d 639, reversed.

2. Oral arguments were heard on April 26, 2006, on Mohawk's petition to dismiss the complaint on the grounds that a single corporation cannot constitute an "enterprise" under the statute and, therefore, is not subject to RICO legislation. The 11th Circuit previously sided with the plaintiffs. On June 5, 2006, the Supreme Court remanded the case to the 11th Circuit for reconsideration in light of the Court's ruling in *Anza v. Ideal Steel Supply Corp.* (04-433) 373 F. 3d 251. The status of the suit remains unsettled at this writing.

3. Hy-Vee is the local supermarket chain with the largest market share, serving a primarily non-Hispanic white clientele.

4. For details, see the U.S. Department of Justice (DOJ) website at http://www.usdoj.gov/opa/pr/2004/July/04_crt_467.htm, last accessed May 3, 2006.

5. DOJ announcement at http://www.usdoj.gov/opa/pr/2004/September/04_crt_615.htm, last accessed May 3, 2006.

Chapter 7

1. Puerto Ricans, as born citizens, face no immigration or formal barriers to political participation. Cubans enjoy a privileged immigration status as a relic of the Cold War face-off with the Castro regime. Mexicans enjoy the benefit of extremely large numbers, but face significant immigration hurdles.

2. The Latino National Survey (LNS) was a fifteen-state plus metro Washington, DC, study of Latinos' public life and attitudes conducted from November 2005 to August 2006. Earlier sections of this book provide more details about the nature and scope of this study.

3. In the LNPS, the perception of common political interests was set up to include all paired combinations (for example, Mexican origin–Puerto Rican, Cuban–Mexican origin). As a result, some pairs had lower levels of perceptions than others.

4. A *tamalada* is a social event built around a large group of people, usually women, getting together to make tamales, a labor-intensive project that, by custom and practicality, begins very early in the morning.

Chapter 8

1. Of course, a competing, Madisonian, tradition suggests that social complexity and group pluralism and competition actually facilitate social and political freedom.

References

Adams, James Thurlow. 1934. *The Epic of America.* Phoenix, AZ: Simon Publications. (2003 paperback edition.)

Alarcón, Rafael. 2002. "The Development of Hometown Associations in the United States and the Use of Social Remittances in Mexico." Working paper.

Alba, Richard, and Victor Nee. 2003. *Remaking the American Mainstream: Assimilation and Contemporary Immigration.* Cambridge, MA: Harvard University Press.

Alba, Richard D., John R. Logan, Brian J. Stults, Gilbert Marzan, and Wenquan Zhang. 1999. "Immigrant Groups in the Suburbs: A Reexamination of Suburbanization and Spatial Assimilation." *American Sociological Review* 64(3):446–460.

Badillo, Herman. 2006. *One Nation, One Standard.* New York: Penguin Group.

Baker, Phyllis L. 2004. "'It Is the Only Way I Can Survive': Gender Paradox among Recent Mexican Immigrants to Iowa." *Sociological Perspectives* 47(4):393–408.

Barbour, Rosaline. 2005. "Making Sense of Focus Groups." *Medical Education* 39:742–750.

Barrera, Mario. 1985. "The Historical Evolution of Chicano Ethnic Goals: A Bibliographic Essay." *Sage Race Relations Abstracts* 10(1):1–48.

Basch, Linda, Nina Glick-Schiller, and Cristina Szanton-Blanc. 1994. *Nations Unbound: Transnational Projects, Postcolonial Predicaments, and Deterritorialized Nation-States.* Basel, Switzerland: Gordon and Breach.

Bischoping, Katherine, and Jennifer Dykema. 1999. "Toward a Social Psychological Programme for Improving Focus Group Methods of Developing Questionnaires." *Journal of Official Statistics* 15(4):495–516.

Blank, Rebecca M., Marilyn Dabady, and Constance F. Citro. 2004. *Measuring Racial Discrimination*. Washington, DC: National Research Council.

Bogardus, Emory S. 1926. "The Group Interview." *Journal of Applied Sociology* 10:372–382.

Bowles, Samuel, and Herbert Gintis. 1976. *Schooling in Capitalist America: Education Reform and the Contradictions of Economic Life*. New York: Basic Books.

Brown, Susan K., and Frank D. Bean. 2006. "Assimilation Models, Old and New: Explaining a Long-Term Process." *Migration Information Source*. Washington, DC: Migration Policy Institute.

Burgdorfer, Bob. 2006. "Cargill Meat Plants to Close Monday for Rally." Reuters News Service, April 25.

Cantú, Lionel. 1995. "The Peripheralization of Rural America: A Case Study of Latino Migrants in America's Heartland." *Sociological Perspectives* 38(3):399–414.

Carnevale, Anthony P. 1999. *Education = Success: Empowering Hispanic Youth and Adults*. Princeton, NJ: Educational Testing Service.

Chubb, John E., and Terry M. Moe. 1990. *Politics, Markets, and America's Schools*. Washington, DC: The Brookings Institution.

Citrin, Jack, Beth Reingold, and Donald Green. 1990. "American Identity and the Politics of Ethnic Change." *Journal of Politics* 52(4):1124–1154.

Conway, Dennis, and Jeffrey Cohen. 1998. "Consequences of Migration and Remittances for Mexican Transnational Communities." *Economic Geography* 71(1):26–44.

Crabtree, Benjamin F., M. Kim Yanoshik, William L. Miller, and Patrick J. O'Connor. 1993. Selecting group or individual interviews. In *Successful Focus Groups: Advancing the State of the Art*, ed. D. L. Morgan. Thousand Oaks, CA: Sage.

Cullen, Jim. 2003. *The American Dream: A Short History of an Idea That Shaped a Nation*. New York: Oxford University Press.

Dawson, Michael C. 1994. *Behind the Mule: Race and Class in African-American Politics*. Princeton, NJ: Princeton University Press.

de la Garza, Rodolfo O., Louis Desipio, F. Chris Garcia, John Garcia, and Angelo Falcon. 1992. *Latino Voices: Mexican, Puerto Rican, and Cuban Perspectives on American Politics*. Boulder, CO: Westview Press.

Delli Carpini, Michael, and Bruce Williams. 1994. "Methods, Metaphors and Media Research: The Uses of Television in Political Conversation." *Communication Research* 21:782–812.

DeMaio, Theresa, Nancy Mathiowetz, Jennifer Rothgeb, Mary Ellen Beach, and Sharon Durant. 1993. *Protocol for Pretesting Demographic Surveys at the U.S. Census Bureau*. Census Bureau Monograph. Washington, DC: U.S. Bureau of the Census.

DeSipio, Louis. 1996. *Counting on the Latino Vote*. Charlottesville, VA: University of Virginia Press.

————. 2000. "Sending Money Home . . . For Now: Remittances and Immigrant Adaptation in the United States." Working paper, Inter-American Dialogue (Washington, DC) and Tomás Rivera Policy Institute (Los Angeles).

Espinosa, Gastón, Virgilio Elizondo, and Jesse Miranda, eds. 2005. *Latino Religions and Civic Activism in the United States.* New York: Oxford University Press.

Espiritu, Yu. 1992. *Asian American Panethnicity: Bonding Institutions and Identities.* Philadelphia: Temple University Press.

Fern, Edward F. 1982. "The Use of Focus Groups for Idea Generation: The Effects of Group Size, Acquaintanceship and Moderator on Response Quantity and Quality." *Journal of Market Research* 19:1–13.

"First National Poll of Latino Reaction to Bush Immigration Proposal. A Public Opinion Survey." 2004. Conducted by Bendixen and Associates. New America Media. Posted January 29. http://news.newamericamedia.org/news/view_article.html?article_id=f9e0a30c7b390794b6469f6e10fcd1db.

Flaccus, Gillian. 2006. "Immigrants Walk Off the Job in Boycott." Associated Press, May 1.

Folch-Lyon, Evelyn, Luis de la Macorra, and S. Bruce Schearer. 1981. "Focus Group and Survey Research on Family Planning in Mexico." *Studies in Family Planning* 12:409–432.

Forsyth, Barbara H., and Judith T. Lessler. 1991. Cognitive Laboratory Methods: A Taxonomy. In *Measurement Errors in Surveys*, ed. Paul Biemer, Robert M. Groves, Lars E. Lyberg, Nancy A. Mathiowetz, and Seymour Sudman, pp. 393–418. New York: Wiley.

Fraga, Luis R., John A. Garcia, Rodney E. Hero, Michael Jones-Correa, Valerie Martinez-Ebers, and Gary M. Segura. 2006a. Latino National Survey (LNS). [Computer File]. ICPSR20862-v1. Miami, FL: Geoscape International [producer], 2006. Ann Arbor, MI: Inter-university Consortium for Political and Social Research [distributor], 2008-05-27.

Fraga, Luis R., John A. Garcia, Rodney E. Hero, Michael Jones-Correa, Valerie Martinez-Ebers, and Gary M. Segura. 2006b. "*Su Casa Es Nuestra Casa*: Latino Politics Research and the Development of American Political Science." *American Political Science Review* 100(4):515–521.

Fraga, Luis R., Kenneth J. Meier, and Robert E. England. 1986. "Hispanic Americans and Educational Policy: Limits to Equal Access." *Journal of Politics* 48(4):850–876.

Fraga, Luis Ricardo, and David Leal. 2004. "Playing the 'Latino Card': Race, Ethnicity, and National Party Politics." *Du Bois Review* 1(2):297–317.

Fraga, Luis Ricardo, and Ricardo Ramírez. 2003. "Latino Political Incorporation in California, 1990–2000." In *Latinos and Public Policy in California: An Agenda for Opportunity*, ed. David Lopez and Andrés Jiménez, pp. 301–335. Berkeley, CA: Berkeley Public Policy Press, Institute of Governmental Studies, University of California, Berkeley.

Gándara, Patricia, and Frances Contreras. 2009. *The Latino Education Crisis: The Consequences of Failed Social Policies.* Cambridge, MA: Harvard University Press.

Gans, Herbert. 1996. *The War against the Poor: The Underclass and Anti-Poverty Policy.* New York: Basic Books.

Garcia, Eugene E. 2001. *Hispanic Education in the United States: Raíces y Alas.* Lanham, MD: Rowman and Littlefield.

Garcia, F. Chris, and Gabriel R. Sanchez. 2007. *Hispanics and the U.S. Political System: Moving into the Mainstream.* Upper Saddle River, NJ: Pearson Prentice Hall.

Garcia, F. Chris, and Rodolfo de la Garza. 1977. *The Chicano Political Experience: Three Perspectives.* North Scituate, MA: Duxbury.

Garcia, John A. 1982. "Ethnic Identification, Consciousness, Identity: Explanations of Measurement and Inter-Relationships." *Hispanic Journal of Behavioral Sciences* (September):295–313.

———. 2003. *Latino Politics: Community, Culture and Interests.* Boulder, CO: Rowman and Littlefield.

Gibson, Margaret. 1988. *Accommodation without Assimilation: Sikh Immigrants in an American High School.* Ithaca, NY: Cornell University Press.

Giles, Michael W., and Kaenan Hertz. 1994. "Racial Threat and Partisan Identification." *American Political Science Review* 88(2):317–326.

Gilliam, Franklin D., Nicholas A. Valentino, and Matthew N. Beckman. 2002. "Where You Live and What You Watch: The Impact of Racial Proximity and Local Television News on Attitudes about Race and Crime." *Political Research Quarterly* 55(4):755–781.

Glick-Schiller, Nina. 1999. Transmigrants and Nation-States: Something Old and Something New in the U.S. Immigrant Experience. In *The Handbook of International Migration: The American Experience*, ed. Charles Hirschman, Philip Kasinitz, and Josh DeWind, pp. 94–119. New York: Russell Sage Foundation.

Glick-Schiller, Nina, and Georges Fouron. 1999. "Terrains of Blood and Nation: Haitian Transnational Social Fields." *Racial and Ethnic Studies* 22:340–366.

Gordon, Milton. 1964. *Assimilation in American Life: The Role of Race, Religion and National Origins.* Oxford: Oxford University Press.

Greene, Jay P., and Marcus A. Winters. 2006. "Leaving Boys Behind: Public High School Graduation Rates." Education Working Paper Archive, University of Arkansas. http://www.uark.edu/ua/der/EWPA/approved/Leaving.

Guarnizo, Luis E. 2000. "Notes on Transnationalism." Paper presented at workshop on Transnational Migration: Comparative Theory and Research Perspectives. Wadham College, University of Oxford, July 2000.

Hajnal, Zoltan L. 2001. "White Residents, Black Incumbents, and a Declining Racial Divide." *American Political Science Review* 95(3):603–618.

Hayes-Bautista, David, and Jorge Chapa. 1987. "Latino Terminology: Conceptual Basis for Standardized Terminology." *American Journal of Public Health* 77(1):61–68.

Henig, Jeffrey. 1994. *School Choice: Limits of the Market Metaphor.* Princeton, NJ: Princeton University Press.

Hernstein, Richard J., and Charles Murray. 1994. *The Bell Curve: Intelligence and the Class Structure.* New York: The Free Press.

Hero, Rodney E. 1992. *Latinos and the U.S. Political System: Two-Tiered Pluralism.* Philadelphia: Temple University Press.

Hochschild, Jennifer L. 1984. *The New American Dilemma: Liberal Democracy and School Desegregation.* New Haven, CT: Yale University Press.

———. 1995. *Facing Up to the American Dream: Race, Class, and the Soul of the Nation.* Princeton, NJ: Princeton University Press.

Hochschild, Jennifer L., and Nathan Scovronick. 2004. *The American Dream and the Public Schools.* New York: Oxford University Press.

Huntington, Samuel P. 1997. "The Erosion of American National Interests." *Foreign Affairs* 76(5):28–49.

———. 2004a. *Who Are We? The Challenges to America's National Identity.* New York: Simon and Schuster.

———. 2004b. "The Hispanic Challenge." *Foreign Policy* (March–April):30–45.

Hurtado, Aida, Patricia Gurin, and Timothy Peng. 1994. "Social Identities—A Framework for Studying the Adaptations of Immigrants and Ethnics: The Adaptations of Mexicans in the United States." *Social Problems* 41(1):129–151.

"International Migration Review, special issue on 'Transnational Migration: International Perspectives.'" 2003 (Fall). *International Migration Review,* ed. Peggy Levitt, Josh DeWind, and Steven Vertovec.

Jones-Correa, Michael. 1998. *Between Two Nations: The Political Predicament of Latinos in New York City.* Ithaca, NY: Cornell University Press.

———. 2007. "Coming to America: Latinos and the Adoption of Identity." Paper presented at the Annual Meeting of the Midwest Political Science Association, Chicago, IL, April 12–15, 2007.

Jones-Correa, Michael, and David Leal. 1996. "Becoming Hispanic: Secondary Pan-ethnic Identity among Latin American Origin Population in the U.S." *Hispanic Journal of Behavioral Sciences* 18(2):214–254.

Kaufmann, Karen M. 2007. "Immigration and the Future of Black Power in U.S. Cities." *DuBois Review* 4(1):79–96.

King, Desmond S., and Rogers M. Smith. 2005. "Racial Orders in American Political Development." *American Political Science Review* 99(1):75–92.

Knodel, John, N. Havanon, and Werasit Sittitrai. 1990. "Family Size and the Education of Children in the Context of Rapid Fertility Decline." *Population and Development Review* 16(1):31–62.

Kreuger, Richard A. 1994. *Focus Groups: A Practical Guide for Applied Research.* 2nd ed. Thousand Oaks, CA: Sage.

Lake Research Partners. 2007. "The American Dream Survey: Toplines." March 2007. http://www.changetowin.org/fileadmin/pdf/topline.CTW .Workers.R.040307.pdf.

Lee, Sharon M., and Barry Edmonston. 2005. "New Marriages, New Families: U.S. Racial and Hispanic Intermarriage." *Population Bulletin* 60(2):1–36.

Levitt, Peggy. 2001. "Transnational Migration: Taking Stock and Future Directions." *Global Networks: A Journal of Transnational Affairs* 1(3): 195–216.

Lien, Pei-te. 2001. *The Making of Asian America through Political Participation.* Philadelphia: Temple University Press.

Macias, Reynaldo F. 1998. *Summary Report of the Survey of the States' Limited English Proficient Students and Available Educational Programs and Services, 1996–97.* Washington, DC: National Clearinghouse for Bilingual Education.

Martinez-Ebers, Valerie, Luis Fraga, Linda Lopez, and Arturo Vega. 2000. "Latino Interests in Education, Health, and Criminal Justice Policy." *Political Science and Politics* 33(3):547–554.

Massey, Douglas, and Jorge Durand. 1992. "Continuities in Transnational Migration: An Analysis of Thirteen National Communities." Paper presented at a conference on New Perspectives on Mexico-U.S. Immigration, University of Chicago, Mexican Studies Program, Chicago, October 23–24.

McClain, Paula D. 2006. "Racial Intergroup Relations in a Set of Cities: A Twenty-Year Perspective." *Journal of Politics* 68(4):757–770.

McClain, Paula D., Niambi M. Carter, Victoria M. DeFrancesco Soto, Monique L. Lyle, Jeffrey D. Grynaviski, Shayla C. Nunnally, Thomas J. Scotto, J. Alan Kendrick, Gerald F. Lackey, and Kendra Davenport Cotton. 2006. "Racial Distancing in a Southern City: Latino Immigrants' Views of Black Americans." *Journal of Politics* 68(3):571–584.

McClain, Paula D., and Joseph Stewart Jr. 2002. *"Can We All Get Along?" Racial and Ethnic Minorities in American Politics,* 3rd ed. Boulder, CO: Westview Press.

Meier, Kenneth J., and Eric Gonzalez Juenke. 2005. Electoral Structure and the Quality of Representation on School Boards. In *Besieged: School Boards and the Future of Education Politics,* ed. William G. Howell, pp. 199–227. Washington, DC: Brookings Institution Press.

Meier, Kenneth J., and Joseph Stewart, Jr. 1991. *The Politics of Hispanic Education: Uno Paso Pa'lante y Dos Pa'tras.* Albany, NY: State University of New York Press.

Merton, Robert, K. M. Fiske, and P. L. Kendall. 1956. *The Focused Interview.* Glencoe, IL: Free Press.

Michelson, Melissa R. 2003. "Getting out the Latino Vote: How Door-to-Door Canvassing Influences Voter Turnout in Rural Central California." *Political Behavior* 25(3):247–263.

Moe, Terry M. 2001. *Schools, Vouchers, and the American Public.* Washington, DC: Brookings Institution Press.

Morgan, David L. 1988. *Focus Groups as Qualitative Research.* Qualitative Research Methods Series, 16. Thousand Oaks, CA: Sage.

———. 1996. "Focus Groups." *Annual Review of Sociology* 22:129–152.

Morgan, David L., ed. 1993. *Successful Focus Groups: Enhancing the State of the Art.* Newbury Park, CA: Sage.

Morgan, David L., and R. A. Kreuger. 1993. When to Use Focus Groups and Why. In *Successful Focus Groups,* ed. David Morgan. London: Sage.

Morowska, Ewa. 2001. Immigrants, Transnationalism and Ethnicization: A Comparison of This Great Wave and the Last. In *E Pluribus Unum? Contemporary and Historical Perspectives on Immigrant Political Incorporation,* ed. Gary Gerstle and John Mollenkopf, pp. 175–212. New York: Russell Sage Foundation.

Nagel, Joan. 1994. *American Indian Ethnic Renewal: Red Power and the Resurgence of Identity and Culture.* New York: Oxford University Press.

National Center for Education Statistics (NCES). 2007. Digest of Education Statistics. Tables and Figures. http.//ncesed.gov/pubs2007/pcscnroll06/tables/table_2.asp.

National Commission on Excellence in Education. 1983. *A Nation at Risk: The Imperative for Education Reform.* Washington, DC: Secretary of Education, U.S. Department of Education.

National League of Cities (NLC). 2004. ""The American Dream in 2004: A Survey of the American People." *NCLC Research Report Series,* September 2004. Washington, DC: NLC.

Oboler, Suzanne. 1992. "The Politics of Labeling: Latino/a Cultural Identities of Self and Others." *Latin American Perspectives* 19(4):18–36.

Omni, Michael, and Howard Winant. 1994. *Racial Transformation in the U.S.: From the 1960s to 1980s.* New York: Routledge and Paul.

Orfield, Gary, and Chungmei Lee. 2004. *Brown at 50: King's Dream or Plessy's Nightmare?* Cambridge, MA: The Civil Rights Project, Harvard University.

Orfield, Gary, and John Yun. 1999. *Resegregation in American Schools.* Cambridge, MA: The Civil Rights Project, Harvard University. http://www.law.Harvard.edu/groups/civilrights/publications/resegregation99.html.

Orozco, Manuel. 2000. "Latino Hometown Associations as Agents of Development in Latin America." Working paper, Inter-American Dialogue and Tomás Rivera Policy Institute.

Padilla, Felix. 1986. *Latino Ethnic Consciousness: Case of Mexican Americans and Puerto Ricans.* Notre Dame, IN: University of Notre Dame Press.

Pantoja, Adrian, Ricardo Ramírez, and Gary M. Segura. 2001. "Citizens by Choice, Voters by Necessity: Patterns in Political Mobilization by Naturalized Latinos." *Political Research Quarterly* 54:729–750.

Park, Robert E. 1950. *Race and Culture.* Glencoe, IL: Free Press.

Patterson, James T. 2002. *Brown v. Board of Education: A Civil Rights Milestone and Its Troubled Legacy.* New York: Oxford University Press.

Peterson, Paul E., and Bryan C. Hassel, eds. 1998. *Learning from School Choice.* Washington, DC: Brookings Institution Press.

Pew Hispanic Center/Kaiser Family Foundation. 2002. "National Survey of Latinos: The Latino Electorate." Washington, DC: Pew Hispanic Center.

————. 2004a. "National Survey of Latinos: Education." January. Washington, DC: Pew Hispanic Center.

————. 2004b. "The 2004 National Survey of Latinos: Politics and Civic Participation." Washington, DC: Pew Hispanic Center.

Portes, Alejandro, and Min Zhou. 1993. "The New Second Generation: Segmented Assimilation and Its Variants." *Annals of the American Academy of Political and Social Sciences* 530(1):74–96.

Portes, Alejandro, and Rubén G. Rumbaut. 2001. *Legacies: The Story of the Immigrant Second Generation.* Los Angeles: University of California Press.

Quiocho, Alice M. L., and Annette M. Daoud. 2006. "Dispelling Myths about Latino Parent Participation in Schools." *The Educational Forum* 70 (Spring):255–267.

Ramirez, Robert R., and Patricia de la Cruz. 2002. "The Hispanic Population in the United States: March 2002." *Current Population Reports,* P20-545. Washington, DC: U.S. Census Bureau.

Riley, Richard W., and Delia Pompa. 1998. *Improving Opportunities: Strategies from the Secretary of Education for Hispanic and Limited English Proficient Students.* Washington, DC: U.S. Department of Education, Office of Bilingual Education and Minority Languages Affairs.

Rodrigues, Helena Alves, and Gary M. Segura. 2007. A Place at the Lunch Counter: Latinos, African-Americans, and the Dynamics of American Race Politics. In *Latino Politics: Identity, Mobilization, and Representation,* ed. Kenneth Meier, Rodolfo Espino, and David Leal. Charlottesville, VA: University of Virginia Press.

Rohe, William M., Shannon Van Zandt, and George McCarthy. 2001. "The Social Benefits and Costs of Homeownership: A Critical Assessment of the Research." Cambridge, MA: Joint Center for Housing Studies, Harvard University. www.jchs.harvard.edu/publications/homeownership/liho01-12.pdf.

Rossi, Peter, and Eleanor Weber. 1996. "The Social Benefit of Home Ownership: Empirical Evidence from National Surveys." *Housing Policy Debate* 7(1):1–36.

Rumbaut, Rubén G. 1997. "Paradoxes (and Orthodoxies) of Assimilation." *Sociological Perspectives* 40(3):483–511.

Saint-Germain, Michelle A., Tamsen L. Bassford, and Gail Montano. 1993. "Surveys and Focus Groups in Health Research with Older Hispanic Women." *Qualitative Health Research* 3:341–367.

San Miguel, Guadalupe. 1987. *Let Them All Take Heed: Mexican Americans and the Campaign for Educational Equality in Texas, 1910–1981.* Austin, TX: University of Texas Press.

Sassler, Sharon L. 2006. "School Participation among Immigrant Youths: The Case of Segmented Assimilation in the Early 20th Century." *Sociology of Education* 29:1–24.

Schildkraut, Debra J. 2007. "Defining American Identity in the Twenty-First Century: How Much 'There' Is There?" *Journal of Politics* 69(3):597–615.

Schlosser, Eric. 2004. "Tyson's Moral Anchor." *The Nation,* July 12.

Secada, Walter G., Rudolfo Chavez-Chavez, Eugene Garcia, Ciprano Munoz, Jeannie Oakes, Isaura Santiago-Santiago, and Robert Slavin. 1998. *No More Excuses: The Final Report of the Hispanic Dropout Project.* Washington, DC: U.S. Department of Education.

Segura, Gary. 2007. "Transnational Linkages, Generational Change and Latino Political Engagement." Paper prepared for presentation at the Annual Meeting of the Midwest Political Science Association, Chicago, April 12–15, 2007.

Segura, Gary M., and Helena Alves Rodrigues. 2006. "Comparative Ethnic Politics in the United States: Beyond Black and White." *Annual Review of Political Science* 9:375–395.

Sigel, Roberta. 1996. *Ambition and Accommodation: How Women View Gender Relations.* Chicago: University of Chicago Press.

Skerry, Peter. 1993. *Mexican Americans: The Ambivalent Minority.* New York: Free Press.

Smith, Michael Peter, and Luis Guarnizo. 1998. *Transnationalism from Below.* New Brunswick, NJ: Transaction Publishers.

Smith, Robert. 1998. Transnational Localities: Community, Technology and the Politics of Membership within the Context of Mexico and U.S. Migration. In *Transnationalism from Below,* ed. Michael Peter Smith and Luis Guarnizo, pp. 196–240. New Brunswick, NJ: Transaction Publishers.

Smith, Rogers M. 1993. "Beyond Tocqueville, Myrdal, and Hartz: The Multiple Traditions in America," *American Political Science Review* 87(3): 549–566.

———. 1997. *Civic Ideals: Conflicting Visions of Citizenship in U.S. History.* New Haven, CT: Yale University Press.

Soss, Joe, Laura Langbein, and Alan Metelko. 2003. "Why Do White Americans Support the Death Penalty?" *Journal of Politics* 65(2):397–421.

Stewart, D. W., and P. N. Shamdasani. 1990. *Focus Groups: Theory and Practice.* Applied Social Research Methods Series, 20. Newbury Park, CA: Sage.

Suro, Roberto. 2006. "A Developing Identity: Hispanics in the United States." *Carnegie Reporter* 3(4):1–5.

Tyack, David. 1974. *The One Best System: A History of American Urban Education.* Cambridge, MA: Harvard University Press.

Tyack, David, and Larry Cuban. 1995. *Tinkering Toward Utopia: A Century of Public School Reform.* Cambridge, MA: Harvard University Press.

U.S. Census Bureau. 2001. "Census 2000: Hispanics in the U.S.A." http://www.census.gov/mso/www/pres_lib/hisorig/sld001.htm.

———. 2002. "National Population Projections. I. Summary Files, Total Population by Age, Sex, Race, and Hispanic Origin." Population Division, Population Projections Branch. Aug. 2. http://www.census.gov/population/www/projections/natsum-T3.html.

———. 2004. "U.S. Interim Projections by Age, Sex, Race, and Hispanic Origin." March 18. http://www.census.gov/population/www/projections/usinterimproj/.

———. 2006. "C03001. Hispanic or Latino Origin by Specific Origin." *American Community Survey.* Washington, DC: U.S. Department of Commerce. http://factfinder.census.gov/servlet/DTTable?_bm=y&-geo_id=01000US&-ds_name=ACS_2007_3YR_G00_&-redoLog=false&-mt_name=ACS_2007_3YR_G2000_B03001.

———. 2007. "The American Community—Hispanics: 2004." American Community Survey Reports. Washington, DC: U.S. Bureau of the Census.

Valdés, Guadalupe. 1996. *Con Respecto, Bridging the Distances between Culturally Diverse Families and Schools: An Ethnographic Portrait.* New York: Teachers College Press.

Valenzuela, Angela. 1999. *Subtractive Schooling: U.S. Mexican Youth and the Politics of Caring.* Albany, NY: State University of New York Press.

Vaughn, Sharon, Jeanne Shay Shumm, and Jane M. Sinagub. 1996. *Focus Group Interviews in Education and Psychology.* Thousand Oaks, CA: Sage.

Villareal, Roberto. 1988. The Politics of Mexican-American Empowerment. In *Latino Empowerment: Progress, Problems, and Prospects*, ed. Roberto E. Villareal, Norma G. Hernandez, and Howard D. Neighbor, pp. 1–10. New York: Greenwood Press.

Waldinger, Roger. 2006. "Immigrant 'Transnationalism' and the Presence of the Past." In *Borders, Boundaries and Bonds: America and Its Immigrants in Eras of Globalization*, ed. Elliott Barkan et al. New York: New York University Press.

———. 2007. "Between Here and There: How Attached Are Latino Immigrants to Their Native Country?" Pew Hispanic Center Report. http://pewhispanic.org/reports/report.php?ReportID=80.

Ward, Victoria M., Jane T. Bertrand, and Lisanne F. Brown. 1991. "Focus Groups and Surveys as Complementary Research Methods: A Case

Example." In *Successful Focus Groups: Advancing the State of the Art*, ed. David Morgan, pp. 118–136. Thousand Oaks, CA: Sage.

Warner. William Lloyd, and Leo Srole. 1945. *The Social Systems of American Ethnic Groups.* New Haven, CT: Yale University Press.

Warren, Elizabeth, and Amelia Warren Tyagi. 2003. *The Two-Income Trap: Why Middle-Class Mothers and Fathers Are Going Broke.* New York: Basic Books.

Williams, L. Susan, Sandra D. Alvarez, and Kevin S. Andrade Hauck. 2002. "My Name Is Not María: Young Latinas Seeking Home in the Heartland." *Social Problems* 49(4):563–584.

Wilkins, David. 2007. *American Indian Politics and the American Political System*, 2nd ed. Lanham, MD: Rowman & Littlefield.

Index

About the Authors

Luis Ricardo Fraga is Associate Vice Provost for Faculty Advancement, Director of the Diversity Research Institute, and Russell F. Stark University Professor in the Department of Political Science at the University of Washington.

John A. Garcia is Professor of Political Science at the University of Arizona.

Rodney E. Hero is the Packey J. Dee Professor of American Democracy in the Department of Political Science at the University of Notre Dame.

Michael Jones-Correa is Professor of Government at Cornell University.

Valerie Martinez-Ebers is Professor of Political Science at the University of North Texas.

Gary M. Segura is Professor of Political Science and Director of Chicana/o Studies in the Center for Comparative Studies of Race and Ethnicity at Stanford University.